Everyone is talking about the...

WORKING SOLO SOURCEBOOK

"If you're planning to go it alone, the good news is you can get all the help you need from the WORKING SOLO SOURCEBOOK. This book is proof positive that we're living smack dab in the middle of the Information Age. It's an invaluable guide to entrepreneurial wisdom."

> —Jay Conrad Levinson
> Author, *Guerrilla Marketing*

"What a fabulous resource! Finally, a comprehensive and easy-to-read reference book for the entrepreneurial businessperson. All you need—organizations, seminars, tax information, books, and more—is right at your fingertips."

> —Leslie Smith
> Associate Director, National Association
> for Female Executives (NAFE)

"Every self-bosser knows you can never have too much time, information, or inspiration. This book points you to the best resources available. If you dream of building an extraordinary business, help starts here."

> —Barbara J. Winter
> Author, *Making a Living Without a Job*

working solo®
SOURCEBOOK

Essential Resources
for Independent Entrepeneurs

Terri Lonier

Portico Press

WORKING SOLO SOURCEBOOK
Essential Resources for Independent Entrepreneurs
by Terri Lonier

Published by:

Portico Press
PO Box 190
New Paltz, NY 12561-0190
914/255-7165
914/255-2116 (fax)

Cover Design: Leslie Newman, Newman Design/Illustration, Seattle
Author photo: Arthur L. Cohen, Arthur Cohen Photography, New York City

Library of Congress Cataloging-in-Publication Data

Lonier, Terri.
    Working Solo Sourcebook: Essential Resources for Independent
Entrepreneurs / by Terri Lonier
        p. cm.
        Includes index.
    ISBN 1-883282-50-0 cloth
    ISBN 1-883282-60-8 trade paper

1. Self-employed—United States—Directories. 2. Entrepreneurship—
United States—Directories. 3. Small business—United States—Directories.
I. Title.
HD8037.U6L652   1995
658'.041—dc20   94-67631

Distributed to the trade by Publishers Group West
800/788-3123

Printed in the United States of America
10 9 8 7 6 5 4 3 2 1

Acknowledgments

One of the joys of working solo is knowing that even though you're operating independently, you never need to work alone. In creating the WORKING SOLO SOURCEBOOK, I have been fortunate to team up with many individuals. Each generously shared ideas, time, and energy to make this volume the complete reference it is.

First, kudos to my two research assistants, Jessica Dubin and Melissa Spinelli, for their superb work in organizing information and tracking down details. Jessica's efforts gave the project its important initial momentum, while Melissa helped pull the final pieces together and assisted in preparing the electronic version of the SOURCEBOOK for its online debut. Their focused energies contributed greatly to the quality of the information gathered here, and I am pleased they could be my partners in this endeavor.

Many librarians and other information professionals assisted with this project, and I am grateful for their guidance and support. Thanks to Resource Development Librarian Terry King at the SUNY College at New Paltz Library and fellow research librarians Fran Seaholm and Shirley Tung. Mary Hujsak, librarian for the American Craft Council, offered help in locating valuable resources for creative professionals. Gratitude also goes to "cybrarian" Karin Sedestrom for her online research assistance. Special appreciation is extended to Margaret Hickey, U.S. Small Business Administration librarian, for sharing her time and expertise while I was conducting research in Washington, D.C.

During the publishing process I was pleased to have a superb team of professionals to guide me through the transformation of my mammoth database into this printed volume. Thanks to Ellen Leanse for her on-target editorial insights and to Nancy Stabile for her skillful copyediting of the introductions and sidebars. It was a pleasure to work with Leslie Newman—who brought her cheerful energy and creative talents to designing the cover, interior layout templates, and icons—and to have her assistant Flora Wong as part of the team. I'm also grateful to techno-wizards Bob Delio, Tim Celeski, and Wayne Wong for providing a safety net with their technical expertise while I pushed the limits of computer-based publishing. Appreciation is also extended to Richard Beatty for his aesthetic talents in turning the icon drawings into a PostScript font.

The WORKING SOLO SOURCEBOOK will soon extend to other media, and I feel fortunate to have found individuals who share the vision of electronic information access, particularly Barbie O'Connor, Suzanne Lassen, Richard Gingras, Christopher Bargeron, Judy Borman, Pete Johnson, and Nora Kim. Thank you, all.

The independent publishing community continues to provide me a wonderful network of colleagues and support. Thanks to Ed and Barbara Morrow, co-owners of the Northshire Bookstore in Manchester Center, Vermont, and to Kieran McKenna, Northshire's Business Books Manager, for their insights and helpful suggestions on how to make the WORKING SOLO SOURCEBOOK an even more valuable tool for entrepreneurs. I'm grateful to Dan Poynter for his publishing guidance, and to fellow publishers Greg Godek, John Kremer, Marilyn Ross, Elaine Floyd, Noelle Allen, and John Hetz for their ideas and feedback. Hats off to the dozens of marketing professionals at publishing houses large and small for their assistance. Thanks, too, to Susan Reich and the team at Publishers Group West for continuing to be an important partner in helping me serve solo entrepreneurs.

Appreciation is also extended to a special corps of individuals who offered ideas, inspiration, and support in so many ways. They include: Bill Allenson, Yvonne Allenson, Janet Attard, Barbara Brabec, Marianne Carroll, Marylyn Dintenfass, Jim Donovan, Jonathan Evetts, Susan Flynn, Gail Freedman, Charlie Gailis, Marian Karpen, Mark Kawakami, Joanne Larrabee, Jay Conrad Levinson, EddieLynn Morgan, Barbara Richardson, Barrie Selack, Fred Showker, Brian Smiga, Kimberly Stanséll, David Tisdale, and Dr. Thomas Zwart. Special thanks goes to Carol Vincie for her ceaseless efforts in promoting my work to others.

Most of all, I'm grateful to my family and my husband, Robert Sedestrom, for their patience in discovering once again how entrepreneurial publishers spend their summers—unfortunately, not on vacation.

Dedication

*Being an entrepreneur is a lot
like leaning out a window.*

*You can reach farther and
take greater risks when
you know that someone you trust
is there to grab onto your ankles
and keep you grounded.*

*This book is dedicated to
my husband, Robert Sedestrom,
for holding on tight as I've wriggled out
the entrepreneurial window.*

Publisher's Note

This book is designed to provide information in regard to the subject matter covered. It is sold with the understanding that the publisher and author are not engaged in rendering legal or financial advice. If legal or other expert assistance is required, the services of a competent professional should be sought.

While every effort has been made to make this book as complete and accurate as possible, information regarding small business and self-employment is constantly changing. Therefore, this book should be used as a general guide and with the understanding that it is not the ultimate source of self-employment information.

Portico Press accepts no payment for listings featured in this publication, and inclusion does not imply endorsement by the publisher or author.

The purpose of this book is to educate and entertain. The author and Portico Press shall have neither liability nor responsibility to any person or entity with respect to any loss or damage caused, or alleged to be caused, directly or indirectly by the information contained in this book.

Any person not wishing to be bound by the above may return this book to the publisher for a refund.

Table of Contents

Introduction

Ask a group of successful entrepreneurs to name the essential elements for success, and chances are they'll agree on two central points: the value of information, and the importance of staying connected. Savvy entrepreneurs understand that you don't need to know all the answers to your questions. What's far more valuable is having *access* to the proper information so you can make informed decisions.

Similarly, entrepreneurs who have achieved success understand that the path to the top is much easier—and far more enjoyable—if you've established a strong network with others. Sharing information and energy creates a dynamic synergy that's impressive in its power. Ideas, solutions, brainstorms, and insights seem to flow easily and effortlessly among entrepreneurial colleagues.

These dual elements of information and networking are the primary goals of the WORKING SOLO SOURCEBOOK: to provide easy access to valuable business resources for entrepreneurs, and to assist them in making connections with others on their path to success.

In these pages you'll find more than 1,200 resources ready to use in your own entrepreneurial endeavors. Perhaps you're seeking to boost your understanding of a particular subject. Or you're on the lookout for a new source of supplies or equipment. Maybe you're wondering if anyone else shares your passion for a specific subject, or you want to connect with like-minded spirits in a seminar or workshop. All these solutions, and much more, await your discovery within these pages.

You can access the information in the WORKING SOLO SOURCEBOOK in several ways. The *Table of Contents* lists more than 40 different subject headings, many of which are cross-referenced within the chapters themselves. Each individual resource listing is accompanied by a small icon indicating what type of resource it is. For example, if you're searching for audiotapes on a variety of subjects, you can flip through the pages and find the graphic showing the individual wearing the Walkman-type headset.

Throughout the book you'll also find sidebars that offer professional tips and practical techniques on how to use these entrepreneurial resources to save you time, energy, and money. The index in the back of the book offers yet another way to find the information you need. With such a variety of access points, we're sure you'll soon discover your own favorite methods of locating and using the wealth of information provided here. To get the most out of your efforts right from the beginning, be sure to read the next section, *How to Use This Sourcebook*. It's filled with advice on how to make your searches pay off.

The WORKING SOLO SOURCEBOOK is designed to be a living document, reflecting the vast reservoir of information available to this growing field. The project grew out of the resource section from my original business guidebook, WORKING SOLO. The flood of positive responses from that 14-page resource collection confirmed my hunch that solo entrepreneurs are—like me—hungry to find and tap into more of these valuable information pools.

The SOURCEBOOK was launched with the realization that it would change and grow over time. This has been true in the first year of research, and I'm certain it will continue that way as each year brings new materials and new individuals to the community of solo entrepreneurs.

As a dynamic resource, the WORKING SOLO SOURCEBOOK will be updated periodically. It also will appear in other formats such as the electronic options of online computer networks or on CD-ROM disk. With this inaugural printed edition, the goal was to gather as complete a survey as possible of resources that would enhance the work lives of solo entrepreneurs. As with most references, there is some information that will change over time. I also know that we might have overlooked some valuable entries—perhaps a favorite resource of yours.

If you'd like to share this information or point us in the direction of a new discovery, we would enjoy hearing from you. A form is included in the back of the book to capture all the information we need. It's my hope that subsequent editions of the WORKING SOLO SOURCEBOOK will reflect the feedback and insights of solo entrepreneurs throughout the country, working in all types of businesses.

Most of all, this book is a celebration of the energy, creativity, and vision of millions of independent entrepreneurs. As we zoom toward the year 2000, the landscape of American business is being dramatically changed by the dual impact of information and entrepreneurship. Technology now allows us to access information with greater speed and in larger quantities than previous generations may have gathered in a *lifetime*. In this same era, more individuals are starting businesses—particularly solo endeavors—than at any other time in our nation's history. Together, these forces create an exciting new world of opportunity for individuals who know how to harness information and use it for their entrepreneurial efforts.

You're likely to be among these solo pioneers creating the new services, products, and markets for the 21st century. Let the WORKING SOLO SOURCEBOOK be your gateway to information and connections on your entrepreneurial journey. May it bring you much success!

How to Use This Sourcebook

The WORKING SOLO SOURCEBOOK is jam-packed with thousands of valuable bits of information to help you on your path to entrepreneurial success. For these resources to be of greatest benefit, however, you need to be able to access, understand, and use them. The following pages highlight some of the numerous ways you can put the SOURCEBOOK to work for your business. The few moments you take to review them will pay off in your ability to maximize the SOURCEBOOK's resources and profit from the many opportunities they present.

A Guide to the Icons

One of the features that sets the WORKING SOLO SOURCEBOOK apart from other directories is the use of icons. These miniature graphic images enable you to scan a listing and immediately know in which format the information is available as well as grasp other basic details about the resource. Here are the icons and a quick summary of what they represent:

 The **book icon** indicates that the resource is printed material available in hardcover, paperback, or binder format. Most listings include the date of the publication and the page count to help you determine the age of the information (some data are more time-sensitive than others) and the extent or depth of the coverage.

 The **magazine icon** represents material published in a serial, or ongoing, way, such as magazines or newsletters. It also is used for pamphlets, booklets, workbooks, and other publications generally less than 80 pages in length.

The **audiotape icon** is the image of the person wearing a headset commonly used with portable cassette players. It signifies that the material is available in recorded form. A listing usually includes details on the length of the tapes and how many may be in a set.

 The **videotape icon** indicates resources that are available in video form (generally in VHS format unless otherwise specified). As with audiotapes, the listings usually include length of time and number of tapes in a set.

 The **computer icon** represents resources that are computer-related, material published in disk-based format (either floppy disks or on CD-ROM), or information available through computer networks.

 The **education icon**, signified by a graduation cap, refers to entrepreneurial training resources. These range from complete programs within university business departments to seminars sponsored by nonprofit or independent organizations and self-study programs.

 The **networking icon** shows two hands clasped in a handshake, a symbol of the dynamic personal interchange that can occur when entrepreneurs get together. Listings include professional associations and networking organizations of all sizes, geographic locations, and professional interests.

 The **conferences icon**, represented by a speaker at a podium, refers to formal gatherings of entrepreneurs at which they discuss common concerns. This icon is most frequently used in conjunction with the networking icon, indicating an organization's sponsorship of an annual meeting, seminar, or conference.

 The **government icon** identifies entrepreneurial and small business information available from local, state, or federal agencies. Listings are located within the *Government Resources* chapter as well as in other related topic-specific sections.

The **supplies and services icon,** signified by an individual carrying a package, indicates companies that provide support to entrepreneurs through the products or services they offer.

Several listings have **multiple icons.** This means the information may be available in more than one format (e.g., a book and audio version of the same material). It can also indicate that the resource includes materials in two formats (e.g., an audiotape accompanied by a booklet or workbook). A resource may also carry two icons if it is related to two different areas (e.g., a government-sponsored book or pamphlet) or if it blends two areas (e.g., a computer-related supply). In some cases it would be appropriate for a listing to carry more than two icons, but space has limited us to a pair as maximum.

 You'll also find a **notebook icon** scattered throughout the book. These sections provide practical tips and insights on how to use the resources to best advantage in your business. They are based on the experiences of entrepreneurs around the country who have been working solo for many years, in all types of businesses.

The Listings

Each listing in the WORKING SOLO SOURCEBOOK is based on providing a set of core information. This includes: the official title of the resource; the author or contact person; a copyright or founding date; the page count, frequency, or duration; the price; the publisher/provider contact information, including complete address and telephone number(s); and a brief description of the resource and its value to entrepreneurs.

Printed materials also carry an ISBN (International Standard Book Number) or an ISSN (International Standard Serial Number). These numbers (ISBN for books, ISSN for periodicals) are unique identification numbers assigned by the publishers. They make tracking down specific resources—particularly ones that have similar names or subjects—much easier.

The capsule summary in each listing is designed to give you an overview of the resource's content and focus. Since individual judgments and taste vary widely, a listing in the SOURCEBOOK does not imply an endorsement of any particular resource. Instead, the listings provide essential information that takes you a big step closer to finding the exact information you need.

How to Locate and Purchase the Resources

Once you have identified resources you would like to obtain, examine more closely, or find more information about, you have several options to pursue. Many of the printed materials can be located in public library collections or at your favorite local bookstore. If not on your bookstore shelves, they can usually be ordered easily by providing the ISBN identification.

Many valuable books are published by smaller presses and sometimes are not available through regular bookstore channels. If that's the case, a quick phone call to the number in the related listing should enable you to make the connection and receive the material quickly via mail order.

Be aware that simply popping a check in the mail for the price of an item featured in a listing may not guarantee its arrival. Addresses change, and many prices do not include shipping costs. These fees generally run $3.00–$5.00, depending on the item's size and weight and the method of shipping it to you. Better that you make contact via a telephone call, letter, or postcard first to save frustration and delays later.

Some organizations may ask that you submit your request in writing, along with a self-addressed stamped envelope (also known as an SASE) with appropriate postage. Many smaller organizations do not have robust budgets, and postage to answer hundreds of inquiries would deplete funds slated for member programs. If you send an SASE, make sure it is at least a business-size (#10) envelope so that there is ample room for the material you requested to be sent back to you.

An easy way to obtain information from a supplier is to call their toll-free number and request a copy of their current catalog. Of course, once you are on their mailing list, you may be deluged with subsequent catalogs for years to come. If you find yourself not using their products anymore, do the environment a favor and give them another call—this time to request that your name be taken *off* their list.

In conducting your searches, keep in mind that new and valuable materials are being developed all the time. By asking a simple question—"Do you have any other resources related to this topic that you think may be of interest to me?"—you may discover brand-new information that could be of great benefit to you and your business.

Sharing Extends Your Resource Collection

As you uncover new resources and locate information that helps your business, I encourage you to share your findings with others. This may be done informally with colleagues, through professional networks and organizations, online via computer networks, in classes and seminars—or through the next edition of the WORKING SOLO SOURCEBOOK. A form in the back of the book gives contact information where you can submit your nominations by mail, by fax, or electronically.

Experienced entrepreneurs know that we are all climbing the same ladder of success. Offering assistance to a colleague today means a helping hand extended to you tomorrow. May the resources gathered here give your business a boost up the success ladder. Along the way, keep your eyes and ears open for information you'd like to share. Together, we all enjoy the climb.

Advertising

See also Direct Marketing; Marketing; Promotion and Public Relations

As part of an overall marketing program, advertising can play an important role in spreading the message about your solo business. A well-executed advertising campaign can reinforce in print your other marketing efforts. The following resources can guide you in making informed advertising decisions. Some can help you analyze marketing goals and determine if advertising is a wise choice. Others highlight the steps to create advertising with impact, and how to use technology to save time and money.

If your solo business is in this field, trade magazines can keep you up to date on this exciting industry, while organizations and networks can help you make connections with other professionals.

Advertising, $1.00. U.S. Small Business Administration, SBA Publications, PO Box 30, Denver, CO 80201-0030. (800) 827-5722; (202) 205-6665. This booklet presents the basics of advertising and offers pointers on how to effectively advertise your products and services.

Advertising Age, by Fred Danzig, Ed., weekly, $76.00/yr. Crain Communications, Inc., 220 E. 42nd St., New York, NY 10017. (800) 678-9595; (212) 210-0111 (fax). This weekly trade publication for the advertising field features industry news and informative articles on trends and effective advertising campaigns.

Advertising From the Desktop, by Elaine Floyd & Lee Wilson, ©1993, 427 pp., ISBN: 1-56604-064-7, $24.95. Ventana Press, PO Box 2468, Chapel Hill, NC 27515. (919) 942-0220; (919) 942-1140 (fax). This book helps desktop publishers master the fundamentals of professional advertising design. Offers sound advice for each step, from creating a sound marketing plan to choosing fonts, selecting illustrations, applying special effects, and more.

Tracking Ad Results

One of the most challenging things about advertising is judging the return on your investment. Experienced professionals track the source of each response by keying each ad with a unique code. This might be a special offer, a department number, a telephone extension, or a series of letters and numbers. By asking customers where they heard about your product or service—and about the code in the ad—you can analyze the effectiveness of your advertising efforts.

 Business Ideas Newsletter, by Dan Newman, 10x/yr., $40.00/yr. Dan Newman Co., 1051 Bloomfield Ave., Clifton, NJ 07012. (201) 778-6677. This publication specifically targets advertising and marketing professionals and provides ideas and resources which can help increase productivity and profits.

 Copywriting Toolkit, by Wally Bock, ©1994, $9.95. RHE Publications, 1441 Franklin St., Ste. 301, Oakland, CA 94612. (800) 648-2677; (510) 835-8531 (fax). This kit, put together by an experienced copywriter, is designed to help you create stronger copy for your advertising and marketing materials. It includes two market/audience analysis forms, two product analysis forms, a copy-building form, the Classic Headline Idea Starter, the Offer Idea Starter, a form for analyzing copy, plus instructions.

 Do-It-Yourself Advertising, by David Ramacitti, ©1992, 192 pp., ISBN: 0-8144-0223-2, $18.95. AMACOM Books, PO Box 1026, Saranac Lake, NY 12983. (800) 262-9699; (518) 891-3653 (fax). This book presents a comprehensive overview of advertising, ranging from why you should advertise and what it can do for your business to tips on creating ads that are most effective for print, radio, or TV.

 Great Ad!, by Carol Wilkie Wallace, ©1990, 353 pp., ISBN: 0-8306-3467-3, $19.95. TAB Books, PO Box 40, Blue Ridge Summit, PA 17294-0850. (800) 233-1128; (717) 794-2191. This book gives readers information and techniques to enable them to create small business advertising on their own.

Guerrilla Advertising, by Jay Conrad Levinson, ©1994, 324 pp., ISBN: 0-395-68718-7, $11.95. Houghton Mifflin Company, Wayside Rd., Burlington, MA 01803. (800) 225-3362. Jay Conrad Levinson applies his guerrilla philosophy in entertaining, informative chapters that cover everything from developing a cost-effective advertising strategy to designing ads and writing copy.

Marketing Without Advertising, by Michael Philips & Salli Rasberry, ©1986, 240 pp., ISBN: 0-87337-019-8, $14.00. Nolo Press, 950 Parker St., Berkeley, CA 94710. (800) 955-4775; (510) 549-1976; (800) 645-0895 (fax). Phillips and Rasberry demolish the myth of advertising effectiveness and outline practical steps for marketing a small business.

The Advertising Handbook for Small Business, by Dell Dennison, ©1994, 296 pp., ISBN: 0-88908-798-9, $10.95. Self-Counsel Press, Inc., 1704 N. State St., Bellingham, WA 98225. (800) 663-3007; (206) 676-4530; (206) 676-4549 (fax). This book explains point-by-point what advertising is, how it works, and how it can work best for your small business. Includes worksheets to help you analyze your company's position in the marketplace.

Which Ad Pulled Best?, by Philip Ward Burton & Scott C. Purvis, ©1994, 172 pp., ISBN: 0-8442-3514-8, $16.95. National Textbook Company, 4255 W. Touhy Ave., Lincolnwood, IL 60646-1975. (800) 323-4900; (708) 679-5500. A collection of 50 case histories of advertising success, presented as matched pairs of ads. The reader is left to determine which ad generated the better response, while learning the creative principles of successful headlines, copy, and product positioning. The answer key with the actual readership scores for all 50 ads is $3.50.

Barter

Business owners throughout the ages have relied on barter—the exchange of products or services with others—as a way to obtain needed goods by bypassing more traditional commercial transactions. On an informal basis, many solo entrepreneurs use barter as a common means of stretching slim budgets or making mutually beneficial trades. In recent years, however, a nationwide network of professional barter exchanges has sprung up. These organizations, which allow individuals and companies to use their goods or services as a barter "currency," have greatly expanded the creative options for trading. This chapter of the WORKING SOLO SOURCEBOOK features some of the leading barter resources around the country. Explore them and discover how you can tap into this innovative trading network.

 Barter Advantage, Lois Dale, Executive Director, 1751 Second Ave., Ste. 103, New York, NY 10128. (212) 534-7500; (212) 534-8145 (fax). This barter exchange, based in New York City, has reciprocal trading agreements with more than 150 companies worldwide. The firm's computerized inventory network allows members to obtain a wide range of products and services, ranging from accounting and legal services to advertising, business equipment, travel, office space, printing, and more. Members receive a monthly newsletter and directory of participants.

 Barter News, quarterly, $40/yr., PO Box 3024, Mission Viejo, CA 92690. (714) 831-0607; (714) 831-9378 (fax). This quarterly magazine, written by industry practitioners, has been the "Bible" of the barter industry since 1979. It reports on news and developments in the industry as well as presenting tips on how businesses of all sizes can profit from bartering. Each issue is 80-100 pages and includes a free 30-word classified ad.

Barter Referral Directory: Small Business Edition, by Barter
Publishing Staff, ©1992, ISBN: 0-911617-64-7, $29.95. Prosperity
& Profits Unlimited, Box 416, Denver, CO 80201-0416. (303) 575-
5676. Ideas on setting up barter arrangements, whom to contact,
and details on how to make it a successful venture are all covered
in this publication, presented in binder format. For a listing of
other related publications, send a self-addressed stamped envelope
to the publisher.

 Barter Telemarketing Script Presentations, by Barter Publishing
Staff, ISBN: 0-911617-42-6, $29.95. Prosperity & Profits Unlimited,
Box 416, Denver, CO 80201-0416. (303) 575-5676. This book, in
binder format, presents sample telemarketing scripts for businesses who would like to barter with others. Covers bartering for
education, lodging, travel, meals, secretarial services, janitorial
services, and more.

 Barter Update, by A. Doyle, Ed., annually, $4.00. Prosperity &
Profits Unlimited, Box 416, Denver, CO 80201-0416. (303) 575-
5676. This annual update, published in January, summarizes press
releases and other materials from companies discussing new ideas
in barter, and new references. Back issues are not available.

The New Look of Barter

*If your notion of barter goes back to Colonial times when
commercial traders exchanged crops for furs on the early frontier,
it's time for an update. Today businesses conduct more than $7
billion in bartered sales each year. Savvy entrepreneurs trade
everything from professional legal, accounting, or design services
to items such as office supplies, airline tickets, or automobiles.*

*In addition to informal barter arrangements, a growing num-
ber of entrepreneurs are taking part in professional barter
associations that use computers to track complex exchanges. Each
participant obtains "trade dollars" for goods or services, which
are advertised in nationwide systems. Many find it the perfect
way to conserve cash while growing their businesses.*

International Reciprocal Trade Association (IRTA), 9513 Beach Mill Rd., Great Falls, VA 22066. (703) 759-1473; (703) 759-0792. Founded in 1979, this organization fosters the common interests of individuals and businesses involved in the commercial barter industry. The IRTA provides a range of services to members wishing to establish a barter exchange in their area, including the IRTA Information Exchange (see listing below), consulting assistance, and educational programs. A fax newsletter and newspaper are published, and annual meetings are held.

 IRTA Information Exchange, National Commerce Exchange of Tampa Bay, Largo, FL 34641. (813) 539-8719; (813) 531-4678 (fax). This information service, operated as a public service to the barter industry by the National Commerce Exchange of Tampa Bay, is a clearinghouse of information for individuals or businesses who want to start a barter exchange. The service maintains a library of sample operations manuals, newsletters, contracts, and other documents, many of which are available to IRTA members at a nominal cost.

 National Association of Trade Exchanges (NATE), Tom McDowell, Executive Director, 27801 Euclid Ave., Ste. 610, Euclid, OH 44132. (216) 732-7171; (216) 732-7172 (fax). This association represents the barter industry and 65 nationwide trade exchanges. Founded in 1984, it offers training, information on tax laws, public relations for the industry, and general support for businesses operating or interested in starting a trade exchange in their region. The organization also act as a referral center for individuals trying to locate a barter exchange near them. An annual conference is held in March, and dues are $295/year.

Bookkeeping and Accounting

See also Financial Matters

Keeping track of financial matters with solid bookkeeping and accounting systems is essential to the success of any small business. Strapped for time, many solo entrepreneurs shuffle these tasks to somewhere on the To-Do list between cleaning off the desk and filing. One reason is that the terminology can be complex and intimidating. The following resources provide ways to master bookkeeping and accounting, and they offer guidance on establishing systems that will put you in control of your financial recordkeeping.

Accounting for the New Business, by Christopher R. Malburg, ©1994, 300 pp., ISBN: 1-55850-349-8, $10.95. Bob Adams, Inc., 260 Center Street, Holbrook, MA 02343. (800) 872-5627; (617) 767-8100; (800) 872-5628 (fax). Written for the nonaccountant business owner, this guide explains the concepts needed to understand, establish, and improve a firm's accounting system.

Accounting Services for Small Service Firms, $0.50. U.S. Small Business Administration, SBA Publications, PO Box 30, Denver, CO 80201-0030. (800) 827-5722; (202) 205-6665. This pamphlet illustrates with real-life examples how an accounting service can help identify trouble spots in your business.

Basic Accounting for the Small Business, by Clive G. Cornish, ©1993, 208 pp., ISBN: 0-88908-938-8, $7.95. Self-Counsel Press, Inc., 1704 N. State St., Bellingham, WA 98225. (800) 663-3007; (206) 676-4530; (206) 676-4549 (fax). This book, written in plain English, provides basic accounting instruction for the small business owner, including handling of sales, cash, receivables, and inventories. Sample financial statements are included.

Bookkeeping Made Easy

One of the easiest ways to control financial recordkeeping is to make sure there's a paper trail behind every business transaction you make. For many solo entrepreneurs, this means buying everything with a check or credit card (along with keeping those receipts). Once a month your printed record arrives in the mail— in the form of your bank statement or credit card bill.

You don't have to invest in a special "business edition" credit card—just assign one of your regular cards to business-only purposes. You'll still need to keep a good set of financial records, but your paper trail will make it a simpler task.

 Dome Bookkeeping Systems, Dome Enterprises, Dome Building, 10 New England Way, Warwick, RI 02887. (800) 432-4352. This company manufactures a wide range of recordkeeping books and booklets to help you establish and maintain a strong accounting system. They also offer a series of financial software programs, currently available in PC versions only.

 Easy Financials for Your Home-Based Business, by Norm Ray, 184 pp., ISBN: 1-887810-92-4, $19.95. Rayve Productions, Inc., PO Box 726, Windsor, CA 95492. (800) 852-4890; (707) 838-2220 (fax). For business owners who lack a financial background and hate accounting jargon, this guide offers a simple, understandable way to manage and control the financial aspects of your business. Written in a friendly tone by an experience CPA, it offers time-saving techniques and 31 ready-to-use worksheets.

 Journal of Small Business Finance, by Rassoul Yazdipour, Ed., quarterly, $90.00/yr. JAI Press, Inc., 55 Old Post Rd., No. 2, Box 1678, Greenwich, CT 06836-1678. (203) 661-7602. This publication focuses on the financial, accounting, and economic concerns of small businesses.

Keeping the Books: Basic Recordkeeping and Accounting for the Small Business, by Linda Pinson & Jerry Jinnett, ©1993, 208 pp., ISBN: 0-936894-47-4, $19.95. Upstart Publishing Co., Inc., 12 Portland St., Dover, NH 03820. (800) 235-8866; (603) 749-5071; (603) 742-9121 (fax). This book provides a basic, hands-on introduction to small business bookkeeping, including record-keeping as well as preparing and analyzing financial statements.

 Quicken, $69.95. Intuit, P.O.Box 3014, Menlo Park, CA 94026. (800) 624-8742. This popular easy-to-use personal finance software has the power and features to handle the bookkeeping tasks of solo businesses of all types. Available in DOS, Macintosh, and Windows formats.

  Record Keeping in a Small Business, $1.00. U.S. Small Business Administration, SBA Publications, PO Box 30, Denver, CO 80201-0030. (800) 827-5722; (202) 205-6665. This booklet provides some basic advice on small business record keeping.

 Small Time Operator: How to Start Your Own Small Business, Keep Your Books, Pay Your Taxes, and Stay Out of Trouble, by Bernard Kamaroff, ©1994, 216 pp., ISBN: 0-917510-10-0, $14.95. Bell Springs Publishing, Box 640 Bell Springs Rd., Laytonville, CA 95454. (707) 984-6746. This classic has sold over 450,000 copies and gone through 19 editions since it was first published in 1976. It provides the reader with a panoramic survey of the start-up and management of a small business, particularly focusing on the financial and tax aspects.

 Step-By-Step Bookkeeping, by Robert Ragan, ©1992, 144 pp., ISBN: 0-8069-8690-5, $7.95. Sterling Publishing Co., Inc., 387 Park Ave. South, New York, NY 10016-8810. (800) 367-9692; (212) 532-7160; (800) 542-7567 (fax). This comprehensive handbook is designed for small business owners who have little familiarity with bookkeeping. Includes clear explanations of the basics of ledgers, balance sheets, tax forms, accounts receivables, and more.

Understanding the Bottom Line, ©1994, 128 pp., ISBN: 1-56414-108-X, $8.95. Career Press, 180 Fifth Ave., PO Box 34, Hawthorne, NJ 07507. (800) CAREER-1; (201) 427-2037 (fax). A clear, concise guide to standard accepted accounting principles for nonfinance professionals, including case studies for small business owners.

Business Philosophy

Savvy solo entrepreneurs know that learning from the "words of wisdom" of others is one of the best ways to avoid time-consuming mistakes and costly errors while building a business. A single idea can generate a remarkable shift in your own thinking and open new avenues of opportunity. The resources below capture the insights of some of America's leading entrepreneurs on topics such as goals, success, and achievement as well as personal and professional fulfillment. The authors share their experiences and offer inspiring examples of how an individual's unique skills and abilities can create a positive impact on the world.

 Career Shifting: Starting Over in a Changing Economy, by William Charland, Jr., ©1993, 252 pp., ISBN: 1-55850-259-9, $9.95. Bob Adams, Inc., 260 Center St., Holbrook, MA 02343. (800) 872-5627; (617) 767-8100; (800) 872-5628 (fax). Insights on using your skills and abilities in America's rapidly changing economy and evolving workplace, by a Senior Fellow at the Center for the New West in Denver.

 For Entrepreneurs Only, by Wilson Harrell, ©1994, 224 pp., ISBN: 1-56414-123-3, $21.95. Career Press, 180 Fifth Ave., PO Box 34, Hawthorne, NJ 07507. (800) CAREER-1; (201) 427-2037 (fax). Thought-provoking, inspiring lessons gleaned from an entrepreneurial lifetime by the former publisher of *Inc.* magazine.

 Goals and Goal Setting, by Larrie Rouillard, ©1993, 85 pp., ISBN: 1-56052-120-1, $8.95. Crisp Publications, 1200 Hamilton Ct., Menlo Park, CA 94025. (415) 323-6100; (415) 323-5800 (fax). This practical book teaches you how to establish and achieve goals more easily both in business and in personal life.

Growing a Business, by Paul Hawken, ©1988, 256 pp., ISBN: 0-671-67164-2, $11.00. Simon & Schuster, Inc., 1230 Avenue of the Americas, New York, NY 10020. (800) 223-2336; (212) 698-7000. A classic on small business—in both practical and philosophical terms—from the founder of the California mail-order firm, Smith & Hawken.

 Living the Seven Habits, by Stephen R. Covey, $59.95. Nightingale Conant, 7300 N. Lehigh Ave., Niles, IL 60714. (800) 525-9000 (orders); (800) 323-3938; (708) 647-7145 (fax). Expanding on his book, *The Seven Habits of Highly Effective People,* Covey shows how the seven habits provide an anchor in a rapidly changing and chaotic world. Includes five audio tapes, a laminated chart, and a workbook.

 Maximum Achievement, by Brian Tracy, ©1993, 352 pp., ISBN: 0-671-86518-8, $22.00. Simon & Schuster, Inc., 1230 Avenue of the Americas, New York, NY 10020. (800) 223-2336; (212) 698-7000. One of America's top professional speakers and business consultants shares his inspirational ideas and insights. Bringing together ideas and methods from the fields of psychology, philosophy, metaphysics, and human potential research for the first time, Tracy offers techniques that help raise self-esteem, improve personal performance, give greater focus to your efforts, and let you enhance your personal and professional life.

 Over the Top, by Zig Ziglar, ©1994, 288 pp., ISBN: 0-7852-7973-3, $19.99. Thomas Nelson Publishers, PO Box 141000, Nashville, TN 37214. (800) 251-4000; (615) 889-9000. America's #1 motivational expert spotlights the eight things people desire most in life: to be happy, healthy, reasonably prosperous, secure, have friends, peace of mind, good family relationships, and hope—and shows how to achieve them.

 Pathways to Success, by Michael D. Ames, ©1994, 275 pp., ISBN: 1-881052-57-5, $16.95. Berrett-Koehler Publishers, Inc., 155 Montgomery St., San Francisco, CA 94104. (800) 929-2929; (415) 288-0260; (415) 362-2512 (fax). This book features a collection of more than 100 letters from successful business leaders describing the values and qualities that are necessary for effective leadership and career success.

Personal Excellence: Where Achievement and Fulfillment Meet, by Kenneth Blanchard, $59.95. Nightingale Conant, 7300 N. Lehigh Ave., Niles, IL 60714. (800) 525-9000 (orders); (800) 323-3938; (708) 647-7145 (fax). In this six-tape set, leading business consultant Ken Blanchard teaches skills that allow individuals to feel more fulfilled by their achievements. A workbook is included in the set.

Powertalk! Strategies for Lifelong Success, by Anthony Robbins, $195.00. Nightingale Conant, 7300 N. Lehigh Ave., Niles, IL 60714. (800) 525-9000 (orders); (800) 323-3938; (708) 647-7145 (fax). This 12-volume library is filled with personal anecdotes, success-building strategies, and thought-provoking commentary. Each volume contains two cassettes, one with commentary and strategies given by Robbins, the other with an interview of his successful guests and a summary of their books. Among the guests are Charles Givens, Bernie Segal, Norman Cousins, Stephen Covey, and Marianne Williamson.

Risk Taking: 50 Ways to Turn Risks Into Rewards, by Marlene Caroselli & David Harris, ©1994, 147 pp., $17.95. SkillPath, Inc., 6900 Squibb Rd., PO Box 2768, Mission, KS 66201-2768. (800) 873-7545; (913) 677-3200; (913) 362-4241 (fax). The authors take readers through 25 low risks, then 25 higher risks, teaching how change can be the key to individual success.

Feeding Your Mind

How do successful solo entrepreneurs stay dedicated to their goals and fresh in their thinking? They're lifelong learners who keep books, videos, and audiotapes close at hand.

Just as good health comes from proper diet and exercise, a thriving solo business is fed by the inspiration and experience of others. Successful entrepreneurs are specialists in their fields but generalists in business—and always hungry for new ideas. They know that by investing in quality resources, they can piggyback on others' achievements and make their journey a more rewarding one.

Second Coming of the Wooly Mammoth, by Ted Frost, ©1991, 288 pp., ISBN: 0-89815-407-3, $11.95. Ten Speed Press, PO Box 7123, Berkeley, CA 94707. (800) 841-BOOK; (510) 845-8414; (510) 524-1052 (fax). A classic small-business survival manual, fully revised for the 1990s.

 The Courage to Live Your Dreams, by Les Brown, $69.95. Nightingale Conant, 7300 N. Lehigh Ave., Niles, IL 60714. (800) 525-9000 (orders); (800) 323-3938; (708) 647-7145 (fax). In this set of six audiotapes, Les Brown, a community activist and nationally recognized public speaker who overcame harsh childhood struggles to become a success, shows how to reach within yourself and find your strengths.

 The Ecology of Commerce, by Paul Hawken, ©1993, 272 pp., ISBN: 0-88730-704-3, $13.00. HarperBusiness, 10 East 53rd St., New York, NY 10022-5299. (800) 982-4377; (212) 207-7000. In this book Paul Hawken ponders the question of whether or not businesses can remain competitive in today's marketplace while being ecologically conscientious and protective of the earth's delicate environment.

 The Magic of Thinking Big, by David Joseph Schwartz, ©1965, 238 pp., ISBN: 0-671-64678-8, $10.00. Simon & Schuster, Inc., 1230 Avenue of the Americas, New York, NY 10020. (800) 223-2336; (212) 698-7000. This inspiring classic—which has sold more than four million copies—offers down-to-earth advice for learning how to control the power of your thinking to create success in every part of your life.

 The Master Key to Success, by Napoleon Hill, $99.95. Nightingale Conant, 7300 N. Lehigh Ave., Niles, IL 60714. (800) 525-9000 (orders); (800) 323-3938; (708) 647-7145 (fax). This inspirational four-video set shows the specific traits and skills that lead to success, including how to improve your self-discipline, communicate powerfully, take control of your mind, and develop leadership.

 The Official Guide to Success, by Tom Hopkins, ©1982, 152 pp., ISBN: 0-446-39112-3, $8.95. Warner Books, 1271 Avenue of the Americas, New York, NY 10019. (800) 222-6747. Multimillion-dollar salesman Hopkins explains his motivational and inspirational techniques to achieve success in this concise best-selling book.

The Psychology of Achievement, by Brian Tracy, $60.00. Brian Tracy International, 462 Stevens Ave., Suite 202, Solana Beach, CA 92075. (800) 542-4252; (619) 481-2977; (619) 481-2445 (fax). This series of six audiotapes and workbook features a motivational expert's techniques on high achievement, including taking charge of your life, developing a powerful self-image, achieving goals, and unlocking the potential of your superconscious mind.

The Psychology of Human Motivation, by Dennis Waitley, $79.95. Nightingale Conant, 7300 N. Lehigh Ave., Niles, IL 60714. (800) 525-9000 (orders); (800) 323-3938; (708) 647-7145 (fax). This eight-tape set explains six types of goal-directed motivation, the power of internal drive, seven guidelines for role modeling, and the importance of perseverance. Includes a 40-page workbook.

The Seven Habits of Highly Effective People, by Stephen R. Covey, ©1994, ISBN: 0-671-68796-4, $9.95. Simon & Schuster, Inc., 1230 Avenue of the Americas, New York, NY 10020. (800) 223-2336; (212) 698-7000. An audio condensation of this popular-selling book on personal management and business success. An expanded version on six audiotapes for $59.95 is available from Nightingale Conant, (800) 525-9000.

Think and Grow Rich, by Napoleon Hill, $59.95. Nightingale Conant, 7300 N. Lehigh Ave., Niles, IL 60714. (800) 525-9000 (orders); (800) 323-3938; (708) 647-7145 (fax). Since 1937 this classic has helped individuals achieve personal and professional success. This set of six tapes provides an audio version of Hill's philosophy and techniques.

Thinkertoys, by Michael Michalko, ©1991, 336 pp., ISBN: 0-89815-408-1, $17.95. Ten Speed Press, PO Box 7123, Berkeley, CA 94707. (800) 841-BOOK; (510) 845-8414; (510) 524-1052 (fax). This book is designed to turn readers into creative thinkers. It teaches how to develop new strategies for better brainstorming, problem solving, business invention, and marketing ideas.

Thinkpak, by Michael Michalko, ©1994, ISBN: 0-89815-607-6, $11.95. Ten Speed Press, PO Box 7123, Berkeley, CA 94707. (800) 841-BOOK; (510) 845-8414; (510) 524-1052 (fax). This pack of brainstorming cards are designed to stimulate creative, innovative ideas to help you make breakthroughs, start new ventures, or solve tough problems. Packed with a brief instruction booklet.

Timing Is Everything, by Denis Waitley, ©1992, 308 pp., ISBN: 0-8407-9163-1, Thomas Nelson, Inc., PO Box 141000, Nashville, TN 37214. (800) 251-4000; (615) 889-9000; (800) 448-8403 (fax). Waitley's philosophy on achieving success focuses on recognizing that everything one does has a season of conception, development, growth, and harvest. He explains how to get the best out of each phase for personal and professional fulfillment.

 We Are All Self-Employed, by Cliff Hakim, ©1994, 225 pp., ISBN: 1-881052-47-8, $24.95. Berrett-Koehler Publishers, Inc., 155 Montgomery St., San Francisco, CA 94104. (800) 929-2929; (415) 288-0260; (415) 362-2512 (fax). The author takes the notion of being self-employed to a new level, explaining that individuals in every sector of the American workplace need to view their career as a lifetime endeavor. It shows how to live with a self-employed attitude even if you are currently working within the framework of a traditional job.

 What the Pros Say About Success, $149.95. SkillPath, Inc., 6900 Squibb Rd., PO Box 2768, Mission, KS 66201-2768. (800) 873-7545; (913) 677-3200; (913) 362-4241 (fax). This 20-cassette program, compiled and published by the American Management Association, brings together experts from a variety of fields. Personal advice from Zig Ziglar, Denis Waitley, Peter Drucker, and many others is included in this inspiring and informative audio set.

 You Are a Natural Champion, by Zig Ziglar, $59.95. Nightingale Conant, 7300 N. Lehigh Ave., Niles, IL 60714. (800) 525-9000 (orders); (800) 323-3938; (708) 647-7145 (fax). Zig Ziglar's 24-step plan for achievement builds on an individual's natural gifts, from taking a positive inventory to what type of reading material is best suited for success. Includes six audio tapes.

Business Planning

See also Managing Your Business; Starting a Business

Taking time to craft a business plan is a step entrepreneurs often bypass in developing their business. In the rush and excitement to make things happen, the quiet, reflective moments required for planning frequently get postponed or ignored. Successful business owners will tell you, however, that time spent planning is some of the most valuable energy you can put into your business. Planning gives direction and purpose to your efforts and expenditures of time, energy, and money. The resources in this section can lead you through the many options of planning your business.

Keep in mind that the most effective business plans are used as dynamic documents—they change as your business, interests, focus, and goals change. If your enterprise has been up and running for a while, it may be time to review your business plan and see if it truly reflects the direction and future of your business.

 All-In-One Business Planning Guide, by Christopher R. Malburg, ©1994, 300 pp., ISBN: 1-55850-347-1, $10.95. Bob Adams, Inc., 260 Center St., Holbrook, MA 02343. (800) 872-5627; (617) 767-8100; (800) 872-5628 (fax). Addressing every major area in the small company, this guide shows how to design company plans and develop them so that they work efficiently.

 Anatomy of a Business Plan, by Linda Pinson & Jerry Jinnett, ©1993, 191 pp., ISBN: 0-7931-0618-4, $17.95. Dearborn Trade, 520 N. Dearborn St., Chicago, IL 60610-4354. (800) 245-2665; (312) 836-4400; (312) 836-1021 (fax). The authors provide clear and concise language to explain how to prepare an effective business plan for starting up a new venture as well as for organizing and implementing strategies for an existing business.

Biz Plan Builder, $139.00. JIAN Tools For Sales Inc., 1975 W. El Camino Real, #301, Mountain View, CA 94040-2218. (800) 346-5426; (415) 254-5600; (415) 254-5640 (fax). This software package presents a strategic business plan template in diskette form that works with any word processor, saving hours of typing and allowing users to edit instead of start from scratch. Available in both PC and Macintosh formats.

 Business Plan for Retailers, $1.00. U.S. Small Business Administration, SBA Publications, PO Box 30, Denver, CO 80201-0030. (800) 827-5722; (202) 205-6665. This booklet teaches you how to develop an appropriate business plan for a retail business, including inventory and start-up issues.

 Business Plan for Small Construction Firms, $1.00. U.S. Small Business Administration, SBA Publications, PO Box 30, Denver, CO 80201-0030. (800) 827-5722; (202) 205-6665. This booklet helps owners/managers of a small construction firm come up with a viable business plan.

 Business Plan for Small Manufacturers, $1.00. U.S. Small Business Administration, SBA Publications, PO Box 30, Denver, CO 80201-0030. (800) 827-5722; (202) 205-6665. This booklet provides the basic information necessary to develop an effective business plan for someone setting up a small manufacturing firm.

 Business Plan for Small Service Firms, $1.00. U.S. Small Business Administration, SBA Publications, PO Box 30, Denver, CO 80201-0030. (800) 827-5722; (202) 205-6665. This booklet outlines the key points involved in developing an effective business plan for a small service business.

 Business Plans That Win $$$, by Stanley R. Rich & David E. Gumpert, ©1987, 224 pp., ISBN: 0-06-091391-6, $12.00. HarperCollins International, 10 E. 53rd St., New York, NY 10022-5299. (800) 982-4377; (212) 207-7641; (800) 822-4090 (fax). Detailed guidance on crafting your business plan, based on lessons from MIT's Enterprise Forum.

Business Plan Toolkit, $150.00. Palo Alto Software, 2641 Colum-bia St., Eugene, OR 97403. (800) 229-7526; (503) 683-6162; (503) 683-6250 (fax). This software package includes computer spread-sheet templates, graphs, and a printed workbook designed to assist in the development of a business plan. The spreadsheets can be customized to work for nearly any business. The workbook provides a sample plan as well as chapter-by-chapter instructions for preparing a professional document. Available in DOS, Win-dows, or Macintosh format. Microsoft Excel is recommended for use with the spreadsheets.

Developing a Strategic Business Plan, $1.00. U.S. Small Business Administration, SBA Publications, PO Box 30, Denver, CO 80201-0030. (800) 827-5722; (202) 205-6665. One of the SBA's best-selling booklets, this publication helps you develop a strategic action plan for your small business.

How to Write a Business Plan, by Mike McKeever, ©1992, 272 pp., ISBN: 0-87337-184-4, $19.95. Nolo Press, 950 Parker St., Berkeley, CA 94710. (800) 955-4775; (510) 549-1976; (800) 645-0895 (fax). Author, teacher, and financial manager Mike McKeever shows how to write the business plan and loan package necessary to finance a new or expanding business. Includes a streamlined method for writing a business plan in one day.

Plan A, $99.95. Mighty Information Company, 184 N. Main St. #158, Champlain, NY 12919. (800) 363-9939; (514) 762-3212; (514) 762-3216 (fax). This software package includes valuable fill-in-the-blank tools to help you create a business plan, a marketing plan, an ad and publicity plan, and a financial plan for your new business. Pre-written documents guide you step-by-step through the process of choosing the right strategies for your company. The software then generates the printed reports and documents. Comes bundled with a free copy of Michael Shane's book, *How to Think Like an Entrepreneur.* Available in DOS, Windows, or Macintosh formats.

Planning and Goal Setting for Small Business, $0.50. U.S. Small Business Administration, SBA Publications, PO Box 30, Denver, CO 80201-0030. (800) 827-5722; (202) 205-6665. This pamphlet introduces you to proven management techniques which can help you plan your business.

A Dynamic Document

A business plan is most effective if you use it as an ongoing road map for your business. Don't let it languish in the back of some desk drawer. Refer to it often, update it as needed, and use it to keep you focused and on target toward your business goals.

 Small Business Decision Making, $1.00. U.S. Small Business Administration, SBA Publications, PO Box 30, Denver, CO 80201-0030. (800) 827-5722; (202) 205-6665. This booklet presents an overview of management approaches used to identify, analyze, and solve business problems.

 The Business Plan: Your Roadmap to Success, $30.00. U.S. Small Business Administration, SBA Publications, PO Box 30, Denver, CO 80201-0300. (800) 827-5722; (202) 205-6665. This video teaches the essentials of developing a business plan that will allow you to obtain capital and maintain profitability.

 The Business Planning Guide: Creating a Plan for Success in Your Own Business, by David H. Bangs, Jr., ©1993, 208 pp., ISBN: 0-936894-39-3, $19.95. Upstart Publishing Co., Inc., 12 Portland St., Dover, NH 03820. (800) 235-8866; (603) 749-5071; (603) 742-9121 (fax). This popular small business classic has been used by hundreds of thousands of entrepreneurs as a guide to putting together a complete and effective business plan and financing proposal. Includes examples, forms, and worksheets. Disk-based computer templates relating to the book are available separately for $12.95 in PC-compatible and Macintosh formats.

 The Successful Business Plan, by Rhonda M. Abrams, ©1994, 352 pp., ISBN: 1-55571-314-9, $21.95. Oasis Press, 300 N. Valley Dr., Grants Pass, OR 97526. (800) 228-2275; (503) 479-9464; (503) 476-1479 (fax). This book offers a start-to-finish guide to writing a business plan, and includes interviews and tips from venture capitalists, bankers, and successful CEOs. Gives a complete sample plan that shows where to put your facts and figures. Includes worksheets for ease in planning and budgeting. Also available in binder format bundled with PC-compatible software for $109.95

Buying and Selling a Business

See also Franchises

While most solo entrepreneurs turn their own ideas and efforts into a business, some individuals choose to buy an existing business as a way to jump-start their ventures. At the other end of the spectrum, longtime entrepreneurs may seek a way to sell their business, either to launch a new endeavor or retire to a less demanding lifestyle. In this section, you'll find resources that can help you with the many steps of buying or selling a business, including the legal aspects as well as the financial details of establishing a value and completing the transactions.

 Buying a Business: Tips for the First-Time Buyer, by Ronald J. McGregor, ©1992, 130 pp., ISBN: 1-56052-166-X, $15.95. Crisp Publications, 1200 Hamilton Ct., Menlo Park, CA 94025. (415) 323-6100; (415) 323-5800 (fax). This book takes the reader through the entire process of selecting and buying a business in a practical, real-life fashion.

 Buying and Selling a Small Business, by Michael M. Coltman, ©1991, 168 pp., ISBN: 0-88908-988-4, $8.95. Self-Counsel Press, Inc., 1704 N. State St., Bellingham, WA 98225. (800) 663-3007; (206) 676-4530; (206) 676-4549 (fax). This book contains vital information regarding the sale or acquisition of a business and pays special attention to the legal aspect of the transaction.

 How to Buy or Sell a Business, $1.00. U.S. Small Business Administration, SBA Publications, PO Box 30, Denver, CO 80201-0030. (800) 827-5722; (202) 205-6665. This booklet discusses several crucial techniques to help you determine the best price to pay when you buy or sell a business.

Institute of Business Appraisers, Raymond C. Miles, PO Box 1447, Boynton Beach, FL 33425-1447. (407) 732-3202; (407) 433-0908 (fax). More than 2,000 professionals involved with the appraisal of businesses and major business assets belong to this association. Membership is $195/year.

 Selling Your Business, by Holmes F. Crouch, ©1994, 224 pp., ISBN: 0-944817-20-3, $16.95. Allyear Tax Guides, 20484 Glen Brae Dr., Saratoga, CA 95070. (408) 867-2628. An experienced tax consultant shares insights on the many tax matters related to selling a business. Techniques are presented for evaluating intangibles such as patents, copyrights, licenses, contracts, customer lists, franchises, and goodwill. Nine methods for pricing the business are presented, together with pointers on preparing the sales contract.

 Small Business Valuation Book, by Lawrence W. Tuller, ©1994, 300 pp., ISBN: 1-55850-355-2, $10.95. Bob Adams, Inc., 260 Center St., Holbrook, MA 02343. (800) 872-5627; (617) 767-8100; (800) 872-5628 (fax). In clear language, this professional guide demystifies the many aspects every business owner should know about valuing a business. It examines the most commonly used methods and shows which approach is best to use in specific business situations.

Building Value in Your Business

Sometimes the most unlikely things in your business can bring significant value when it comes time to sell. Intangible items such as goodwill and your company's reputation can make it much more attractive to potential buyers. Similarly, good financial records and well-maintained mailing lists of customers and suppliers can become important business assets.

As you're building your business—even if you think you would never sell it—always keep in mind the value that your actions and recordkeeping might bring. You'll be creating a stronger enterprise, and your efforts might pay off one day in an increased selling price.

The Complete Guide to Selling a Business, by Michael Semanik & John Wade, ©1994, 172 pp., ISBN: 0-8144-0223-2, $22.95. AMACOM Books, PO Box 1026, Saranac Lake, NY 12983. (800) 262-9699; (518) 891-3653 (fax). A straightforward guide to selling a business that uses a four-step approach, from deciding to sell to dealing with the separation.

 The Purchase and Sale of Small Businesses: Forms, by Marc J. Lane, ©1991, 407 pp., ISBN: 0-471-52085-3, $112.50. John Wiley & Sons, Inc., 605 Third Ave., New York, NY 10158-0012. (800) CALL-WILEY; (212) 850-6000; (212) 850-8641 (fax). Includes all the necessary forms to complete the purchase or sale of a small, private-held business.

 The Purchase and Sale of Small Businesses: Tax and Legal Aspects, by Marc J. Lane, ©1991, 781 pp., ISBN: 0-471-52084-5, $112.50. John Wiley & Sons, Inc., 605 Third Ave., New York, NY 10158-0012. (800) CALL-WILEY; (212) 850-6000; (212) 850-8641 (fax). A comprehensive book covering the tax and legal considerations involved in the purchase and/or sale of small, private-held businesses.

 The Secrets to Buying and Selling a Business, by Ira N. Nottonson, ©1994, 250 pp., ISBN: 1-55571-327-0, $19.95. Oasis Press, 300 N. Valley Dr., Grants Pass, OR 97526. (800) 228-2275; (503) 479-9464; (503) 476-1479 (fax). This book is designed to give the average businessperson the necessary tools to buy or sell a small business. It shows how to estimate the value, productivity, and potential of small businesses, and gives advice on the risks, financing, and protection of small business investments.

 Valuing Small Businesses and Professional Practices, by Shannon P. Pratt, ©1993, 600 pp., ISBN: 1-55623-551-8, $90.00. Irwin Professional Publishing, Inc., 1333 Burr Ridge Pkwy., Burr Ridge, IL 60521. (800) 634-3961; (708) 789-4000. A comprehensive guide to assist business owners in assessing the true value of a business or practice as they consider buying or selling.

Choosing a Business

See also Starting a Business

Deciding the focus of your solo business is one of the most creative aspects of being an independent entrepreneur. The aim is to assess your talents and skills, match them with a market, and offer a product or service that is unique enough to establish your identity yet broad enough to ensure a strong customer base.

This section, one of the most extensive in the WORKING SOLO SOURCEBOOK, features two general categories of resources. First are items that can guide you through the self-discovery phase. These resources help you decide if self-employment is a good match for your interests and personality, and can assist you in determining in which areas you should focus. The second part includes resources that provide details on running specific businesses, including some that require specialized skills.

The chapter on *Starting a Business* also contains valuable resources to assist you in the early stages of your business development.

Career and Self-Assessment Resources

 Career Research & Testing, Inc., 2005 Hamilton Ave., Ste. 250, San Jose, CA 95125. (800) 888-4945; (408) 559-4945. This professional career counseling center produces a mail order catalog that offers a large selection of books, software, videos, assessment instruments, and other resources for career counselors and job changers. They also host an information-packed one-day workshop on starting your own private career counseling practice several times each year.

Careering and Re-Careering for the 90's, by Dr. Ronald L. Krannich, ©1993, 383 pp., ISBN: 0-942710-75-4, $13.95. Impact Publications, 9104 N. Manassas Dr., Manassas, VA 22111. (800) 462-6420; (703) 361-7300; (703) 335-9486 (fax). This book outlines the key job and career issues facing Americans today and contains practical how-to advice regarding skill assessment, networking, interviewing, letter writing and research.

 Checklist for Going into Business, $1.00. U.S. Small Business Administration, SBA Publications, PO Box 30, Denver, CO 80201-0030. (800) 827-5722; (202) 205-6665. This booklet highlights the important factors you should consider before deciding to start a business of your own.

 Discover What You're Best At, by Barry and Linda Gale, ©1982, 171 pp., ISBN: 0-671-69589-4, $10.95. Fireside, Simon & Schuster Bldg., Rockefeller Center, 1230 Avenue of the Americas, New York, NY 10020. (800) 223-2336; (212) 698-7000. This book's series of self-tests enable you to identify your interests, talents, and potential skills, then match them to profiles of more than 1,100 careers described in detail.

 Do What You Love, The Money Will Follow, by Marsha Sinetar, ©1987, 195 pp., ISBN: 0-8091-2874-8, $7.95. Paulist Press, 997 Macarthur Blvd., Mahwah, NJ 07430. (201) 825-7300; (800) 836-3161 (fax). This book is one of the classics on "right livelihood," the concept of work being consciously chosen, filled with self-expression and commitment, and the path that can ultimately leading to personal fulfillment and enlightenment.

 Finding the Hat That Fits, by John Caple, ©1993, 240 pp., ISBN: 0-452-26996-2, $10.00. Dutton, 120 Woodbine St., Bergenfield, NJ 07621. (800) 253-6476. This book focuses on finding a career based upon the needs of the individual.

 Finding Your Purpose: A Guide to Personal Fulfillment, by Barbara Braham, ©1992, 103 pp., ISBN: 1-56052-072-8, $8.95. Crisp Publications, 1200 Hamilton Ct., Menlo Park, CA 94025. (415) 323-6100; (415) 323-5800 (fax). Practical exercises in this book lead readers to personal investigation and to discover insights about the way they think and behave. Also available on audiotape.

Finding Your Work, Loving Your Life, by Nanette V. Hucknall, ©1992, 141 pp., ISBN: 0-87728-749-X, $10.95. Samuel Weiser, Inc., Box 612, York Beach, ME 03910. (207) 363-4393; (207) 363-5799 (fax). A spiritual guide to discovering and attaining your true vocation through visualization and meditation exercises.

Follow Your Bliss, by Hal Zina Bennett, Ph.D & Susan J. Sparrow, ©1990, 240 pp., ISBN: 0-380-75893-8, $7.95. Avon Books, 1350 Avenue of the Americas, New York, NY 10019. (800) 238-0658; (800) 6633-1607 (in TN); (212) 261-6800. The authors show how fleeting moments of intense personal joy can lead you to discover a more creative and fulfilling life.

From Executive to Entrepreneur, by Gil Zoghlin, ©1991, 192 pp., ISBN: 0-8144-5010-5, $24.95. AMACOM Books, PO Box 1026, Saranac Lake, NY 12983. (800) 262-9699; (518) 891-3653 (fax). Advice on making the transition from the corporate setting to the entrepreneurial life.

Have You Got What It Takes?, by Douglas A. Gray, ©1993, 200 pp., ISBN: 0-88908-285-5, $12.95. Self-Counsel Press, Inc., 1704 N. State St., Bellingham, WA 98225. (800) 663-3007; (206) 676-4530; (206) 676-4549 (fax). This practical guide helps the individual assess his or her entrepreneurial potential. Checklists, quizzes, and worksheets help you evaluate your suitability as an entrepreneur and to chart a step-by-step plan for action.

How to Find Your Mission in Life, by Richard Bolles, ©l994, 60 min., ISBN: 0-89815-702-1, $9.95. Ten Speed Press, PO Box 7123, Berkeley, CA 94707. (800) 841-BOOK; (510) 845-8414; (510) 524-1052 (fax). Originally created as a segment of the popular job-hunting book *What Color Is Your Parachute?*, this material was recently recorded on audiotape by author Richard Bolles. He wrote it to answer one of the questions most often asked by new career seekers.

I Could Do Anything if I Only Knew What it Was, by Barbara Sher with Barbara Smith, ©1994, 322 pp., ISBN: 0-385-30788-8, $19.95. Delacorte Press, 1540 Broadway, New York, NY 10036. (800) 323-9872; (212) 354-6500. Written by the author of *Wishcraft*, this book helps you discover exactly what you want from life and suggests some innovative ways to get it.

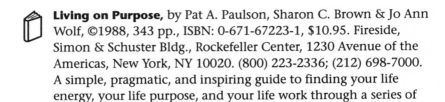

Living on Purpose, by Pat A. Paulson, Sharon C. Brown & Jo Ann Wolf, ©1988, 343 pp., ISBN: 0-671-67223-1, $10.95. Fireside, Simon & Schuster Bldg., Rockefeller Center, 1230 Avenue of the Americas, New York, NY 10020. (800) 223-2336; (212) 698-7000. A simple, pragmatic, and inspiring guide to finding your life energy, your life purpose, and your life work through a series of real-life examples and exercises.

Making Your Dreams Come True, by Marcia Wieder, ©1993, 288 pp., ISBN: 0-942361-78-4, $9.95. MasterMedia Limited, 17 E. 89th St., Ste. 7D, New York, NY 10128. (800) 334-8232; (212) 260-5600; (212) 546-7638 (fax). This book presents an easy, straightforward approach for getting clear about what you want, developing strategies to get you there, removing obstacles in your path, and realizing your career and life interests. It is filled with real-life stories, helpful exercises, and a personal workbook.

The Boostrap Entrepreneur, by Steven C. Bursten, ©1993, 284 pp., ISBN: 0-8407-9185-2, $18.99. Thomas Nelson Publishers, PO Box 141000, Nashville, TN 37214. (800) 251-4000; (615) 889-9000; (800) 448-8403 (fax). A down-to-earth guide to help you decide if you want to be an independent business owner, and how to make your business a success on limited capital.

The Self-Employment Test, by Steve Kahn, ©1987, 95 pp., ISBN: 0-681-40124-9, $4.50. Longmeadow Press, 201 High Ridge Rd., Stamford, CT 06904. (203) 352-2910; (203) 352-2190 (fax). This slim guide offers 64 probing questions to determine if self-employment is a good choice for you.

The Small Business Test, by Colin Ingram, ©1990, 96 pp., ISBN: 0-89815-516-9, $9.95. Ten Speed Press, PO Box 7123, Berkeley, CA 94707. (800) 841-BOOK; (510) 845-8414; (510) 524-1052 (fax). Through a series of questions, readers have the chance to test their interests and likelihood of success in a small business.

What Color Is Your Parachute?, by Richard Bolles, ©1995, 480 pp., ISBN: 0-8915-632-7, $14.95. Ten Speed Press, PO Box 7123, Berkeley, CA 94707. (800) 841-BOOK; (510) 845-8414; (510) 524-1052 (fax). This classic, entertaining, and caring guide for career changers has been helping people discover meaningful life/work options for 25 years. A new audio edition of the book is available, with nearly 11 hrs. of recorded information ($50.00).

Choose with Your Heart

Chances are there will be one business idea that makes you say "Yes!" inside. Listen to that voice.

It may seem silly to base an important decision on such an approach, but there are practical reasons to choosing with your heart. Your passion will sustain you during the long hours and inevitable challenges of start-up. Your enthusiasm will also turn you into a natural salesperson, an important ingredient for your success. Most of all, your business will reflect you—and bring a much deeper level of personal and professional fulfillment.

 What Do You Want to Be When You Grow Up: A Creative Approach to Choosing Your Life's Goals, by Margo Chevers, ©1993, 128 pp., ISBN: 0-9636202-0-7, $14.95. Grand Publishing, PO Box 1584, Plainville, MA 02762. (800) 858-0797; (508) 643-2978 (fax). Interactive exercises help individuals discover what they want from their lives, what steps are needed to attain it, and how to achieve these personal and professional goals.

 Whole Work Catalog, New Careers Center, 1515 23rd St., Box 339-CT, Boulder, CO 80306. (800) 634-9024; (303) 447-1087; (303) 447-8684 (fax). This mail order firm sells a fine selection of books and other resources—many which are hard to find elsewhere—on alternative careers, self-employment, home-based opportunities, and new work options.

 Wishcraft, by Barbara Sher with Annie Gottlieb, ©1979, 278 pp., ISBN: 0-345-31100-0, $5.95. Ballantine Books, 201 East 50th St., New York, NY 10022. (800) 733-3000; (212) 751-2600. This best-selling book presents Sher's down-to-earth, practical advice on finding the life work that fulfills your dreams.

 Work with Passion: How to Do What You Love for a Living, by Nancy Anderson, ©1993, $9.95. New World Library, 58 Paul Dr., San Rafael, CA 94903. (415) 472-6131; (415) 472-6131 (fax). The author presents nine "passion secrets" that successful people know and use to make their lives personally and professionally creative, balanced, and fulfilling.

Zen and the Art of Making a Living, by Laurence G. Boldt, ©1991, 599 pp., ISBN: 0-14-019469-X, $16.00. Penguin/Arkana, 120 Woodbine St., Bergenfield, NJ 07621. (800) 253-6476. A practical guide to discovering and creating the career—and the life—you want. Includes more than 500 quotations from writers, sages, and philosophers as well as 120 easy-to-use worksheets.

Resources for Specific Businesses

100 Best Retirement Businesses, by Lisa Angowski Rogak with David H. Bangs, Jr., ©1994, 408 pp., ISBN: 0-936894-54-7, $15.95. Upstart Publishing Co., Inc., 12 Portland St., Dover, NH 03820. (800) 235-8866; (603) 749-5071; (603) 742-9121 (fax). This book offers retirees information on entrepreneurial options, including details on the most interesting and most lucrative businesses. Covers ease of start-up, financial investment requirements, time commitments, pros and cons of each business, and sources for additional information.

1001 Businesses You Can Start From Home, by Daryl Allen Hall, ©1992, 292 pp., ISBN: 0-471-55849-4, $14.95. John Wiley & Sons, Inc., 605 Third Ave., New York, NY 10158-0012. (800) CALL-WILEY; (212) 850-6000. A comprehensive collection of home-based business ideas, including details on estimated start-up costs, whether it is good for urban or rural locations, and opportunities for the physically challenged.

101 Best Businesses to Start, by Sharon Kahn & Philip Leiff, ©1992, 456 pp., ISBN: 0-385-24180-1, $15.00. Doubleday and Company, Inc., 1540 Broadway, New York, NY 10036. (800) 323-9872; (212) 354-6500. A collection of 101 potential businesses, with guidelines on starting and operating costs, profit projections, and staffing needs for each venture. Also includes real-life stories that present both the pitfalls and rewards of starting a business.

199 Great Home Businesses You Can Start (and Succeed in) for Under $1,000, by Tyler G. Hicks, ©1994, 288 pp., ISBN: 1-55958-224-3, $12.95. Prima Publishing, PO Box 1260, Rocklin, CA 95677-1260. (916) 632-7400; (916) 632-7668 (fax). How to choose the best home business based on your personality type.

250 Home-Based Jobs, by Scott C. Olson, ©1990, 235 pp., ISBN: 0-13-934050-5, $9.95. Simon & Schuster, Inc., 1230 Avenue of the Americas, New York, NY 10020. (800) 223-2336; (212) 698-7000. This book presents 250 innovative business opportunities, along with details on how to get started, what training and/or equipment is needed, what it will cost, and sources for additional information for each business.

 555 Ways to Earn Extra Money, by Jay Conrad Levinson, ©1982, 422 pp., ISBN: 0-8050-1459-4, $12.95. Henry Holt and Company, Inc., 115 W. 18th St., New York, NY 10011. (800) 488-5233; (212) 886-9200. This book is filled with hundreds of ideas for part-time or full-time businesses, organized by personal interest areas (e.g., if you like to work with people, with things, in artistic endeavors). Includes a detailed resource section.

 900 Know-How: How to Succeed with Your Own 900 Number Business, by Robert Mastin, ©1994, 320 pp., ISBN: 0-9632790-6-8, $19.95. Aegis Publishing Group, 796 Aquidneck Ave., Newport, RI 02842. (800) 828-6961; (401) 849-4200. This book presents an overview of essential details on setting up your own business selling information via the telephone. It shows how to launch your own pay-per-call firm using 900 numbers, and includes tips on avoiding common mistakes, how to target a market, and how to track costs. An extensive resource section offers information on trade associations, service providers, and government regulations.

 Best Home Businesses for the 90's, by Paul & Sarah Edwards, ©1991, 268 pp., ISBN: 0-87477-633-3, $11.95. Putnam Publishing Group, 200 Madison Ave., New York, NY 10016. (800) 631-8571; (212) 951-8400. Details on 70 home-based businesses, including skills you need to have, start-up costs, advantages and disadvantages, pricing, potential earnings, best ways to get business, franchises, first steps, and where to get further information.

Bookkeeping on Your Home-Based PC, by Linda Stern, ©1993, 240 pp., ISBN: 0-8306-4304-4, $14.95. Windcrest/McGraw-Hill, 111 W. 19th St., New York, NY 10017. (800) 822-8158; (212) 337-5002. This is a turn-key guide for the person who wants to start of home-based bookkeeping business. Successful bookkeepers offer their advice on every aspect of the business: winning and retaining clients, using accounting software, branching out into related businesses, and more.

Catering Like a Pro, by Francine Halvorsen, ©1994, 288 pp., ISBN: 0-471-59522-5, $16.95. John Wiley & Sons, Inc., 605 Third Ave., New York, NY 10158-0012. (800) CALL-WILEY; (212) 850-6000; (212) 850-8641 (fax). For first-time caterers and seasoned professionals, this book covers all the bases of operating a catering business, from budgeting, legal, and sanitation issues to menu and event planning and landing new accounts.

 Cleaning Up for a Living, by Don Aslett and Mark Browning, ©1991, 208 pp., ISBN: 1-55870-206-7, $12.95. Betterway Books, 1507 Dana Avenue, Cincinnati, OH 45207. (800) 289-0963; (513) 531-4082 (fax). Everything you need to know to become a successful building service contractor. Includes charts, forms, and an equipment list.

 Crafting As a Business, by Wendy Rosen, ©1994, 160 pp., ISBN: 0-8019-8632-X, $19.95. Chilton Book Company, One Chilton Way, Radnor, PA 19089. (800) 695-1214; (610) 964-4745 (fax). Written by a leading figure in the contemporary craft field, this book provides a blueprint for starting and growing a successful business in the crafts. It features details on every step of the process, from drafting a sound business plan to handling daily management challenges. Includes profiles of successful craftspeople and resource listings.

 Desktop Publishing Success: How to Start and Run a Desktop Publishing Business, by Felix Kramer & Maggie Lovaas, ©1991, 350 pp., ISBN: 1-55623-424-4, $29.95. DTP Success, PO Box 844 Cathedral Station, New York, NY 10025. (800) 634-3961 (Irwin Professional Publishing). This book, written by two professionals who have run their own desktop publishing (DTP) business for years, provides a solid look at what it takes to create a successful business in the field. Filled with tips on how to increase productivity, ideas for how to charge and bill for work, and profiles of successful entrepreneurs.

 Ecopreneuring, by Steven J. Bennet, ©1991, 288 pp., ISBN: 0-471-53074-3, $19.95. John Wiley & Sons, Inc., 605 Third Ave., New York, NY 10158-0012. (800) CALL-WILEY; (212) 850-6000; (212) 850-8641 (fax). This comprehensive book discusses entrepreneurial options in the environmental field, including recycling, safe foods and food packaging, green products, green travel services, environmental publishing, and dozens more.

Empire-Building by Writing and Speaking, by Gordon Burgett, ©1987, 190 pp., ISBN: 0-910167-02-8, $12.95. Communication Unlimited, PO Box 6405, Santa Maria, CA 93456. (805) 937-8711; (805) 937-3035 (fax). The author presents an easy-to-follow, 15-step process for taking core information and building a thriving business around disseminating it through articles, books, talks, seminars, audio and/or video tapes, newsletters, or consulting.

 Flowers for Sale, by Lee Sturdivant, ©1994, 216 pp., ISBN: 0-9621635-1-1, $14.95. San Juan Naturals, Box 642, Friday Harbor, WA 98250. (206) 378-2648. This guide provides a step-by-step plan for those who want to grow and sell cut flowers. Includes details on pricing, taxes, and displays, as well as information on how to grow, sell, and buy the flowers.

 Herbs for Sale, by Lee Sturdivant, ©1994, 256 pp., ISBN: 0-9621635-2-X, $14.95. San Juan Naturals, Box 642, Friday Harbor, WA 98250. (206) 378-2648. A practical guide to the many small business opportunities involving herbs, including growing culinary herbs, manufacturing herbal extracts, opening a small herb farm, blending medicinal herbal teas, and more. Includes references for supplies and materials sources.

 How to Become a Successful Weekend Entrepreneur, by Jennifer Bayse, ©1993, 208 pp., ISBN: 1-55958-288-X, $10.95. Prima Publishing, Box 1260, Rocklin, CA 95677-1260. (916) 632-7400; (916) 632-7668 (fax). Tips on creating an income-producing business that operates only on Saturdays and Sundays.

 How to Make $100,000 a Year in Desktop Publishing, by Thomas A. Williams, ©1990, 280 pp., ISBN: 0-55870-160-5, $18.95. Betterway Books, 1507 Dana Ave., Cincinnati, OH 45207. (800) 289-0963; (513) 531-4082 (fax). A nuts-and-bolts guide on running a DTP business, including how to deal with printers, price for profit, and market your products and services.

 How to Make $50,000 a Year or More as a Freelance Business Writer, by Paul D. Davis, ©1994, 320 pp., ISBN: 1-55958-221-9, $14.95. Prima Publishing, Inc., PO Box 1260, Rocklin, CA 95677-1260. (916) 632-7400; (916) 632-7668 (fax). A comprehensive guide for aspiring business writers, including how to find business, keep clients happy, and manage time effectively.

Sometimes a Business Finds You

Defining a solo business is an evolutionary process for many entrepreneurs. Your business may be up and running when one day you discover tasks or customers that bring a new sense of satisfaction—and a whole new business focus is born. Or a client may ask you to perform a job that's related to your current offerings but stretches you in exciting new directions, and you find that other customers want these new goods or services, too.

It's not unusual for a solo business to evolve, but you must stay aware or the opportunities will pass you by.

 How to Make Money in Your Ceramic Business, by Dale Swant, ©1993, 100 pp., ISBN: 0-916809-63-3, $5.00. Scott Publications, PO Box 828, Sidney, OH 45365-4129. (513) 498-0802; (513) 498-0808 (fax). This book focuses on issues of special concern to potters and ceramists and provides tips and insight into creating a profitable business.

 How to Open and Operate a Bed & Breakfast Home, by Jan Stankus, ©1994, 320 pp., ISBN: 1-56440-269-X, $14.95. Globe Pequot Press, PO Box 833, Old Saybrook, CT 06475. (800) 243-0495; (203) 395-0440; (203) 395-0312 (fax). A comprehensive manual for individuals thinking of entering the growing field of running a Bed and Breakfast inn. Includes details on what it takes to run a successful B&B, getting started, publicizing your business, pricing your rooms, screening guests, and more.

 How to Open and Operate a Home-Based Catering Business, by Denise Vivaldo, ©1994, 224 pp., ISBN: 1-56440-240-1, $14.95. Globe Pequot Press, PO Box 833, Old Saybrook, CT 06475. (800) 243-0495; (203) 395-0440; (203) 395-0312 (fax). A complete, step-by-step guide to setting up and running a successful home-based catering business. Written as an interactive handbook, this book incorporates checklists for plans and goals.

How to Open and Operate a Home-Based Crafts Business, by Kenn Oberrecht, ©1994, 224 pp., ISBN: 1-56440-485-4, $14.95. Globe Pequot Press, PO Box 833, Old Saybrook, CT 06475. (800) 243-0495; (203) 395-0440; (203) 395-0312 (fax). The author, a home-based woodworker, shares details on how to turn an interest or pastime in the crafts into a successful part-time or full-time business. Covers all the considerations that must be addressed, and includes helpful worksheets and checklists.

 How to Open and Operate a Home-Based Day Care Business, by Shari Steelsmith, ©1994, 224 pp., ISBN: 1-56440-580-X, $14.95. Globe Pequot Press, PO Box 833, Old Saybrook, CT 06475. (800) 243-0495; (203) 395-0440; (203) 395-0312 (fax). This book offers a candid, complete overview of the business of caring for children. Includes details on how to construct a business plan to obtain financing, how to become licensed, and tips for success and problem-solving techniques.

 How to Open and Operate a Home-Based Landscaping Business, by Owen E. Dell, ©1994, 224 pp., ISBN: 1-56440-451-X, $14.95. Globe Pequot Press, PO Box 833, Old Saybrook, CT 06475. (800) 243-0495; (203) 395-0440; (203) 395-0312 (fax). A complete guide to establishing a landscaping business, from how to decide if its a good choice for you to dealing with clients, subcontractors, taxes, zoning, financial matters, and other business concerns.

 How to Open and Operate a Home-Based Photography Business, by Kenn Oberrecht, ©1994, 224 pp., ISBN: 1-56440-241-X, $14.95. Globe Pequot Press, PO Box 833, Old Saybrook, CT 06475. (800) 243-0495; (203) 395-0440; (203) 395-0312 (fax). A blueprint for setting up a photography business, from the decision to take the plunge to the establishment of a successful independent enterprise. Includes interactive workbook-style pages.

 How to Open and Operate a Home-Based Secretarial Services Business, by Jan Melnik, ©1994, 248 pp., ISBN: 1-56440-398-X, $14.95. Globe Pequot Press, PO Box 833, Old Saybrook, CT 06475. (800) 243-0495; (203) 395-0440; (203) 395-0312 (fax). Details on what it takes to run a successful freelance secretarial service from your home, including tips on how to get started; marketing your services; dealing with taxes, zoning and insurance; setting up your office; and building a client base. Includes an appendix and bibliography with helpful resources.

How to Open and Operate a Home-Based Writing Business, by Lucy V. Parker, ©1994, 329 pp., ISBN: 1-56440-396-3, $14.95. Globe Pequot Press, PO Box 833, Old Saybrook, CT 06475. (800) 243-0495; (203) 395-0440; (203) 395-0312 (fax). Down-to-earth advice on establishing a home-based writing and/or desktop publishing business. Features profiles of 10 successful home-based professionals, as well as handy worksheets, checklists, and forms. Includes a bibliography and resource directory.

 How to Start and Operate a Home-Based Word Processing or Desktop Publishing Business, by Michele Loftus, ©1990, 192 pp., ISBN: 1-55850-854-6, $9.95. Bob Adams, Inc., 260 Center St., Holbrook, MA 02343. (800) 872-5627; (617) 767-8100; (800) 872-5628 (fax). This how-to book focuses on the variety of opportunities available for people interested in home-based desktop publishing and word processing careers.

 How to Start Your Own Business On a Shoestring and Make Up to $500,000 a Year, by Tyler G. Hicks, ©1994, 272 pp., ISBN: 1-55958-564-1, $12.95. Prima Publishing, PO Box 1260, Rocklin, CA 95677-1260. (916) 632-7400; (916) 632-7668 (fax). More than 1,000 businesses you can start from your home, including tips on day-to-day business operations.

 Make Money Reading Books, by Bruce Fife, ©1993, 208 pp., ISBN: 0-941599-20-5, $12.95. Picadilly Books, P.O. Box 25203, Colorado Springs, CO 80936. (719) 548-1844; (719) 548-1844 (fax). Written by an independent book publisher who hires and works with many freelance readers, this book shows you how to make reading a business.

 Make Money with Your PC, by Lynn Walford, ©1994, 96 pp., ISBN: 0-89815-606-8, $7.95. Ten Speed Press, PO Box 7123, Berkeley, CA 94707. (800) 841-BOOK; (510) 845-8414; (510) 524-1052 (fax). Distilled wisdom, careful advice, and hundreds of ideas on starting a successful business with your personal computer.

 Making $70,000 a Year as a Self-Employed Manufacturer's Representative, by Leigh Silliphant & Sureleigh Silliphant, ©1988, 224 pp., ISBN: 0-89815-241-0, $12.95. Ten Speed Press, PO Box 7123, Berkeley, CA 94707. (800) 841-BOOK; (510) 845-8414; (510) 524-1052 (fax). An step-by-step guide to creating a business as a sales representative for manufacturing firms.

Making It On Your Own, by Norman Feingold & Leonard Perlman, ©1991, 320 pp., ISBN: 0-87491-941-X, $12.95. Acropolis Books, 415 Wood Duck Dr., Sarasota, FL 34236. (813) 953-5214; (813) 366-0745 (fax). An overview of starting your own business, including details on 397 potential ventures. Includes practical tips for women, young adults, minorities, disabled individuals, and older adults seeking to launch an entrepreneurial effort. A self-test helps readers learn what ingredients are needed for success and how best to avoid failure.

 Making Money Writing Newsletters, by Elaine Floyd, ©1994, 132 pp., ISBN: 0-9630222-1-0, $29.95. EF Communications, 6614 Pernod Ave., St. Louis, MO 63139-2149. (800) 264-6305 (orders only); (314) 647-6788; (314) 647-1609 (fax). This book shares the secrets the author discovered while building a $250,000-a-year newsletter writing and designing service. It shows low-cost and no-cost start-up and promotional techniques, and how to hand-pick top clients. Included are reporting, interviewing, and proofreading checklists, as well as 39 copy-ready forms.

 On Your Own as a Computer Professional, by Richard H. Rachals, ©1994, 188 pp., ISBN: 0-9641054-0-3, $24.95. Turner House Publications, RD1, Box 85A, Groton, VT 05046. (800) 639-8488; (802) 592-3328; (802) 592-3438 (fax). Written by a professional with 28 years of experience, this information-packed book explains in a clear, easy-to-read style how to get started, how to survive, and how to succeed as an independent. Covers deciding what services to offer, getting your first jobs, setting yourself apart from the competition, screening potential customers, pricing, estimating, contracts, agreements, and more.

 Owning and Managing a Bed and Breakfast, by Lisa Angowski Rogak, ©1994, 250 pp., ISBN: 0-936894-65-2, $15.95. Upstart Publishing Co., Inc., 12 Portland St., Dover, NH 03820. (800) 235-8866; (603) 749-5071; (603) 742-9121 (fax). This guide presents an overview of the many aspects of running a B&B, including how to select the best location, deciding whether to hire staff, the reality of living with guests in your home, and the details of zoning, permits, licenses, and more.

Owning and Managing a Desktop Publishing Service, by Dan Ramsey, ©1994, 250 pp., ISBN: 0-936894-68-7, $15.95. Upstart Publishing Co., Inc., 12 Portland St., Dover, NH 03820. (800) 235-8866; (603) 749-5071; (603) 742-9121 (fax). Details on running a professional desktop publishing service, including financial requirements, choosing equipment, problem solving, setting rates, working with service bureaus, and more.

 Owning and Managing a Resume Service, by Dan Ramsey, ©1994, 250 pp., ISBN: 0-936894-69-5, $15.95. Upstart Publishing Co., Inc., 12 Portland St., Dover, NH 03820. (800) 235-8866; (603) 749-5071; (603) 742-9121 (fax). Features guidelines on operating a professional resume service, including details on opportunities and requirements for starting a service, pricing issues, marketing tactics, day-to-day operations, and more.

 Owning and Managing an Antiques Business, by Lisa Angowski Rogak, ©1994, 250 pp., ISBN: 0-936894-66-0, $15.95. Upstart Publishing Co., Inc., 12 Portland St., Dover, NH 03820. (800) 235-8866; (603) 749-5071; (603) 742-9121 (fax). This book provides information for prospective antiques dealers, including the different types of antiques businesses, pricing issues, repair and restoration services, buying from dealers or estates, and the business details of sales tax, zoning, insurance, and licensing.

 Publishing Your Art as Cards, Posters & Calendars, by Harold Davis, ©1993, 152 pp., ISBN: 0-913069-42-6, $19.95. The Consultant Press, Ltd., 163 Amsterdam Ave., Ste. 201, New York, NY 10023. (212) 838-8640; (212) 873-7065 (fax). This practical guide gives advice on creating, designing, and marketing art for commercial uses. Covers the economics of publishing, tips on dealing with printers, advice on image selection, managing your business, working with sales reps, projecting royalties, and more. Contains helpful resource sections and a glossary.

 Quality Child Care Makes Good Business Sense, $2.00. U.S. Small Business Administration, SBA Publications, PO Box 30, Denver, CO 80201-0030. (800) 827-5722; (202) 205-6665. This manual explains the academic, business, and legal dimensions of running a child care center.

Sell What You Sow: The Growers Guide to Successful Produce Marketing, by Eric Gibson, ©1994, 304 pp., ISBN: 0-9632814-0-2, $22.50. New World Publishing, 3701 Clair Dr., Carmichael, CA 95608. (916) 944-7932. This book offers farmers and market gardeners practical how-to guidance on making a living from the land. Subjects include: making a marketing plan; selecting crops for maximum return; selling through direct as well as wholesale marketing channels; pricing, regulations and insurance; promotion and advertising; and more. An extensive resource section is included.

 Sit and Grow Rich, by Patricia A. Doyle, ©1993, 160 pp., ISBN: 0-936894-48-2, $16.95. Upstart Publishing Co., Inc., 12 Portland St., Dover, NH 03820. (800) 235-8866; (603) 749-5071; (603) 742-9121 (fax). A step-by-step guide on how to start a petsitting and/or housesitting service. Includes more than 90 pages of forms and worksheets.

 So You Want to Open A Profitable Day Care Center, by Patricia C. Gallagher, ©1994, 128 pp., ISBN: 0-943135-53-2, $19.95. Young Sparrow Press, Box 265, Worcester, PA 19490. (215) 364-1945. This book contains a wealth of information and resources on how to start a day care business. Covers how to begin, legal and financial concerns, educational plans and activities, developmental needs, equipment and supplies, program cautions, and more. Includes advice and tips from experienced directors.

 So You Want to Open a Tea Shop, by Martha J. Jones, ©1993, 72 pp., ISBN: 0-9635241-0-0, $10.95. Proper Tea, 1717 Apalachee Pkwy. #429, Tallahassee, FL 32301. This book gives the account of a woman who designed and opened a tea shop/bakery business and the ups and downs she encountered in the process.

 Start and Run a Profitable Bed and Breakfast, by Monica & Richard Taylor, ©1992, 216 pp., ISBN: 0-88908-989-2, $14.95. Self-Counsel Press, Inc., 1704 N. State St., Bellingham, WA 98225. (800) 663-3007; (206) 676-4530; (206) 676-4549 (fax). An easy-to-read guide describing the necessary steps in beginning your own Bed and Breakfast inn.

Start and Run a Profitable Catering Business, by George Erdosh, ©1994, 176 pp., ISBN: 0-88908-772-5, $14.95. Self-Counsel Press, Inc., 1704 N. State St., Bellingham, WA 98225. (800) 663-3007; (206) 676-4530; (206) 676-4549 (fax). All that you need to know about running a catering business, whether from inside your home or from another location.

 Start and Run a Profitable Craft Business, by William G. Hynes, ©1993, 120 pp., ISBN: 0-88908-760-1, $12.95. Self-Counsel Press, Inc., 1704 N. State St., Bellingham, WA 98225. (800) 663-3007; (206) 676-4530; (206) 676-4549 (fax). This book provides a wealth of information about making and selling craft items.

 Start and Run a Profitable Home Day Care, by Catherine Pruissen, ©1993, 160 pp., ISBN: 0-88908-294-4, $14.95. Self-Counsel Press, Inc., 1704 N. State St., Bellingham, WA 98225. (800) 663-3007; (206) 676-4530; (206) 676-4549 (fax). This book offers a step-by-step plan for individuals interested in operating a home-based day care business.

 Start and Run a Profitable Retail Business, by Michael M. Coltman, ©1993, 168 pp., ISBN: 0-88908-767-9, $12.95. Self-Counsel Press, Inc., 1704 N. State St., Bellingham, WA 98225. (800) 663-3007; (206) 676-4530; (206) 676-4549 (fax). An overview of what you need to know about running and maintaining a retail-based business.

 Start and Run A Profitable Travel Agency, by Richard Cropp & Barbara Braidwood, ©1993, 168 pp., ISBN: 0-88908-277-4, $13.95. Self-Counsel Press, Inc., 1704 N. State St., Bellingham, WA 98225. (800) 663-3007; (206) 676-4530; (206) 676-4549 (fax). This book is directed at readers interested in making their livelihood as independent travel agents.

 Start Your Own At-Home Child Care Business, by Patricia C. Gallagher, ©1994, 160 pp., ISBN: 0-943135-08-7, $19.95. Young Sparrow Press, Box 265, Worcester, PA 19490. (215) 364-1945. This handbook offers advice from an experienced entrepreneur who established her own successful home-based child care business. Addresses legal, zoning, health, and safety concerns as well as the nuts-and-bolts business issues of finances, marketing, and daily operations. Also includes dozens of play-and-learn activities and plans.

Starting Your Small Graphic Design Studio, by Michael Fleishman, ©1993, 128 pp., ISBN: 0-89134-466-7, $21.95. North Light Books, 1507 Dana Ave., Cincinnati, OH 45207. (800) 289-0963; (513) 531-4082 (fax). A step-by-step overview of the details of launching a small design studio. Includes 21 case histories and start-up worksheets.

 The Complete Photography Careers Handbook, by George Gilbert, ©1992, 307 pp., ISBN: 0-913969-41-8, $19.95. The Consultant Press, Ltd., 163 Amsterdam Ave., Ste. 201, New York, NY 10023. (212) 838-8640; (212) 873-7065 (fax). More than 75 different career options, many suitable for self-employed entrepreneurs, are presented in this book. Includes an overview of each specific career, typical assignments, required training, salary range, resources, and more.

 The Independent Medical Transcriptionist, by Donna Avila-Weil & Mary Glaccum, ©1994, 512 pp., ISBN: 1-887810-22-3, $32.95. Rayve Productions, Inc., PO Box 726, Windsor, CA 95492. (800) 852-4890; (707) 838-2220 (fax). This definitive guidebook is a step-by-step manual for setting up and successfully running a home-based business that performs medical transcription services for hospitals, medical offices, and clinics. Includes detailed information on more than 300 independent medical transcriptionist topics, resource lists, and a glossary.

 Tradesmen in Business, by Bob Rowan & Melvin Fenn, ©1988, 226 pp., ISBN: 1-55870-103-6, $14.95. Betterway Books, 1507 Dana Avenue, Cincinnati, OH 45207. (800) 289-0963; (513) 531-4082 (fax). A comprehensive business guide and handbook for the skilled tradesman.

 Write and Sell Great Fiction, by Michael Levin, ©1994, $44.95. Altimus Audio, 4 Orne St., Marblehead, MA 01945. (617) 631-8121. This series of four audiotapes offers tips and techniques on how to create and sell fiction.

Communication Skills

See also Marketing; Promotion and Public Relations

When you're working solo, the line between your identity and the product or service you offer can be very thin. As a result, strong communication skills—as you present yourself professionally or make sales proposals—become a vital ingredient to your success. In this section you'll find resources to help you strengthen your abilities to communicate in person, in print, and on the telephone, as well as ways to improve your listening skills. If your solo business focuses on the communications field, be sure to explore the listed associations and networks that can enable you to connect with other professionals.

 American Society of Journalists and Authors, Alexandra Cantor, 1501 Broadway, Ste. 302, New York, NY 10036. (212) 997-0947; (212) 768-7414 (fax). Established in 1948, this association includes 900 freelance nonficition writers whose bylines appear on books and in leading periodicals. They publish a monthly newsletter and hold educational seminars throughout the year. An annual meeting takes place in June. Membership is $165/year.

 Association of Professional Writing Consultants, Lee C. Johns, 3924 S. Troost, Tulsa, OK 74105-3329. (918) 743-4793. More than 200 consultants, trainers, writers, and editors are members of this association. It promotes writing consulting as a profession, publishes a quarterly newsletter and membership directory, and offers a referral service and networking opportunities. Annual meetings are held in March. Membership is $35/year.

Business Etiquette, by Jacqueline Dunckel, ©1992, 160 pp., ISBN: 0-88908-531-5, $9.95. Self-Counsel Press, Inc., 1704 N. State St., Bellingham, WA 98225. (800) 663-3007; (206) 676-4530; (206) 676-4549 (fax). A primer on etiquette and manners in conducting business, including what to do in tricky situations such as accepting gifts from clients or when firing an employee.

 Business Etiquette in Brief, by Anne Marie Sabath, ©1993, 144 pp., ISBN: 1-55850-254-8, $7.95. Bob Adams, Inc., 260 Center St., Holbrook, MA 02343. (800) 872-5627; (617) 767-8100; (800) 872-5628 (fax). A concise review of the dos and don'ts for aspiring professionals.

 Business Letters That Get Results, by J. Hamilton Jones, ©1993, 228 pp., ISBN: 1-55850-042-1, $9.95. Bob Adams, Inc., 260 Center St., Holbrook, MA 02343. (800) 872-5627; (617) 767-8100; (800) 872-5628 (fax). A step-by-step guide to improve the effectiveness of business letters and other correspondence.

Business Writing for Results Seminar, 1 day, $149.00. Fred Pryor Seminars, 2000 Shawnee Mission Pkwy., Shawnee Mission, KS 66205. (800) 938-6330; (913) 722-8580 (fax). This seminar shows how to improve your writing and communication skills. Participants learn to develop a crisper and more personal writing style and how to write effective memos, letters, and business reports.

 Communication Arts, 8x/yr., $98.00/yr. Communication Arts, PO Box 10300, Palo Alto, CA 94303. (800) 258-9111; (415) 326-1648 (fax). This high-quality magazine is targeted to graphic designers, photographers, illustrators, and other communication professionals.

 Communication Briefings, monthly, $69.00/yr. Communication Briefings, 700 Black Horse Pike, Ste. 110, Blackwood, NJ 08012. (800) 888-2084; (609) 232-8286; (609) 232-8245 (fax). This publication provides communication ideas and techniques for small and large businesses as well as individuals.

Communication Skills Seminar, 1 day, $59.00. Fred Pryor Seminars, 2000 Shawnee Mission Pkwy., Shawnee Mission, KS 66205. (800) 938-6330; (913) 722-8580 (fax). This seminar focuses on strategies and skills for improving both verbal and nonverbal communication skills that can impact your business success.

Dealing Effectively with the Media, by John Wade, ©1993, 90 pp., ISBN: 1-56052-116-3, $8.95. Crisp Publications, 1200 Hamilton Ct., Menlo Park, CA 94025. (415) 323-6100; (415) 323-5800 (fax). This book can help all types of readers handle direct communication with the media comfortably and effectively. It provides tips on how to prepare for interviews, what to wear, the interview itself, and how to maintain reliable media contacts.

 Dealing with Conflict and Confrontation Seminar, 1 day, $49.00. CareerTrack, 3085 Center Green Dr., Boulder, CO 80301-5408. (800) 334-1018; (800) 832-9489 (fax). This seminar instructs you in remaining cool, standing your ground, and reaching for positive solutions when conflicts arise in the workplace.

 Effective Business Communications, $0.50. U.S. Small Business Administration, SBA Publications, PO Box 30, Denver, CO 80201-0030. (800) 827-5722; (202) 205-6665. This pamphlet offers information regarding communication skills in business and the important role they play.

 Effective Listening Skills and How to Listen Powerfully, by Ron Meiss, 4 hrs., $59.95. CareerTrack, 3085 Center Green Dr., Boulder, CO 80301-5408. (800) 334-1018; (800) 832-9489 (fax). Learn to master the art of listening, a sorely neglected yet powerful technique that can improve your business. Also on video (2 volumes, 2.5 hrs.) for $149.95. Video includes 32-page workbook.

 Effective Speaking for Business Success, by Jacqueline Dunckel & Elizabeth Parnham, ©1993, 216 pp., ISBN: 0-88908-276-6, $8.95. Self-Counsel Press, Inc., 1704 N. State St., Bellingham, WA 98225. (800) 663-3007; (206) 676-4530; (206) 676-4549 (fax). This book focuses on how to write and deliver a dynamic and persuasive business presentation that will cause people to really listen.

 Effective Telephone Techniques Bulletin, monthly, Dartnell, 4660 N. Ravenswood Avenue, Chicago, IL 60640-4595. (800) 621-5436; (312) 561-3801 (fax). This bulletin can be sent monthly to you or your employees. It consists of articles, tips, and techniques pertaining to telephone customer service. Subscriptions are annual or semiannual. Prices vary according to the number of issues ordered.

Everything You Need to Know to Talk Your Way to Success, by Burton Kaplan, ©1994, 288 pp., ISBN: 0-13-289067-4, $11.95. Prentice Hall, Career & Personal Development, Paramount Publishing, 200 Old Tappan Rd., Old Tappan, NJ 07675. (800) 922-0579; (800) 445-6991 (fax). This book presents specific solutions, step-by-step advice, and real-life examples of how to face communication challenges. Includes advice on language, body communication, and dozens of troubleshooting tips to pinpoint and solve communication problems.

 Execards: Business to Business Message Cards, PSI Research, 300 N. Valley Dr., Grants Pass, OR 97526. (800) 228-2275; (503) 476-1479; (503) 476-1479 (fax). These preprinted cards with more than 125 message options allow easy, professional communication with other businesses. You can choose from many styles and colors, all printed to order, with messages that thank, acknowledge, remind, or follow-up with others who have expressed interest in your business.

 Freelance Editorial Association, Ruth Rautenberg, PO Box 380835, Cambridge, MA 02238. (617) 729-8164. This nonprofit national organization works to promote the interests of editorial freelancers, including editors, indexers, proofreaders, writers, and translators as well as those involved in project management and desktop publishing. They publish and market the Code of Fair Practice, a Yellow Pages of members, and newsletters. Monthly networking meetings are held. Membership is $45/year.

 Grammar for Business Professionals, 6 hrs., $59.95. CareerTrack, 3085 Center Green Dr., Boulder, CO 80301-5408. (800) 334-1018; (800) 832-9489 (fax). Communication expert Pat Cramer demystifies the world of grammar, word usage, punctuation, and syntax, and teaches you to present polished, professional documents. Includes a 64-page workbook. Also on video (2 volumes, 2.75 hrs.) for $199.95.

 Great Connections, by Anne Baber & Lynne Waymon, ©1992, 194 pp., ISBN: 0-942710-81-9, $11.95. Impact Publications, 9104 N. Manassas Dr., Manassas Park, VA 22111. (800) 462-6420; (703) 361-7300; (703) 335-9486 (fax). This unique book reveals how the use of small talk can make great connections that are vital for business success in the 1990s.

How to Be a Great Communicator—In Person, On Paper and On the Podium, by Nido Qubein, $59.95. Fred Pryor Seminars, 2000 Shawnee Mission Pkwy., Shawnee Mission, KS 66205. (800) 938-6330; (913) 722-8580 (fax). Qubein, a master communicator, reveals his practical and proven system of self-expression, including the fundamentals of effective, attention-getting body language, power words, and perceptive listening.

 How to Gain Power and Influence with People, by Tony Alessandra, $59.95. Nightingale Conant, 7300 N. Lehigh Ave., Niles, IL 60714. (800) 525-9000 (orders); (800) 323-3938; (708) 647-7145 (fax). In this six-tape set, Tony Alessandra shows how people fit into four behavioral types, and how to communicate with each to gain the cooperation you need to achieve your goals.

 How to Handle Conflict and Manage Anger, by Dennis Waitley, $59.95. Nightingale Conant, 7300 N. Lehigh Ave., Niles, IL 60714. (800) 525-9000 (orders); (800) 323-3938; (708) 647-7145 (fax). This audio seminar reveals the skills essential to working more effectively with others and existing more comfortably within yourself. Includes six audiotapes and a workbook.

 How to Interview, by Paul McLaughlin, ©1990, 256 pp., ISBN: 0-88908-872-1, $9.95. Self-Counsel Press, Inc., 1704 N. State St., Bellingham, WA 98225. (800) 663-3007; (206) 676-4530; (206) 676-4549 (fax). This book focuses on effective interviewing skills and working with the media, and features anecdotal advice from famous interviewers such as George Plimpton and Robert MacNeil.

What Do You Really Think?

Before you do a presentation to a group or over the telephone, take time to write out your thoughts. Even if no one else will ever see your words in print, the process of putting ideas on paper (or a computer screen!) will help clarify your thinking.

When it's time to verbally deliver, don't read a script. Instead, refer to key points and let the spontaneous part of you take over. Fully prepared, you can make a confident link with your audience and achieve the communication results you want.

How to Make Presentations with Confidence and Power Seminar, 1 day, $199.00. Fred Pryor Seminars, 2000 Shawnee Mission Pkwy., Shawnee Mission, KS 66205. (800) 938-6330; (913) 722-8580 (fax). This seminar provides a collection of innovative tips, techniques, and strategies that enable you to speak with power, confidence, and skill.

How to Speak with Confidence, by Bert Decker, 46 min., $69.95. Nightingale Conant, 7300 N. Lehigh Ave., Niles, IL 60714. (800) 525-9000 (orders); (800) 323-3938; (708) 647-7145 (fax). In this video Bert Decker reveals the key techniques for grabbing any listener's attention. The program offers a step-by-step explanation of how to deliver intelligent, witty, and captivating presentations.

How to Take the Fog Out of Business Writing, by Robert Gunning & Richard A. Kallan, ©1994, 150 pp., ISBN: 0-85013-232-0, $10.95. Probus Publishing, Inc., 1925 N. Clyburn Ave. #401, Chicago, IL 60614. (800) PROBUS-1; (312) 868-6250 (fax). Principles and systems to resolve the most common writing problems from experienced teachers of effective business writing seminars.

How to Write Complaint Letters that Work, by Patricia H. Westheimer & Jim Mastro, ©1994, 247 pp., ISBN: 1-57112-063-7, $12.95. JIST Works, Inc., 720 North Park Ave., Indianapolis, IN 46202-3430. (800) 648-5478; (317) 264-3720; (800) 547-8329 (fax). This informative book explains how to write results-oriented complaint letters, including advice on finding the right person to address, deciding when a complaint letter is appropriate, and determining the proper tone. Includes a detailed listing of third-party organizations and agencies that assist in dispute resolution.

Human Relations in Small Business, by Elwood N. Chapman, ©1992, 227 pp., ISBN: 1-56052-185-6, $15.95. Crisp Publications, 1200 Hamilton Ct., Menlo Park, CA 94025. (415) 323-6100; (415) 323-5800 (fax). This book provides practical techniques, checklists, and exercises for developing better interpersonal skills in business relationships.

I Can See You Naked, by Ron Hoff, ©1992, 326 pp., ISBN: 0-8362-8000-8, $9.95. Andrews and McMeel, 4900 Main St., Kansas City, MO 64112. (800) 826-4216; (816) 932-6700. This book on making strong presentations is filled with practical tips blended with lighthearted, real-life stories and humorous illustrations.

Incentive Products, Successories, 919 Springer Dr., Lombard, IL 60148. (800) 535-2773 (orders); (800) 235-4217 (customer service); (708) 953-1229 (fax). Successories sells products that promote and reward quality teamwork and excellence, including items such as mugs, posters, and gift baskets.

 International Association of Business Communicators (IABC), Norman Leaper, 1 Hallidie Plaza, #600, San Francisco, CA 94102-2818. (415) 433-3400; (415) 362-8762 (fax). More than 12,000 communication and public relations professionals are members of the IABC. A monthly newsletter is published and annual meetings are held in June. Membership: $190/first year; $150/year thereafter.

 Leading Workshops, Seminars and Training Sessions, by Helen Angus, ©1993, 120 pp., ISBN: 0-88908-279-0, $12.95. Self-Counsel Press, Inc., 1704 N. State St., Bellingham, WA 98225. (800) 663-3007; (206) 676-4530; (206) 676-4549 (fax). This book provides the reader with clear-headed advice about how to organize and deliver workshops, seminars, and training sessions.

 Managing Your Mouth, by Robert L. Genua, ©1992, 192 pp., ISBN: 0-8144-7803-4, $17.95. AMACOM Books, PO Box 1026, Saranac Lake, NY 12983. (800) 262-9699; (518) 891-3653 (fax). A guide to help control what you say in every business situation.

 Memory Skills in Business, by Madelyn Burley-Allen, 80 pp., ISBN: 0-931961-56-4, $8.95. Crisp Publications, 1200 Hamilton Ct., Menlo Park, CA 94025. (415) 323-6100; (415) 323-5800 (fax). This book explains how the human memory works and provides several effective techniques to improve its function and capacity. Also available as a video/audiotape program for $95.00.

 National Speakers Association, Barbara Nivala, 1500 S. Priest Dr., Tempe, AZ 85281. (602) 968-2552; (602) 968-0911 (fax). This national organization serves more than 3,000 professional speakers, trainers, and other individuals involved with the speaking industry. They sponsor a national meeting each summer, mid-year educational workshops, and monthly meetings through active regional chapters. Members receive a magazine and informative audiotapes ten times a year, and can participate in an annual directory sent to meeting planners. Membership is $250/year, plus a $175 initiation fee (which includes a voucher for a $100 discount off a member's first conference).

Your Five-Minute Brag

For solo entrepreneurs, professional communication skills include the ability to speak spontaneously and confidently about themselves and their businesses. This verbal business card—something I've dubbed a "Five-Minute Brag"—is a series of prepared phrases that pop out of your mouth when someone asks, "What do you do?" In contrast to turning you into a resounding bore, it prepares you to speak concisely (or up to a full five minutes if a situation warrants) in an interesting, engaging manner.

It takes practice to develop your own verbal presentation, and to nimbly adjust it to match an appropriate business or social situation. Once prepared, however, a Five-Minute Brag often turns into a natural extension of your everyday conversations. It also becomes a way to showcase your business or to turn casual encounters into valuable learning exchanges.

 On the Air, by Al Parinello, ©1991, 190 pp., ISBN: 0-934829-85-3, $12.95. Career Press, Inc., 180 Fifth Ave., PO Box 34, Hawthorne, NJ 07507. (800) CAREER-1; (201) 427-2037 (fax). How to get on television and radio talk shows, and what to do when you get there, written by a longtime radio host. Includes a list of more than 800 national radio and TV talk shows.

 Powerful Presentation Skills, ©1994, ISBN: 1-56414-109-8, Career Press, 180 Fifth Ave., PO Box 34, Hawthorne, NJ 07507. (800) CAREER-1; (201) 427-2037 (fax). Key techniques to overcoming anxiety and stage fright, so you can make confident, dynamic presentations and generate audience interest.

 Powerful Proofreading and Editing Skills, by Michelle Fairfield Poley, $59.95. SkillPath, Inc., 6900 Squibb Rd., PO Box 2768, Mission, KS 66201-2768. (800) 873-7545; (913) 677-3200; (913) 362-4241 (fax). Learn to create flawless and functional documents by understanding the essential aspects of proofreading and editing. Set includes six tapes and a workbook.

Proofreading and Editing Skills, 3 hrs., $199.95. CareerTrack, 3085 Center Green Dr., Boulder, CO 80301-5408. (800) 334-1018; (800) 832-9489 (fax). Learn to catch and correct both common and uncommon errors, modify writing without altering intent, correct spelling and grammar, and express ideas more efficiently. A 44-page workbook is included with the three-volume video set.

Relationship Strategies, by Jim Cathcart & Tony Alessandra, $59.95. Fred Pryor Seminars, 2000 Shawnee Mission Pkwy., Shawnee Mission, KS 66205. (913) 722-8580 (fax). In this program, listeners learn to identify and understand the true nature of the people with whom they come in contact. Six audiotapes plus a Behavior Style Evaluation guide.

Small Business Model Letter Book, by Wilbur Cross, ©1992, 336 pp., ISBN: 0-13-718602-9, $16.95. Prentice-Hall, Inc., 113 Sylvan Ave., Englewood Cliffs, NJ 07632. (800) 922-0579; (210) 592-2281. This book features templates for hundreds of common business letters that can save you time and energy in creating your own business correspondence.

Telephone Terrific!, by David Dee, ©1994, 160 pp., ISBN: 0-85013-226-6, $10.95. Probus Publishing, Inc., 1925 N. Clyburn Ave. #401, Chicago, IL 60614. (800) PROBUS-1; (312) 868-6250 (fax). Facts, fun, and 103 "how-to" tips for using the phone as a business tool for success.

The Polished Professional, ©1994, 128 pp., ISBN: 1-56414-146-2, $8.95. Career Press, 180 Fifth Ave., PO Box 34, Hawthorne, NJ 07507. (800) CAREER-1; (201) 427-2037 (fax). All the dos and don'ts of business etiquette.

The Prima Guide to Better Business Letters, by Michael & Candace Fitzgerald, ©1994, 224 pp., ISBN: 1-55958-448-3, $19.95. Prima Publishing, PO Box 1260, Rocklin, CA 95677-1260. (916) 632-7400; (916) 632-7668 (fax). This book includes a computer disk containing more than 100 letter templates and sample letters for businesses on topics such as business development, financial matters, customer service, and letters to suppliers and vendors. Disk available for PC format only.

The Sound of Your Voice, by Carol Fleming, $59.95. Nightingale Conant, 7300 N. Lehigh Ave., Niles, IL 60714. (800) 525-9000 (orders); (800) 323-3938; (708) 647-7145 (fax). Communications expert Dr. Carol Fleming teaches you how to modify regional accents, avoid verbal mannerisms, and add strength, depth, and vitality to your voice.

 The Winning Image, by James Gray, Jr., ©1993, 208 pp., ISBN: 0-8144-7745-3, $17.95. AMACOM Books, PO Box 1026, Saranac Lake, NY 12983. (800) 262-9699; (518) 891-3653 (fax). Advice on improving your image, from wardrobe to conversation topics, including sections on intercultural communications.

 Think on Your Feet, by Dr. Keith Spicer, $99.95. Center for Video Education, PO Box 635, North White Plains, NY 10603. (800) 621-0043; (914) 428-0180 (fax). This video features tips, techniques, and drills to help you speak confidently without notes in front of others, whether making a formal presentation in front of a large group or sharing your ideas informally.

 Verbal Advantage Plus, by Mary Ann Easley, $179.95. Fred Pryor Seminars, 2000 Shawnee Mission Pkwy., Shawnee Mission, KS 66205. (913) 722-8580 (fax). This program aims to expand your vocabulary as well as provide valuable instruction regarding spelling, public speaking, writing, diction, and grammar usage. Twelve audiotapes plus a guidebook.

 Visual Aids in Business, by Claire Raines, ©1993, 88 pp., ISBN: 0-931961-77-7, $8.95. Crisp Publications, 1200 Hamilton Ct., Menlo Park, CA 94025. (415) 323-6100; (415) 323-5800 (fax). This manual teaches you how to design, make, and use visual aids easily and effectively.

 Why Didn't I Say That?!, by Donald H. Weiss, ©1994, 208 pp., ISBN: 0-8144-0209-7, $21.95. AMACOM Books, PO Box 1026, Saranac Lake, NY 12983. (800) 262-9699; (518) 891-3653 (fax). What to say and how to say it in tough situations on the job, including actual sample dialogs tailor-made for specific problems.

Computers and Technology

The wonders of our electronic age have contributed greatly to the freedom, flexibility, and success of solo entrepreneurs. At the same time, these technological marvels have created new levels of complexity and confusion. Use the resources in this section to expand your skills and understanding of how technology can be a powerful partner for your solo efforts. Books often present a topic in greater detail, while magazines, online networks, and associations provide access to more up-to-date information on this ever-changing industry.

If you're wary of diving in, take heart in knowing that *everyone* was a novice once and that no one can master every aspect of today's digital spectrum. The goal is to be always on the lookout for technology tools that can help you maximize your time, energy, and financial resources.

General Technology Resources

  Association for Women in Computing, Judith A. Andrews, 41 Sutter St., Ste. 1006, San Francisco, CA 94104. (415) 905-4663. This association promotes the interests of women in the field of computing from entry level to highest management through 17 chapters nationwide. Technical and training conferences are held annually. Individual membership is $10/year.

 Byte, Dennis Allen, Ed., monthly, $29.95. McGraw-Hill, Inc., One Phoenix Mill Lane, Peterborough, NH 03458. (603) 924-9281; (603) 924-2550 (fax). This mammoth monthly publication covers all computing platforms, but specializes in the PC arena. It features news, product announcements, reviews, and other industry information.

CD-ROM World, monthly, $29.00. Mecklermedia, 11 Ferry Lane W., Westport, CT 06880. (203) 226-6967; (203) 454-5840 (fax). This magazine presents the latest news and reviews of CD-ROM products and services.

 Educorp, 7434 Trade St., San Diego, CA 82121-2410. (800) 843-9497; (619) 536-9999; (619) 536-2345 (fax). Educorp is one of the leading direct-mail firms for CD-ROM products. They frequently offer "bundles" that include CD-ROM drives and disks at a special price. Most items are for Macintosh or Windows-based computers, although a few will run on DOS-equipped machines.

 Infopreneurs: Turning Data Into Dollars, by H. Skip Weitzen, ©1991, 240 pp., ISBN: 0-471-52824-2, $17.95. John Wiley & Sons, Inc., 605 Third Ave., New York, NY 10158-0012. (800) CALL-WILEY; (212) 850-6000; (212) 850-8641 (fax). A complete guide to the business opportunities available in gathering, organizing, and disseminating information.

 InfoWorld, weekly, $110/yr. InfoWorld Publishing Co., 155 Bovet Rd., Ste. 800, San Mateo, CA 94402. (415) 572-7341. This tabloid-format weekly magazine presents news, reviews, product comparisons, columns by industry pundits, gossip, and more. Covers the entire computer industry, but the primary focus is on the PC arena.

 International Cartridge Recycling Association (ICRA), William E. Kelley, 1200 Nineteenth St., NW, Ste. 300, Washington, DC 20036. (202) 857-1154; (202) 223-4579 (fax). ICRA members are companies involved in the remanufacturing of laser toner cartridges, ribbons, ink jets, and other computer products. A bimonthly publication is produced and semiannual meetings are held in the spring and fall. Membership is $300/year.

 Jargon: An Informal Dictionary of Computer Terms, by Robin Williams & Steve Cummings, ©1993, 688 pp., ISBN: 0-938151-84-3, $22.00. Peachpit Press, 2414 Sixth St., Berkeley, CA 94710. (800) 283-9444; (510) 548-4393; (510) 548-5991 (fax). This straightforward guide explains more than 1,200 of the most useful computer terms in a way that readers can understand. Covers both PC and Macintosh environments.

Small Business Systems, monthly, $39.00/yr. Charles Moore Associates, Inc., PO Box 6, South Hampton, PA 18966. (215) 355-6084; (215) 364-2212 (fax). Designed for the small business owner, this publication provides pertinent information regarding small computer system technology and use.

 Software: What's Hot! What's Not! 1994 Edition, by Cheryl Currid & Company, ©1994, 400 pp., ISBN: 1-55958-386-X, $16.95. Prima Publishing, Inc., PO Box 1260, Rocklin, CA 95677-1260. (916) 632-7400; (916) 632-7668 (fax). This lively and entertaining overview ranks and catalogs a selection of more than 100 Windows software products, citing magazine reviews and industry experts. It is updated on a yearly basis.

 Telecommunications Industry Association (TIA), Matthew J. Flanigan, 2001 Pennsylvania Ave., N.W., Ste. 800, Washington, DC 20006-1813. (202) 457-4912; (202) 457-4939 (fax). TIA is a full-service trade organization of both large and small companies that provide telecommunications materials, products, systems, distribution, and professional services. TIA represents the telecommunications industry in association with the Electronic Industries Association. The organization produces a monthly publication, and annual meetings are held in the spring.

 The CD-ROM Directory, 1,000 pp., ISBN: 1-870889-37-1, $139.00. Pemberton Press, Inc., 462 Danbury Rd., Wilton, CT 06897-2126. (800) 248-8466; (203) 761-1466; (203) 761-1444 (fax). A comprehensive directory of more than 6,000 CD-ROM titles and 3,800 companies who produce them. Also includes information on hardware, software, conferences and exhibitions, books and journals related to the industry. Also available in CD-ROM format for PC-compatibles for $99.00/single disk, or a two-disk annual subscription for $149.00.

 The Underground Guide to Laser Printers, by the editors of *Flash Magazine,* ©1993, 180 pp., ISBN: 1-56609-045-8, $12.00. Peachpit Press, 2414 Sixth St., Berkeley, CA 94710. (800) 283-9444; (510) 548-4393; (510) 548-5991 (fax). This book shows how to save money on supplies and repairs for your laser printer. Also includes tips for doing unusual things with your laser printer, such as printing on mugs and T-shirts, making plate-ready negatives, and other creative uses.

Upside, Eric Nee, Ed., ©1994, monthly, $48.00/yr. Upside Publications, PO Box 469023, Escondido, CA 92046-9944. (619) 745-2809 (customer service); (415) 377-0950; (415) 377-1961 (fax). This magazine's mission statement captures its spirit: "Upside is a provocative, insightful magazine that delivers an unflinchingly honest perspective on the people and companies creating the digital revolution. Upside readers are technology's elite—the impact players who build companies and build products."

 Wired, Louis Rossetto, Ed., monthly, ISSN: 1059-1028, $39.95/yr. Wired Ventures Ltd., 544 Second St., San Francisco, CA 94107. (800) SO WIRED; (415) 904-0660; subscriptions@wired.com (Internet). This technologically "hip" magazine, in both content and format, covers trends, opinions, and news about the digital world of computers, online networks, multimedia, and entertainment.

PC-Specific Resources

 PC Magazine, Michael J. Miller, Ed., monthly, $45.00/yr. Ziff-Davis Publishing Co., One Park Ave., New York, NY 10016-5255. (212) 503-5255. A monthly magazine that offers news, reviews, product announcements, and product tests for PC computer users.

 PC Week, Daniel Farber, Ed., weekly, $160.00. Ziff-Davis Publishing Co., 10 President's Landing, Medford, MA 02155. (609) 829-0667 (subscriptions); (617) 393-3700. A weekly tabloid publication that includes news, reviews, industry insights, and other information for PC users and buyers.

 PC World, Philip Lemmons, Ed., monthly, $29.90/yr. PCW Communications Inc., 501 Second St. #600, San Francisco, CA 94107. (415) 243-0500. This monthly magazine features news, information, product reviews, and hands-on articles to help PC users get the most from their computer equipment.

 Windows Magazine, Fred Langa, Ed., monthly, $25.00/yr. CMP Publications, One Jericho Plaza, Jericho, NY 11753. (800) 829-9150; (516) 733-8300. This monthly magazine focuses solely on products for computers running Windows. It presents news, product announcements, reviews, and other articles related to Windows-based computing.

Macintosh-Specific Resources

 MacUser, Maggie Canon, Ed., ISSN: 0884-0997, $19.97/yr. Ziff-Davis Publishing Company, 950 Tower Lane, 18th fl., Foster City, CA 94404. (800) 627-2247; (415) 378-5600. A monthly magazine featuring news, viewpoints, product testing, and reviews for Macintosh computer users.

 MacWeek, Rick LePage, Ed., weekly, ISSN: 0892-8118, $125.00/yr. Ziff-Davis Publishing Company, 301 Howard St., 15th fl., San Francisco, CA 94105. (415) 243-3500. A tabloid-format weekly that covers the latest news, trends, product announcements, reviews, and gossip about the Macintosh.

 Macworld, Adrian Mello, Ed., monthly, $30.00/yr. Macworld Communications Inc., 501 Second St., 5th fl., San Francisco, CA 94107. (415) 243-0505. A monthly magazine that presents news, industry pundits, product announcements, reviews, consumer viewpoints, and advice for Macintosh computer users.

Insights on Technology

 Investing in the Technologies of Tomorrow, by Gregory Georgiou, ©1993, 250 pp., ISBN: 1-55738-493-2, $24.95. Probus Publishing, Inc., 1925 N. Clyburn Ave. #401, Chicago, IL 60614. (800) PROBUS-1; (312) 868-6250 (fax). This book uncovers the technologies that will change the way we live in the 21st century and identifies the businesses that will bring these technologies to commercial fruition.

  Technotrends: How To Use Technology to Go Beyond Your Competition, by Daniel Burrus with Roger Gittines, ©1993, 400 pp., ISBN: 0-88730-700-0, $14.00. HarperBusiness, 10 E. 53rd St., New York, NY 10022-5299. (800) 982-4377; (212) 207-7000. Insights on how to creatively apply the new tools of technology to create the exciting new products, services, markets, and businesses of the 21st century, written by one of America's leading technology forecasters. Also available in an audiotape edition (3 hrs.) for $17.00.

Getting Started with Your Computer

How to Get Started with a Small Business Computer, $0.50. U.S. Small Business Administration, SBA Publications, PO Box 30, Denver, CO 80201-0030. (800) 827-5722; (202) 205-6665. This booklet helps you hone in on your computer needs, evaluate the alternatives, and select the appropriate computer system for your business.

Mac Home Journal, by Sandra Anderson, Ed., $19.95/yr. 544 Second St., San Francisco, CA 94107. (800) 800-6542; (415) 957-1911. A monthly publication for consumers and home-based/solo business owners who use a Macintosh computer. Noted for its down-to-earth style free of computer jargon. Features news, product reviews, and tips on using the Mac for business, education, and home uses.

PC Novice, monthly, $24.00/yr. PC Novice, PO Box 85380, Lincoln, NE 68501-9807. (800) 472-4100; (402) 477-9252 (fax). This magazine, written in plain English and free of computer jargon, is designed to reach computer users, not technical wizards. It provides information about software and hardware, computing basics, and updating older systems.

Personal Training Systems, $59.95. 173 Jefferson Dr., Menlo Park, CA 94025. (800) 832-2499; (415) 462-2100; (415) 462-2101 (fax). This company develops and markets interactive, self-paced audiotape and CD-ROM-based tutorials for software applications running in the Macintosh, Windows, and DOS environments. Each tutorial includes a 90-minute audiotape and a practice disk with examples that guide you through the learning process. Individuals can listen to the tape on headphones and learn in private at their own pace. Programs are available for novice through advanced levels of dozens of software applications.

The Little Mac Book, by Robin Williams, ©1993, 336 pp., ISBN: 1-56606-052-0, $16.00. Peachpit Press, 2414 Sixth St., Berkeley, CA 94710. (800) 283-9444; (510) 548-4393; (510) 548-5991 (fax). This guide covers the basics of operating a Macintosh computer in straightforward, easy-to-understand language, laced with a dose of humor. Also includes a tutorial for new users and a section on computer jargon.

The Little PC Book, by Larry Magid, ©1993, 384 pp., ISBN: 0-938151-54-1, $17.95. Peachpit Press, 2414 Sixth St., Berkeley, CA 94710. (800) 283-9444; (510) 548-4393; (510) 548-5991 (fax). This guide offers a painless way to become PC-literate, without being treated like a moron or buried in details. Includes two step-by-step cookbooks explaining how to perform 134 common tasks with DOS or Windows.

The MicroMastery Series, $149.95. Center for Video Education, PO Box 635, North White Plains, NY 10603. (800) 621-0043; (914) 428-0180 (fax). This series of audiotape/disk/workbook study system helps individuals master common business computer software programs at their own pace. Available for word processing, spreadsheet, databases, and system management programs, in both PC and Macintosh formats. Each program includes a disk, audiotape, and study guide.

Buying Computers and Supplies

American Computer Exchange (AmCoEx), (800) 786-0717. This company acts as a nationwide matching service between buyers and sellers of used computer systems and printers. To be listed, the equipment must be more than $200 in value. The seller pays 10% of the final selling price as a fee. Prospective buyers and sellers can also call to determine the current pricing for equipment they own.

Business World's Guide to Computers, $19.98. MPI Home Video, 15825 Rob Roy Dr., Oak Forest, IL 60452. (708) 687-7881; (708) 687-3797 (fax). Several business leaders provide information on choosing and maintaining the right computer system for your business needs.

CompUSA Inc., 14951 Dallas Parkway, Dallas, TX 75240. (800) COMP-USA. This nationwide superstore chain carries more than 5,000 computer products, including hardware, software, peripherals, and supplies at a discount. They also sell through a mail-order catalog. By calling their toll-free number you can find the location of the store nearest you.

Computer Shopper, John Blackford, Ed., monthly, $29.97. Coastal Associates Publishing L.P., One Park Ave., 11th fl., New York, NY 10016. (212) 503-3900; (212) 503-3999 (fax). This chunky, tabloid newsprint publication is, as its name says, a shopper's delight. A typical issue features news, reviews, and volumes of display and classified advertising for computers, peripherals, software, and employment. Each issue also usually includes a list of computer user groups. The publication is primarily PC in focus.

Computer Mail-Order Firms

There are dozens of mail-order firms that sell computer hardware, software, and supplies. To locate the ones that will serve your needs best, refer to the list below and ask fellow computer users who are members of your local user group (see p. 84).

The mail-order software business has become very competitive, which has led to increasingly better customer service. For example, most firms offer overnight shipping for only a few dollars, and many offer a full money-back guarantee on your purchases for 60 or 90 days.

Global Computer Supplies
(800) 845-6225; (516) 625-6200 (in NY State)

MacConnection	**PC Connection**
(800) 800-2222	(800) 800-0005
MacWarehouse	**MicroWarehouse**
(800) 255-6227	(800) 367-6808
MacZone	**PC Zone**
(800) 248-0800	(800) 258-2088

NEBS Computer Forms and Software
(800) 225-6380; (800) 234-4324 (fax)
NEBS markets a wide range of custom-order computer forms, stationery, and labels that work with leading software packages. They also publish a catalog that lists more than 800 software programs that work with their preprinted forms.

Rocky Mountain Computer Outfitters
(800) 817-0009

Major Technology Firms

Acer, Inc.
401 Charcot Ave.
San Jose, CA 95131
(800) 585-ACER

Apple Computer, Inc.
1 Infinite Loop
Cupertino, CA 95013
(408) 996-1010

Canon Computer Systems
123 East Paularino Ave.
Costa Mesa, CA 92628
(800) 848-4123

Compaq Computer Corp.
PO Box 692000
Houston, TX 77269
(800) 345-1518

Dell Computer Corp.
9505 Arboretum Blvd.
Austin, TX 78759
(800) 426-5150

Epson America, Inc.
23530 Hawthorne Blvd.
Torrance, CA 90505
(800) 922-8911

Gateway 2000, Inc.
610 Gateway Dr.
N. Sioux City, SD 57049
(800) 846-2000

Hewlett-Packard
19310 Pruneridge Ave.
Cupertino, CA 95014
(800) 752-0900

Hitachi America, Ltd.
3617 Parkway Lane, Ste. 100
Norcross, GA 30092
(404) 446-8820

IBM Corp.
1 Old Orchard Rd.
Armonk, NY 10504
(800) 426-2468

Mitsubishi International
1500 Michael Dr.
Wood Dale, IL 60191
(708) 860-4200

**Panasonic
Communications Systems**
Two Panasonic Way
Secaucus, NJ 07094
(201) 348-7000

Sharp Electronics Corp.
Sharp Plaza
Mahwah, NJ 07430
(201) 529-8200

Sony Corp. of America
1 Sony Dr.
Park Ridge, NJ 07656
(800) 222-7669

Texas Instruments, Inc.
PO Box 202230
Austin, TX 78720
(800) 527-3500

**Toshiba America
Information Systems, Inc.**
9740 Irvine Blvd.
Irvine, CA 92718
(800) 457-7777

Online Resources

 Cyberpower Alert!, by Wally Bock, $95.00/yr. electronic format; $120.00/yr. printed format. RHE Publications, 1441 Franklin St., Ste. 301, Oakland, CA 94612. (800) 648-2677; (510) 835-8531 (fax); bocktalk@aol.com (Internet). This monthly newsletter keeps you up-to-date on new services, developments, and techniques in the online world. Each issue features one in-depth story on an aspect of doing business online, as well as news, professional techniques, money-saving tips, and answers to frequently asked questions. Delivery can be via online service or by mail. A typical printed issue runs approximately 14 pages.

 Cyberpower for Speakers, Trainers, and Consultants, by Wally Bock, ©1993, 58 pp., $24.95. RHE Publications, 1441 Franklin St., Ste. 301, Oakland, CA 94612. (800) 648-2677; (510) 835-8531 (fax); bocktalk@aol.com (Internet). This special report, written by one of the leading authorities on online resources, shows how independent entrepreneurs can use the power of computer networks. Topics covered include: what equipment you'll need, which services are best, how to get connected, how to minimize your costs, basic research strategies, and more. Readers also receive coupons and special offers worth more than $300 for related products and services.

 Cyberpower Prospecting: How to Get More & Better Clients, by Wally Bock, ©1994, 30 min., $12.95. RHE Publications, 1441 Franklin St., Ste. 301, Oakland, CA 94612. (800) 648-2677; (510) 835-8531 (fax); bocktalk@aol.com (Internet). This audiotape shows you how to find just the prospects you want—quickly and easily—by using online resources. Learn how to get detailed profiles of prospects and clients in minutes that will help you serve them better.

 The Virtual Community: Homesteading the Electronic Frontier, by Howard Rheingold, ©1993, 325 pp., ISBN: 0-201-60870-7, $22.95. Addison-Wesley Publishing Company, One Jacob Way, Reading, MA 01867. (800) 367-7198; (617) 944-3700. An inside look at the community of individuals who are subscribers to computer online services, as told by a longtime "resident." Rheingold points out the myths and potential for our future as we become part of an ever-expanding electronically linked global network.

Making the Online Connection

A vast source of information and numerous business opportunities await entrepreneurs who tie into the worldwide network of electronic online services. This "information highway" links computers of all sizes at sites throughout the world via common telephone lines. Once connected, solo entrepreneurs can send messages instantly to colleagues, access statistical data, obtain free software, conduct research, make purchases of supplies, exchange ideas, pose questions to other entrepreneurs—or even create a "virtual company" of individuals who may live thousands of miles apart yet work on projects together.

Individuals usually connect to the information highway in one of three ways: through local bulletin board systems (BBSs), through commercial online services, or direct to the Internet. All offer, to different degrees, electronic mail, special interest groups, access to public domain software, and other information services. Local BBSs are generally regional systems operated at no charge by volunteers. The connection is a local phone call and your neighborhood computer store can provide details. Commercial online services often come with easy-to-use software and charge for connect time; the main service providers are listed below. The Internet, originally started by university and government researchers, has an estimated 20 million users and forms the backbone of the electronic highway. Internet details are found on page 82.

Commercial Online Services

America Online (AOL), America Online, 8619 Westwood Center Dr., Ste. 200, Vienna, VA 22182. (800) 827-6364; (703) 448-8700. AOL is one of the most popular computer online services, and solo entrepreneurs can network in Microsoft's Small Business Center, a forum hosted by small business author Janet Attard. Software is available in DOS, Macintosh, and Windows formats.

AppleLink, AppleLink Account Administration, PO Box 10600, Herndon, VA 22070-0600. (408) 974-3305. This online service connects Apple's extended "family," including worldwide employees, consultants, user groups and other enthusiasts.

CompuServe, CompuServe, PO Box 20212, Columbus, OH 43220. (800) 848-8199; (614) 457-8600. CompuServe is the granddaddy of online services, and offers a mind-boggling array of information. Subscribers can search extensive business databases, or network with other entrepreneurs in the Entrepreneur Forum, the Public Relations and Marketing Forum, or the Working From Home Forum (hosted by authors Paul & Sarah Edwards). Software available for DOS, Windows or Macintosh.

Delphi Internet, Delphi Internet Services Corp., 1030 Massachusetts Ave., Cambridge, MA 02138. (800) 695-4005; (617) 491-3342. Delphi, a longtime online services provider, has recently shifted their focus to offering inexpensive Internet access. The service is available to DOS, Macintosh, or any ASCII-based personal computer system. A Windows interface is in development.

eWorld, Apple Computer, Inc., 1 Infinite Loop, Cupertino, CA 65014. (408) 996-1010. Apple's newest online service has one of the easiest user interfaces. It is home to the WORKING SOLO Online Business Forum, which includes an electronic version of this book as well as libraries of business information. The WORKING SOLO Café features real-time conferences with guests, and a message board allows solo entrepreneurs to network with their peers. Currently available only in Macintosh format; a Windows-based version is in development.

GEnie, GEnie, 401 N. Washington St., Rockville, MD 20850. (800) 638-9636; (301) 340-5397; (301) 340-4488 (fax). GEnie offers several popular meeting places for solo entrepreneurs. In the Home Office/Small Business Roundtable, the Tax RoundTable, and the WorkPlace RoundTable (all hosted by author Janet Attard), subscribers can share information and find answers to business questions. The Business Resource Directory is a searchable database of information resources. Available to computers running DOS or Macintosh system software, or any ASCII-based PC.

Prodigy, Prodigy Information Services, 445 Hamilton Ave., White Plains, NY 10601. (800) 776-3449; (914) 993-8000. Formed by a business alliance between Sears and IBM, Prodigy has a large subscriber base. The Home Office and Entrepreneurs' Exchange bulletin boards are the liveliest networking areas for solo entrepreneurs. Works with DOS, Windows, or Macintosh systems.

Internet Resources

Internet Business Companion, by David Angell & Brent Heslop, ©1994, 304 pp., ISBN: 0-201-40850-3, $19.95. Addison-Wesley Publishing Company, One Jacob Way, Reading, MA 01867. (800) 367-7198; (617) 944-3700. This book takes a pragmatic look at how businesses should strategically plan their Internet futures. It explains what the Internet is, how to assess online opportunities, ways to get connected, and techniques on making the connection a profitable experience. The authors also explain how to use the Internet to accomplish important business tasks, such as conducting research, offering product support, catalog publishing, and marketing.

Internet Membership Kit, $69.95. Ventana Media, PO Box 2468, Chapel Hill, NC 27515. (800) 209-3342; (919) 942-0220; (919) 942-1140 (fax). This kit features a valuable collection of tools and resources to connect you to the Internet, including: software that puts a graphical interface on the Internet; a disk of software utilities to help you easily navigate and retrieve information; a copy of the best-selling book, *The Internet Tour Guide*; a copy of *The Internet Yellow Pages,* a 440-page listing of thousands or resources on the Internet; and free trial Internet access through CERFnet, a leading Internet service provider. Available in Macintosh or Windows format.

Internet Starter Kit, by Adam C. Engst, ©1994, $29.95. Hayden Books, Macmillan Computer Publishing, 201 W. 103rd St., Indianapolis, IN 46290. (800) 545-5914; (317) 581-3500. This book/disk combination includes a complete guide to connecting to the Internet, and once there, getting the most out of it. Includes coupons and offers worth more than $100 and a collection of popular software utilities on disk. Available in both Macintosh and Windows versions.

Internet Newsgroups are worldwide discussion groups on the Internet that carry messages, news, and freeflowing commentary from participants on thousands of topics. Newsgroups of particular value to entrepreneurs include: alt.business, alt.business.misc, clari.biz.products, clari.biz.misc, and misc.entrepreneurs.

Protecting Your Equipment

 A Small Business Guide to Computer Security, $1.00. U.S. Small Business Administration, SBA Publications, PO Box 30, Denver, CO 80201-0030. (800) 827-5722; (202) 205-6665. This booklet helps you to understand the important details of computer security and minimize the risks for your own computer systems.

 Panamax Surge Protectors, 150 Mitchell Blvd., San Rafael, CA 94903-2057. (800) 472-5555; (415) 499-3900; (415) 472-5540 (fax). Panamax manufactures and markets a full line of surge protectors—devices designed to protect computers and other delicate electronic equipment from destructive power surges. They come with a lifetime warranty as well as a $25,000 guarantee to replace any equipment damaged by a power surge while it was properly connected to a Panamax surge protector.

 Safeware, The Insurance Agency, Inc., 2929 N. High St., PO Box 02211, Columbus, OH 43202. (800) 848-3469. Safeware offers a variety of computer insurance packages, including theft, repair coverage for mechanical breakdowns, travel coverage, and policies for data loss.

Telephone Headsets

 Hello Direct, 5884 Eden Park Pl., San Jose, CA 95138-1859. (800) 444-3556; (408) 972-1990; (408) 972-8155 (fax). Hello Direct offers a full line of telephone headsets and productivity tools, including answering systems, pagers, mobile phones, telephone office products, and more.

 Plantronics, Inside Sales Department, PO Box 635, Santa Cruz, CA 95061-0635. (800) 544-4660 x1776. Plantronics sells lightweight and comfortable telephone headsets which improve your efficiency and leave your hands free to do other things while you're on the phone.

Digital Birds of a Feather

One of the best ways to ensure that you're getting the most out of your technology investment is to join a computer user group. These organizations of computer enthusiasts are devoted to helping members increase their understanding and enjoyment of their systems. Groups range in size from a few people who gather once a month in someone's living room to megagroups of 10,000 members or more who sponsor weekly events in large auditoriums. Meetings are a great place to connect with other entrepreneurs, find solutions to your computing problems, learn new tips, or sort out buying decisions.

There are user groups for nearly every brand of computer and computing interest area. The hotlines listed below can connect you with a group near you. A call to your local computer store can also provide you with information on groups in your area.

User Groups

 Association of Personal Computer User Groups, 1730 M St. NW, Washington, DC 20036. (914) 876-6678. This umbrella organization for PC computer users maintains a database of user groups around the country. They can help you find one nearby, or assist you in starting your own.

User Group Connection, PO Box 67249, Scotts Valley, CA 95067-7249. (800) 538-9696, ext. 500; (408) 461-5700; (408) 461-5701. This independent organization offers information and support to the more than 2,100 Apple Computer user groups nationwide. They publish a bimonthly newsletter highlighting Apple news and offering management advice to group leaders. Groups are also eligible to receive discounts on computer products and supplies through programs negotiated with industry vendors. Call the toll-free number to locate the user group closest to you.

Consulting Information

For many individuals, consulting is the perfect solo business. A consultancy usually involves little initial financial investment and generally can be operated with low overhead costs. Establishing oneself as a successful consultant, however, requires more than being an authority on a particular subject. Successful consultants have a mastery of marketing, proposal writing, negotiating, networking, and other professional skills. Let the following resources guide you in establishing yourself as the expert in your field who has valuable information and services to offer.

 American Consultants League, Hubert Bermont, 1290 N. Palm Ave., Ste. 112, Sarasota, FL 34236. (813) 952-9290; (813) 925-3670 (fax). This association of more than 1,000 members assists consultants in setting up and managing their business through the Consultants Institute, an educational division. An annual directory and bimonthly newsletter are produced. Dues are $96/year.

 Consultant's National Resource Center, Steve Lanning, PO Box 430, Clear Spring, MD 21722. (301) 791-9332. The center provides consultants and professional service marketers with vertical marketing courses and helps them start and/or build their practice. It also offers courses, software, and publications expressly for professional service marketing.

 How to Become a Successful Consultant In Your Own Field, by Hubert Bermont, ©1994, 224 pp., ISBN: 1-55958-119-0, $21.95. Prima Publishing, PO Box 1260, Rocklin, CA 95677-1260. (916) 632-7400; (916) 632-7668 (fax). Tips from an experienced pro on what it takes to be a consultant, how to get hired, what to charge, and how to operate a successful business.

How to Make at Least $100,000 Every Year as a Successful Consultant in Your Own Field, by Jeffrey Lant, ©1993, 315 pp., $39.50 (postpaid). JLA Publications, PO Box 38-2767, Cambridge, MA 02238. (617) 547-6372; (617) 547-0061 (fax). This is Lant's complete guide to succeeding in the advice business, designed for the consultant who has mastered the basics. Includes details on raising fees, landing retainer contracts, developing a nationwide business by phone, and expanding your reach through books, audiotapes, special reports, and other income-producing avenues.

 Marketing Your Consulting or Professional Services, by David Karlson, ©1993, 108 pp., ISBN: 0-931961-40-8, $8.95. Crisp Publications, 1200 Hamilton Ct., Menlo Park, CA 94025. (415) 323-6100; (415) 323-5800 (fax). A tactical handbook for consultants that teaches how to define a market, build an effective marketing plan, articulate objectives, evaluate competition, identify unique strengths, and promote yourself successfully.

  Professional and Technical Consultants Association (PATCA), Catherine Tornbom, Executive Director, PO Box 4143, Mountain View, CA 94040-4143. (800) 286-8703; (415) 903-8305; (415) 967-0995 (fax). PATCA is a nonprofit organization of independent technical consultants and small consulting firms. It is dedicated to enhancing the professionalism, integrity, objectivity, and business competence of its members, and to promoting the profession of consulting. The association publishes a monthly newsletter, an annual directory, and a biennial survey of rates and business practices. Membership is $295/year.

 Selecting and Working With Consultants, by Thomas J. Ucko, ©1993, 100 pp., ISBN: 0-931961-87-4, $8.95. Crisp Publications, 1200 Hamilton Ct., Menlo Park, CA 94025. (415) 323-6100; (415) 323-5800 (fax). This book is full of practical advice concerning the selection, fee negotiation, and evaluation of the appropriate consultant for any job.

 Start and Run a Profitable Consulting Business, by Douglas A. Gray, ©1990, 232 pp., ISBN: 0-88908-897-7, $14.95. Self-Counsel Press, Inc., 1704 N. State St., Bellingham, WA 98225. (800) 663-3007; (206) 676-4530; (206) 676-4549 (fax). A succinct, well-organized overview about starting a consulting business.

A Consultant's Niche

One of the challenges that new consultants face is establishing the "width" of their specialization. If you market your services as a generalist who covers too broad a subject area, you may be considered not proficient enough to address specific needs. In contrast, if you limit your field to a very narrow focus, you may find there is not enough of a market to sustain you.

Most consultants resolve this dilemma by selecting a somewhat broad category within one specialty—for example, desktop publishing or direct-mail marketing. As their practices develop and they find work they enjoy and in which they excel, they narrow their focus. (The desktop publisher might specialize in pre-press services; the direct-mail marketer could develop into the guru of mailing list selection.) Once they become recognized masters in their niche, they can be more selective in their clients, charge higher fees, and build their businesses to new levels.

The Complete Guide to Being an Independent Contractor, by Herman Holtz, ©1995, 304 pp., ISBN: 0-7931-0889-6, $24.95. Dearborn Trade, 520 N. Dearborn St., Chicago, IL 60610-4354. (800) 245-2665; (312) 836-4400; (312) 836-1021 (fax). The author, a longtime professional consultant, offers guidance that can help new and prospective contractors start, build, and manage their ventures successfully and profitably. Includes tips and strategies on marketing, winning and negotiating contracts, pricing, tax planning, and a dozen model contracts and letters of agreement.

The Complete Guide to Consulting Success, by Howard L. Shenson & Ted Nicholas, ©1994, 304 pp., ISBN: 0-79310-492-0, $29.95. Dearborn Trade, 520 N. Dearborn St., Chicago, IL 60610-4354. (800) 245-2665; (312) 836-4400; (312) 836-1021 (fax). The late Howard Shenson, one of the country's top consultants, and direct-marketing pro Ted Nicholas reveal their practical secrets on how to create a successful consulting business in any field. Includes sample contracts, agreements, and letters.

The Consultant's Calling, by Geoffrey M. Bellman, ©1992, 264 pp., ISBN: 1-55542-411-2, $16.95. Jossey-Bass Publishers, 350 Sansome St., San Francisco, CA 94104-1310. (415) 433-1767; (415) 433-0499 (fax). This book is designed for those who want to know whether consulting can really be a career and way of life. The author presents the practical issues of managing time, clients, and money as well as broader issues of how to balance work and life.

 The Consultant's Handbook, by Stephan Schiffman, ©1989, 252 pp., ISBN: 0-937860-93-X, $12.95. Bob Adams, Inc., 260 Center St., Holbrook, MA 02343. (800) 872-5627; (617) 767-8100; (800) 872-5628 (fax). This book offers a detailed breakdown of the pros and cons of entering the consulting field, an outline of common problems encountered by beginning consultants, and tips on making the most financially rewarding strategy decisions.

 The Consultant's Kit: Establishing and Operating Your Successful Consulting Business, by Jeffrey Lant, ©1991, 208 pp., $38.50 (postpaid). JLA Publications, PO Box 38-2767, Cambridge, MA 02238. (617) 547-6372; (617) 547-0061 (fax). In his sassy, straightforward style, Jeffrey Lant delivers solid advice on launching your consulting business. Covers defining your specialty, developing a contact network, marketing and promoting your expertise, writing contracts, setting up shop, incorporating, handling bookkeeping, accounting, tax matters, and more.

 The Independent Consultant's Q & A Book, by Lawrence W. Tuller, ©1993, 300 pp., ISBN: 1-55850-117-7, $10.95. Bob Adams, Inc., 260 Center St., Holbrook, MA 02343. (800) 872-5627; (617) 767-8100; (800) 872-5628 (fax). Details proven methods for dealing with each area of a consulting business, and provides creative, authoritative solutions to problems encountered in starting or operating any type of consulting business.

Customers

See also Advertising; Communication Skills; Marketing;
Promotion and Public Relations

Customers are the most valuable element of any business—a fact that is particularly important when you're working solo. Without customers, solo businesses can't exist. Since it takes approximately *eight times* as much effort and expense to find a new customer as it does to serve an existing one, savvy entrepreneurs know that good customers are like money in the bank, and they value them accordingly. This section of the WORKING SOLO SOURCEBOOK focuses on resources that will help you understand how to polish your customer relations, stay in touch with them, and be responsive to their needs.

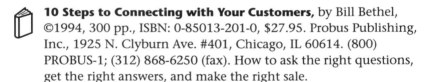 **10 Steps to Connecting with Your Customers,** by Bill Bethel, ©1994, 300 pp., ISBN: 0-85013-201-0, $27.95. Probus Publishing, Inc., 1925 N. Clyburn Ave. #401, Chicago, IL 60614. (800) PROBUS-1; (312) 868-6250 (fax). How to ask the right questions, get the right answers, and make the right sale.

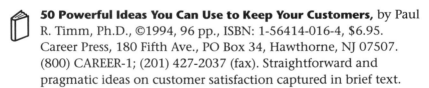 **50 Powerful Ideas You Can Use to Keep Your Customers,** by Paul R. Timm, Ph.D., ©1994, 96 pp., ISBN: 1-56414-016-4, $6.95. Career Press, 180 Fifth Ave., PO Box 34, Hawthorne, NJ 07507. (800) CAREER-1; (201) 427-2037 (fax). Straightforward and pragmatic ideas on customer satisfaction captured in brief text.

50 Ways to Win New Customers, by Paul R.Timm, Ph.D., ©1994, 96 pp., ISBN: 1-56414-722-5, $8.95. Career Press, 180 Fifth Ave., PO Box 34, Hawthorne, NJ 07507. (800) CAREER-1; (201) 427-2037 (fax). Fast, simple, and inexpensive ways to attract new customers to your business.

Close to the Customer, by James H. Donnelly, Jr., ©1991, 214 pp., ISBN: 1-55623-569-0, $20.00. Irwin Professional Publishing, Inc., 1333 Burr Ridge Pkwy., Burr Ridge, IL 60521. (800) 634-3961; (708) 789-4000. This book provides how-to tips and encourages readers to establish close relationships with their customers to ensure better communications and more profitable returns.

 Customers as Partners: Building Relationships That Last, by Chip R. Bell, ©1994, 250 pp., ISBN: 1-881052-54-0, $24.95. Berrett-Koehler Publishers, Inc., 155 Montgomery St., San Francisco, CA 94104. (800) 929-2929; (415) 288-0260; (415) 362-2512 (fax). This practical how-to guide is written with the passion and humor of a great novel. It presents step-by-step guidelines for enhancing long-term customer loyalty, and delves into issues such as spirit, service, passion, trust, and faith in building lasting relationships.

 Delivering Knock Your Socks Off Service, by Kristin Anderson & Ron Zemke, ©1991, 130 pp., ISBN: 0-8144-7777-1, $15.95. AMACOM Books, PO Box 1026, Saranac Lake, NY 12983. (800) 262-9699; (518) 891-3653 (fax). A practical, witty guide to creating and maintaining excellent customer service with many small business examples.

 Exceptional Customer Service Seminar, 1 day, $99.00. Fred Pryor Seminars, 2000 Shawnee Mission Pkwy., Shawnee Mission, KS 66205. (800) 938-6330; (913) 722-8580 (fax). This seminar teaches how to work easily with others, including ways to communicate with customers in person and over the phone, helpful skills for dealing with angry customers, tactics for keeping your composure under stress, how to build customer goodwill, and more. Also available on six audiotapes with a workbook for $59.95.

  How to Provide Excellent Customer Service, by Linda Frascatti, $59.95. SkillPath, Inc., 6900 Squibb Rd., PO Box 2768, Mission, KS 66201-2768. (800) 873-7545; (913) 677-3200; (913) 362-4241 (fax). In this set of six audiotapes and a workbook, listeners learn how to treat customers well and to get the most out of every customer contact.

Keeping Customers for Life, by Joan K. Cannie & Donald Caplin, ©1992, 288 pp., ISBN: 0-8144-7812-3, $14.95. AMACOM Books, PO Box 1026, Saranac Lake, NY 12983. (800) 262-9699; (518) 891-3653 (fax). Hands-on, 12-step strategy about customer relations augmented by a number of charts and worksheets.

 Keeping Customers Happy, by Jacqueline Dunckel & Brian Taylor, ©1994, 184 pp., ISBN: 0-88908-790-3, $8.95. Self-Counsel Press, Inc., 1704 N. State St., Bellingham, WA 98225. (800) 663-3007; (206) 676-4530; (206) 676-4549 (fax). This book offers advice and tips for developing a program to keep your customers happy and coming back.

 People Pleasing Seminars, 1 day, $99.00-129.00. Dunn & Bradstreet Business Education Services, PO Box 5100, New York, NY 10150-5100. (212) 692-6600; (212) 692-6456 (fax). A series of three workshops: The How-To's of Outstanding Customer Service; The How-To's of Good Customer Service; and Developing Excellent Customer Service by Telephone. These seminars present practical, ready-to-use techniques on improving specific aspects of customer relations, and each is offered at sites around the country.

Creating "Golden" Customers

Customers define a solo business—both with the income they bring now and with feedback and suggestions that can impact your business future. Their recommendations carry weight no marketing budget can match, while requests for customized products or services can lead to exciting new business avenues.

Let your customers know how much they mean to you. Often it's the little things that can make a big difference in your relations with them. Give them a phone call to say thanks, drop them a postcard, offer them a special premium or discount for bringing you repeat business. They are casting their vote for your business with their checkbook—don't ever underestimate their value to your business success.

Positively Outrageous Service and Showmanship, by T. Scott Gross, ©1993, 200 pp., ISBN: 0-942361-82-2, $12.95. MasterMedia Limited, 17 E. 89th St., Ste. 7D, New York, NY 10128. (800) 334-8232; (212) 260-5600; (212) 546-7638 (fax). Customer service guru T. Scott Gross reveals his secrets to adding personality to any product or service. Focusing on nontraditional marketing techniques, this books shows how the customer experience can become a competitive edge in your business.

 Power of Customer Service, 45 min., $95.00. Nightingale Conant, 7300 N. Lehigh Ave., Niles, IL 60714. (800) 525-9000; (708) 647-0300; (708) 647-7145 (fax). This video program provides professional tips and ideas on improving customer relations.

Professional Telephone Skills Seminar, half-day, $49.00. CareerTrack, 3085 Center Green Dr., Boulder, CO 80301-5408. (800) 334-1018; (800) 832-9489 (fax). This seminar shows how to use telephone skills to improve your business image and keep customers coming back.

 Seeking and Keeping Customers with Field Guide to Marketing, by Benson P. Shapiro & John J. Sviokla, ©1994, ISBN: 0-87584-442-1, $49.95. Harvard Business School Press, McGraw-Hill, Inc., 11 W. 19th St., New York, NY 10011. (800) 822-8158. This three-in-one electronic sourcebook contains the text of two best-selling books and a glossary of marketing terms. Because of its format, it also offers features such as the ability to find words or phrases in an instant, copy and paste text, add margin comments, highlight text, mark pages, and move easily throughout the volumes. Designed especially for Macintosh PowerBook computers, but can be used on any Mac with a hard drive and large display. Comes on two 1.4MB high-density floppy disks.

 The Survey Genie, $149.95. Oasis Press, 300 N. Valley Dr., Grants Pass, OR 97526. (800) 228-2275; (503) 479-9464; (503) 476-1479 (fax). This software allows you to create, administer, and analyze any type of survey. It can help you learn how your customers feel about your advertising, customer service, image, physical environment, pricing, product image, product quality, and telephone service. Requires DOS 3.3 or higher, hard disk, 640KB RAM, and a graphics card.

Total Quality Customer Service, by Jim Temme, ©1994, 141 pp., $17.95. SkillPath, Inc., 6900 Squibb Rd., PO Box 2768, Mission, KS 66201-2768. (800) 873-7545; (913) 677-3200; (913) 362-4241 (fax). This practical, hands-on guide includes 22 exercises to help you check your progress, growth, and success in offering customers quality service.

 Tough Customers, by Dartnell, ©1994, 150 pp., ISBN: 0-85013-210-X, $12.95. Probus Publishing, Inc., 1925 N. Clyburn Ave. #401, Chicago, IL 60614. (800) PROBUS-1; (312) 868-6250 (fax). This book teaches how to deal with tough customers, particularly on the telephone.

 What Do Your Customers Really Want?, by John F. Lytle, ©1994, 240 pp., ISBN: 1-55738-829-6, $19.95. Probus Publishing, Inc., 1925 N. Clyburn Ave. #401, Chicago, IL 60614. (800) PROBUS-1; (312) 868-6250 (fax). Insights into common misconceptions about customers' needs and how to overcome them. Includes how to create a company in your customers' image and how to keep customers for life.

 Why Customers Leave and How to Get Them to Stay, by Lisa Ford & Jeff Salzman, 38 min., $79.95. CareerTrack, 3085 Center Green Dr., Boulder, CO 80301-5408. (800) 334-1018; (800) 832-9489 (fax). In this video program, service expert Lisa Ford shares her insights, experience and candid advice about the impact of customer relations.

Direct Marketing

See also Advertising; Marketing; Promotion and Public Relations

Direct marketing focuses on reaching potential customers with a "direct" contact, primarily through the mail with printed materials such as brochures or catalogs. Seasoned pros in the mail-order field explain that the system for success can almost be seen as a science, with specific results generated from tightly designed programs. Others view it more akin to an art form, with a subtle blend of the printed materials, the offer, and the mailing list. Either way, direct mail can be a powerful marketing tool for solo entrepreneurs, even on a small scale using an in-house mailing list of current customers. The following resources provide both an overview and the details of what it takes to conduct successful direct-mail campaigns.

 101 Tips for More Profitable Catalogs, by Maxwell Sroge, 122 pp., ISBN: 0-8442-3660-8, $29.95. National Textbook Company, 4255 W. Touhy Ave., Lincolnwood, IL 60646-1975. (800) 323-4900; (708) 679-5500; (708) 679-2494 (fax). Profit-producing tips culled by direct-marketing legend Sroge from the pages of his successful newsletter. Includes advice on creative techniques, mailing lists, merchandising, production, advertising, telemarketing, and fulfillment.

 A Small Business Guide to Direct Mail, by Lin Grensing, ©1991, 192 pp., ISBN: 0-88908-976-0, $9.95. Self-Counsel Press, Inc., 1704 N. State St., Bellingham, WA 98225. (800) 663-3007; (206) 676-4530; (206) 676-4549 (fax). This user-friendly guide takes the needs of small business seriously and shows how to produce an inexpensive, high-impact direct-mail marketing plan.

Beyond 2000: The Future of Direct Marketing, by Jerry I.
Reitman, ©1994, 288 pp., ISBN: 0-8442-3450-8, $34.95. National
Textbook Company, 4255 W. Touhy Ave., Lincolnwood, IL 60646-
1975. (800) 323-4900; (708) 679-5500; (708) 679-2494 (fax).
Twenty-eight of the world's leading direct-marketing experts
predict the changes that will impact you and your company in
the coming years.

 Building Your Business with Direct Marketing, by John E.
Groman, 6 hrs., $149.00. John A. Knight Smith, Marketing
Education Department, Epsilon/American Express, World Financial Center, 200 Vesey St., 34th fl., New York, NY 10285-3400. (212)
619-9666 (fax). This five-tape seminar is part of the live Merchant
Training program American Express offers to small businesses. In
an easy-to-follow approach, it covers the basic principles and
techniques of successful direct marketing. Topics include: direct-
marketing strategy and uses; developing offers; structuring
packages and costs; developing databases and lists; testing programs; analyzing results; and more. Includes two handouts.

 Direct Hit, by Dave Majure, ©1994, 250 pp., ISBN: 1-55738-821-0,
$22.95. Probus Publishing, Inc., 1925 N. Clyburn Ave. #401,
Chicago, IL 60614. (800) PROBUS-1; (312) 868-6250 (fax). This
book presents real-world insights and common-sense advice from
a direct-marketing pro.

 Direct Marketing Association, Bette Lawler, 11 W. 42nd St.,
New York, NY 10036-8096. (212) 768-7277; (212) 768-4546 (fax).
More than 6,500 individuals and 3,600 companies are members of
this association dedicated to furthering the field of direct marketing. They hold 17 annual conferences nationwide, and offer one
of the largest selections of books on direct marketing in the
country. A monthly newsletter keeps members informed on
government activities regarding direct mail and the association's
lobbying efforts.

 Direct Marketing Checklists, by John Stockwell & Henry Shaw,
©1994, 208 pp., ISBN: 0-8442-3224-6, $19.95. National Textbook
Company, 4255 W. Touhy Ave., Lincolnwood, IL 60646-1975.
(800) 323-4900; (708) 679-5500; (708) 679-2494 (fax). This
resource distills the important fundamentals of direct marketing
into 99 ready-to-use checklists, charts, and forms to save you
time, cut costs, and boost your response rates.

Do-It-Yourself Direct Marketing: Secrets for Small Business, by Mark S. Bacon, ©1994, 288 pp., ISBN: 0-471-00876-1, $26.95. John Wiley & Sons, Inc., 605 Third Ave., New York, NY 10158-0012. (800) CALL-WILEY; (212) 850-6000; (212) 850-8641 (fax). A complete guide to the latest inexpensive, high-impact direct-marketing techniques and strategies for entrepreneurs and small business owners.

Home-Based Catalog Marketing, by William J. Bond, ©1993, ISBN: 0-07-006596-9, $14.95. McGraw-Hill, Inc., 11 W. 19th St., New York, NY 10011. (800) 822-8158. Based on the author's 25 years of experience, this book presents upbeat, practical tips on starting up and running a successful catalog business from home.

How to Create Successful Catalogs, by Maxwell Sroge, 460 pp., ISBN: 0-8442-3661-6, $79.95. NTC Business Books, 4255 W. Touhy Ave., Lincolnwood, IL 60646-1975. (800) 323-4900; (708) 679-5500; (708) 679-2494 (fax). Insights on every phase of catalog creation, from shooting product to writing copy, guarantees, and order forms. Includes examples from hundreds of successful catalogs, compiled by a master in the industry and 39 other pros.

Mining Your List

Direct-marketing pros are quick to point out that one of the most valuable assets in a direct-mail campaign is your customer list. By maintaining accurate records of your customers—including details on their buying habits and interests—you can more effectively target your message and get a better return on your marketing dollar. Fortunately, computers make this task easier than ever before.

Staying in regular contact with customers allows you to create an ongoing bond as well as keep address information current. Even if customers don't buy again immediately, it may be worth it to conduct a mailing or survey to maintain their link with you. When it's time to drop them from your list, you can encourage them to buy before they lose the valuable connection you've established.

How You Too Can Make at Least $1 Million in the Mail-Order Business, by Gerardo Joffe, ©1992, 384 pp., ISBN: 0-88908-283-9, $11.95. Self-Counsel Press, Inc., 1704 N. State St., Bellingham, WA 98225. (800) 663-3007; (206) 676-4530; (206) 676-4549 (fax). This book shows how to build an effective mail-order business from start to finish.

 Introduction to Mail Order, quarterly, $10.00/yr. G & B Records, 23735 Olive St. Box 10150, Terra Bella, CA 93270-0150. (209) 535-5722. This publication provides information for the new and continuing mail-order entrepreneur.

 Mail Order Moonlighting, by Cecil C. Hoge, Sr., ©1988, 416 pp., ISBN: 0-89815-222-4, $9.95. Ten Speed Press, PO Box 7123, Berkeley, CA 94707. (800) 841-BOOK; (510) 845-8414; (510) 524-1052 (fax). A complete course on mail-order success by one of the masters in the industry.

 Mail Order Success Secrets, by Tyler G. Hicks, ©1994, 320 pp., ISBN: 1-55958-144-1, $12.95. Prima Publishing, PO Box 1260, Rocklin, CA 95677-1260. (916) 632-7400; (916) 632-7668 (fax). Down-to-earth advice from a longtime business owner who built a successful mail-order empire.

 Money In Your Mailbox, by L. Perry Wilbur, 240 pp., ISBN: 0-471-57330-2, $12.95. John Wiley & Sons, Inc., 605 Third Ave., New York, NY 10158-0012. (800) CALL-WILEY; (212) 850-6000; (212) 850-8641 (fax). Professional tips and techniques on how to start and operate a mail-order business.

 National Infomercial Marketing Association International, Helene Blake, 1201 New York Ave. NW, Ste. 1000, Washington, DC 20005. (800) 962-9796; (202) 962-8342; (202) 962-8300 (fax). This association represents the interests of the infomercial, home shopping, and direct response spot industry.

 Sell Anything by Mail, by Frank Jefkins, ©1990, 144 pp., ISBN: 1-55850-942-9, $6.95. Bob Adams, Inc., 260 Center St., Holbrook, MA 02343. (800) 872-5627; (617) 767-8100; (800) 872-5628 (fax). This how-to book provides a direct and functional approach to the mail-order business.

Selling by Mail Order, $1.00. U.S. Small Business Administration, SBA Publications, PO Box 30, Denver, CO 80201-0030. (800) 827-5722; (202) 205-6665. This booklet provides basic information on how to start and run a successful mail-order business, including product selection, pricing, testing, and writing effective ads.

Successful Direct Marketing Methods, by Bob Stone, ©1994, 640 pp., ISBN: 0-8442-3510-5, 39.95. National Textbook Company, 4255 W. Touhy Ave., Lincolnwood, IL 60646-1975. (800) 323-4900; (708) 679-5500; (708) 679-2494 (fax). An updated fifth edition of the industry classic by a pro with more than 40 years experience. It covers every step of the process, from selecting an offer to evaluating responses as well as details on new developments such as interactive computer vehicles and business-to-business strategies.

The Complete Direct Marketing Sourcebook, by John Kremer, ©1992, 276 pp., ISBN: 0-471-55387-5, $19.95. John Wiley & Sons, Inc., 605 Third Ave., New York, NY 10158-0012. (800) CALL-WILEY; (212) 850-6000; (212) 850-8641 (fax). This comprehensive sourcebook is an easy-to-use, hands-on guide to organizing and managing a successful direct-marketing program. It includes more than 40 blank worksheets, checklists, and sample letters to help anyone—from mail-order neophytes to seasoned professionals—make the most of their direct-marketing promotions.

The Golden Mailbox, by Ted Nicholas, 212 pp., ISBN: 0-7931-0486-6, $39.95. Dearborn Trade, 520 N. Dearborn St., Chicago, IL 60610-4354. (800) 245-2665; (312) 836-4400; (312) 836-1021 (fax). In this classic, direct-marketing pro Nicholas shares his secrets for success, including selecting products, pricing, choosing lists and ad media, evaluating copy and layout, managing costs, fulfilling orders, and more.

Education

Many feel that while entrepreneurial *instinct* cannot be taught, entrepreneurial *skills* can be learned by nearly anyone. (Whether success depends on some magical combination of the two is still being debated—and likely will be for years.) In response to increased interest, a growing number of private and public colleges and universities have expanded their traditional business departments to offer classes in entrepreneurship. In addition to these nationally acclaimed universities, local junior colleges and adult education centers frequently offer innovative courses.

A common trait of successful entrepreneurs is their commitment to lifelong learning. Explore the resources below as well as the educational offerings in your area to expand your own knowledge and abilities.

Center for Entrepreneurial Studies at Babson College, William D. Bygrave, Executive Director, Babson College, Babson Park, Wellesley, MA 02157. (617) 239-4332, (617) 239-5272 (fax). Babson is consistently rated as one of the leading entrepreneurial education centers in the U.S. It offers a full range of undergraduate and graduate courses, conducts and publishes research, and sponsors an outreach program to encourage and honor entrepreneurship and assist other colleges in starting entrepreneurial studies' programs.

The Entrepreneurial Center, Inc., Marge Lovero, Executive Director, The Centre at Purchase, 1 Manhattanville Rd., Purchase, NY 10577. (800) MY-START; (914) 694-4947; (914) 694-6498 (fax). This nonprofit educational center offers innovative programs for both emerging and established entrepreneurs. The Center also publishes a quarterly newsletter, hosts regular networking forums, provides counseling, and maintains a library. Annual membership is $125.00.

Colleges and Universities

Ball State University
School of Business
Muncie, IN 47306
(317) 289-1241

Baylor University
Baugh Center for
Entrepreneurship
Waco, TX 76798-8011
(817) 755-1011
(817) 755-2265

Boise State University
School of Business
1910 University Dr.
Boise, ID 83725
(208) 385-1011

Bradley University
School of Business
1501 W. Bradley Avenue
Peoria, IL 61625
(309) 676-7611

Brigham Young University
School of Business
Provo, UT 84602
(801) 378-1211

**California State
Polytechnic Institute**
School of Business
3801 W. Temple Ave.
Pomona, CA 91768
(714) 869-7659

**California State University,
Bakersfield**
College of Business
9001 Stockdale Hwy.
Bakersfield, CA 93311
(805) 823-2011

**California State University,
Fullerton**
College of Business
800 N. State College Blvd.
Fullerton, CA 92631
(714) 773-2011

**California State University,
Hayward**
College of Business
Hayward, CA 94542
(415) 881-3000

**California State University,
Los Angeles**
College of Business
5151 State University Dr.
Los Angeles, CA 90032
(213) 343-3000

**Central Michigan
University**
School of Business
Mount Pleasant, MI 48859
(517) 774-4000

Clemson University
School of Business
101 Sikes Hall
Clemson, SC 29634
(803) 656-3311

Cornell University
School of Business
401 Thurston Avenue
Ithaca, NY 14850
(607) 255-2000

East Carolina University
School of Business
East 5th St.
Greenville, NC 27858
(919) 757-6131

Eastern Michigan University
School of Business
Ypsilanti, MI 48197
(313) 487-1849

Farleigh Dickenson University
School of Business
223 Montross Avenue
Rutherford, NJ 07070
(201) 460-5000

Ferris State University
School of Business
901 S. State St.
Big Rapids, MI 49307
(616) 796-0461

Florida International University
School of Business
Tamiami Trail
Miami, FL 33199
(305) 554-2000

Florida State University
School of Business
600 W. College St.
Tallahassee, FL 32306
(904) 644-2525

Harvard University
Business School
Soldiers Field Rd.
Boston, MA 02163
(617) 495-6000

Indiana University at Bloomington
School of Business
Bloomington, IN 47405
(812) 332-0211

Kean College of New Jersey
School of Business
Morris Avenue
Union, NJ 07083
(908) 527-2000

Long Island University
College of Business
Northern Blvd.
Greenvale, NY 11548
(516) 299-0200

Louisiana State University
Office of the Dean
College of Business
Baton Rouge, LA 70803
(504) 388-3211

Louisiana Tech University
College of Business
700 W. California
Ruston, LA 71272
(318) 257-0211

Colleges and Universities *(continued)*

Marquette University
School of Business
517 N. 14th St.
Milwaukee, WI 53233
(414) 288-7700

Metropolitan State College
School of Business
1006 11th St.
Denver, CO 80204
(303) 556-2400

Northeastern University
School of Business
360 Huntington Ave.
Boston, MA 02115
(617) 373-2000

Northern Arizona University
School of Business
PO Box 4096
Flagstaff, AZ 86011
(602) 523-9011

Northern Illinois University
School of Business
DeKalb, IL 60115
(815) 753-1000

Ohio University
Dept. of Small Business &
Entrepreneurship
Haning 121
Athens, OH 45701
(614) 593-1000

Portland State University
School of Business
631 S.W. Harrison
Portland, OR 97214
(503) 725-3000

Saint Mary's College
Business Administration
and Entrepreneurial Studies
Notre Dame, IN 46556
(219) 284-4000

San Francisco State University
College of Business
1600 Holloway Ave.
San Francisco, CA 94132
(415) 338-1111

Southeast Missouri State University
School of Business
1 University Plaza
Cape Girardeau, MO 63701
(314) 651-2000

Stanford University
Ctr. for Entrepreneurship
Graduate School of Business
Stanford, CA 94305
(415) 723-2146

St. Louis University
Jefferson Smurfit Ctr. for
Entrepreneurial Studies
3674 Lindell Blvd.
St. Louis, MO 63108
(314) 658-3896

St. Mary's University
School of Business
1 Camino Santa Maria
San Antonio, TX 78228
(512) 436-3011

Texas A & M University
School of Business
College Station, TX 77843
(409) 845-3211

University of Alabama at Tuscaloosa
School of Business
Fergusson Center
University Post Office
Tuscaloosa, AL 35401
(205) 348-6010

University of Arizona
School of Business
Tucson, AZ 85721
(602) 621-2211

University of Arkansas
School of Business
Fayettville, AR 72701
(501) 575-2000

University of Colorado
School of Business
Campus Box 419
Boulder, CO 80306
(303) 492-1807

University of Connecticut
School of Business
368 Fairfield Rd.
Storrs, CT 06268-2041
(203) 486-2315 (BA)
(203) 486- 2872 (MBA)

University of Georgia
School of Business
114 Academic Building
Athens, GA 30602
(706) 542-3132

University of Illinois at Urbana-Champaign
School of Business
Rm. 350 Commerce West
1206 S. 6th St.
Champaign, IL 61801
(217) 333-1000

University of Miami
School of Business
Coral Gables, FL 33177
(305) 284-4641

University of Minnesota
School of Business
267 19th Ave. S.
Minneapolis, MN 55455
(612) 625-5000

University of Montana
School of Business
Missoula, MT 59812
(406) 243-0211 x4831

University of New Mexico
Anderson School of Business
University Hill N.E.
Albuquerque, NM 87131
(505) 277-0111

Colleges and Universities *(continued)*

University of North Texas
College of Business
PO Box 13677
Denton, TX 76203
(817) 565-2000

**University of
Northern Iowa**
College of Business
1222 W. 27th St.
Cedar Falls, IA 50614
(319) 273-6240

University of Pennsylvania
Wharton School of
Business
Entrepreneurial Center
3733 Spruce St.
Vance Hall, 4th fl.
Philadelphia, PA 19104
(215) 898-4856

University of Rhode Island
School of Business
Kingston, RI 02881
(401) 792-1000

**University of
South Carolina**
School of Business
Columbia, SC 29208
(803) 777-7000

**University of Southern
California**
The Entrepreneurship
Program
USC School of Business
Administration
Bridge Hall, Rm. 6
Los Angeles, CA 90089
(213) 740-0641

**University of Texas at
Austin**
College of Business
Administration
Austin, TX 78712
(512) 471-1000 (BA)
(512) 471-7612 (MBA)

University of Tulsa
School of Business
600 S. College Ave.
Tulsa, OK 74104
(918) 631-2000

**University of Wisconsin at
LaCrosse**
College of Business
1725 State St.
LaCrosse, WI 54601
(608) 785-8000

**University of Wisconsin at
Oshkosh**
College of Business
Administration
800 Algoma Blvd.
Oshkosh, WI 54901
(414) 424-1234

University of Wisconsin at Whitewater
School of Business
800 W. Main St.
Whitewater, WI 53190
(414) 472-1234

Virginia Commonwealth University
School of Business
1015 Floyd Ave.
PO Box 844000
Richmond, VA 23284
(804) 828-1595

Wayne State University
School of Business Administration
5201 Cass Ave.
Detroit, MI 48202
(313) 577-2424

Wichita State University
Center for Entrepreneurship
1845 Fairmount Ave.
Wichita, KS 67260-0147
(316) 698-3000

Xavier University
College of Business
7325 Palmetto St.
New Orleans, LA 70125
(504) 486-7411

Youngstown State University
College of Business
Williamson Hall
Youngstown, OH 44555
(216) 742-3000

Employees

See also Managing Your Business

Most solo entrepreneurs have chosen an independent business structure because they don't want or need employees. As a result, developing skills in working with others often takes a back seat to more pressing concerns. Yet as an enterprise grows, the need for managing others and even—heaven forbid!—hiring an assistant may be inevitable. In this section you'll find resources for developing your skills in supervising others as well as guidance on finding and hiring part-time and full-time employees. Even if hiring employees is not in your plans, the information and techniques on working with others can be of great value to your solo efforts.

 A Small Business Guide to Employee Selection, by Lin Grensing, ©1991, 176 pp., ISBN: 0-88908-959-0, $7.95. Self-Counsel Press, Inc., 1704 N. State St., Bellingham, WA 98225. (800) 663-3007; (206) 676-4530; (206) 676-4549 (fax). This book teaches you how to define the needs of your business in regard to hiring the best possible employees. Also available on audiotape.

 Assertiveness for Managers, by Diana Cawood, ©1992, 168 pp., ISBN: 0-88908-996-5, $12.95. Self-Counsel Press, Inc., 1704 N. State St., Bellingham, WA 98225. (800) 663-3007; (206) 676-4530; (206) 676-4549 (fax). This book explores the importance and effectiveness of assertive management techniques, and how to develop skills to communicate and delegate among colleagues and assistants.

 Checklist for Developing a Training Program, $0.50. U.S. Small Business Administration, SBA Publications, PO Box 30, Denver, CO 80201-0030. (800) 827-5722; (202) 205-6665. This pamphlet describes a step-by-step manner in which you can set up an effective employee training program.

Employee Benefits for Small Business, by Jane White, ©1991, ISBN: 0-13-273939-9, $25.00. Prentice Hall, 15 Columbus Circle, New York, NY 10023. (212) 373-8500; (212) 698-8059 (fax). This book discusses a variety of options available to small business owners interested in providing benefits to their employees.

 Employees: How to Find and Pay Them, $1.00. U.S. Small Business Administration, SBA Publications, PO Box 30, Denver, CO 80201-0030. (800) 827-5722; (202) 205-6665. This booklet helps you discover and hire the right people for your business, and advises on compensation.

 Hiring the Best, by Ann M. Magill, ©1993, 100 pp., ISBN: 1-55623-865-7, $10.00. Irwin Professional Publishing, Inc., 1333 Burr Ridge Pkwy., Burr Ridge, IL 60521. (800) 634-3961; (708) 789-4000. How to find and hire the best possible employees for your business.

 How to Delegate Work and Ensure It's Done Right, by Dick Lohr, $49.95. CareerTrack, 3085 Center Green Dr., Boulder, CO 80301-5408. (800) 334-1018; (800) 832-9489 (fax). This program teaches delegating skills that really work in an easy to follow, step-by-step program. Also available on video for $119.95.

 How to Get Results Through People, by William H., $59.95. SkillPath, Inc., 6900 Squibb Rd., PO Box 2768, Mission, KS 66201-2768. (800) 873-7545; (913) 677-3200; (913) 362-4241 (fax). Learn from professional managers how to achieve top performance from your support staff. This set, based on a live seminar presentation, contains six tapes.

 How to Handle People with Tact and Skill Seminar, 1 day, $39.00. CareerTrack, 3085 Center Green Dr., Boulder, CO 80301-5408. (800) 334-1018; (800) 832-9489 (fax). This seminar teaches specific strategies for dealing with difficult people in the business environment.

 How to Supervise People, 1 day, $99.00. Fred Pryor Seminars, 2000 Shawnee Mission Pkwy., Shawnee Mission, KS 66205. (800) 938-6330; (913) 722-8580 (fax). This seminar teaches how to motivate, manage, and take charge of projects and people. It covers creating a plan, delegating, working under pressure, training new employees, developing your own style of leadership, and more. A related video program is also available for $95.00.

Delegating with Clarity

When a solo enterprise grows and it's time to take on assistants, many entrepreneurs face unexpected challenges in delegating tasks. Accustomed to working independently, we often lack the skills of effectively communicating how we want a job completed. Our previous experience was an internal dialogue —and we always understood what we wanted accomplished!

One of the best ways of successfully delegating any task is to explain the end result the work is trying to achieve. With the final goal clearly in mind, both parties can strategize how best to reach it.

 Managing Employee Benefits, $1.00. U.S. Small Business Administration, SBA Publications, PO Box 30, Denver, CO 80201-0030. (800) 827-5722; (202) 205-6665. This booklet discusses the role of employee benefits as part of an overall compensation package and the proper way to manage them.

 Managing People, by Sara P. Noble, Ed., ©1992, 191 pp., ISBN: 1-880394-02-2, $12.95. Inc. Publishing, 38 Commercial Wharf, Boston, MA 02110-3883. (800) 468-0800 x4760; (617) 248-8000. A collection of 101 proven ideas for making you and your staff more productive, gathered from interviews with leading small business owners and articles from *Inc.* magazine. Topics include: hiring, motivation, communications, productivity, incentives, salary and bonuses, long-term compensation, benefits, performance reviews, firing, and the law.

 People, Common Sense & the Small Business, by Patricia Tway, ©1992, 224 pp., ISBN: 1-55870-245-8, $9.95. Betterway Books, 1507 Dana Avenue, Cincinnati, OH 45207. (800) 289-0963; (513) 531-4082 (fax). Provides how-to advice on developing motivated and successful workers, emphasizing the responsibility of the business owner.

Simplified Employee Pensions: What Small Businesses Need to Know, ©1988, 12 pp., ISBN: 0-16-004561-4, $1.00. U.S. Small Business Administration, New Orders, Superintendent of Documents, PO Box 371954, Pittsburgh, PA 15250-7954. (202) 783-3238; (202) 512-2250 (fax). SEPs were created by Congress in 1978 and make it easy for small companies to offer retirement savings plans to their employees. This pamphlet describes what they are, how to establish one, and provides answers to commonly asked questions.

 Supervising Part-Time Employees: A Guide to Better Productivity, by Elwood M. Chapman, ©1994, 85 pp., ISBN: 1-56052-243-7, $8.95. Crisp Publications, 1200 Hamilton Ct., Menlo Park, CA 94025. (415) 323-6100; (415) 323-5800 (fax). Learn to utilize your part-time staff, delegate specific jobs, and evaluate the contributions of part-time employees.

 Techniques for Productivity Improvement, $1.00. U.S. Small Business Administration, SBA Publications, PO Box 30, Denver, CO 80201-0030. (800) 827-5722; (202) 205-6665. This booklet teaches the small business owner motivational concepts to increase worker productivity, and how to tailor benefit packages to meet employee needs.

 Training Methods That Work, by Lois B. Hart, ©1993, 96 pp., ISBN: 1-56052-082-5, $8.95. Crisp Publications, 1200 Hamilton Ct., Menlo Park, CA 94025. (415) 323-6100; (415) 323-5800 (fax). This book describes specific innovative training methods and guidelines on how to select, conduct, and evaluate the best ones.

Financial Matters

See also Bookkeeping and Accounting; Taxes

Here is a collection of resources that can assist all entrepreneurs in gaining a better understanding and control of their business finances. Every aspect of financial management is represented, from budgeting, collections, and cash flow to pricing, financial reports, and applying for loans. Several items are designed for business owners with little or no financial background—a good place to start if you're feeling overwhelmed by the jargon and methods. Even if you rely on an outside financial advisor to assist you in most of your business dealings, the resources featured in this section will empower you by providing you with a better grasp of a key element of solo business success—your finances.

General Financial Management

 Analyze Your Records to Reduce Costs, $0.50. U.S. Small Business Administration, SBA Publications, PO Box 30, Denver, CO 80201-0030. (800) 827-5722; (202) 205-6665. This pamphlet teaches you how to relate expenses to sales, inventories, and profits, and how to utilize your money more efficiently.

 Buying for Retail Stores, $1.00. U.S. Small Business Administration, SBA Publications, PO Box 30, Denver, CO 80201-0030. (800) 827-5722; (202) 205-6665. This booklet covers the latest trends in retail buying patterns, offers guidance on making buying decisions, and includes a bibliography for further private and public sources of information on the topic.

Finance and Accounting for Nonfinancial Managers, by Richard L. and Keith A. Lymon, $165.00. Fred Pryor Seminars, 2000 Shawnee Mission Pkwy., Shawnee Mission, KS 66205. (800) 938-6330; (913) 722-8580 (fax). This practical program offers an understanding of financial and accounting terms, techniques, and practices—even if you have no financial background. Covers interpreting financial statements, calculating inventory costs, determining profitability, managing cash flow, and more.

Finance for Non-Financial Professionals, 4 hrs., $249.95. CareerTrack, 3085 Center Green Dr., Boulder, CO 80301-5408. (800) 334-1018; (800) 832-9489 (fax). This program is designed to teach you business finance quickly and easily. It increases your knowledge of financial language and helps you prepare and analyze financial statements. A 48-page workbook is included with the three-volume video package.

Financial Basics of Small Business Success, by James O. Gill, ©1993, 175 pp., ISBN: 1-56052-167-8, $15.95. Crisp Publications, 1200 Hamilton Ct., Menlo Park, CA 94025. (415) 323-6100; (415) 323-5800 (fax). This book helps new business owners decide which financial reports are needed to control the business, and how to read, understand, and use these tools effectively.

Financial Templates for Small Business, ©1994, $69.95. Oasis Press, 300 N. Valley Dr., Grants Pass, OR 97526. (800) 228-2275; (503) 479-9464; (503) 476-1479 (fax). This collection of 28 financial templates includes spreadsheets to help you forecast and track your business, chart cash flow, evaluate income, project sales, analyze break-even points, and more. Works with Lotus 1-2-3 and Microsoft Excel for DOS. Comes with one 3.5" disk and instruction manual.

Graphic Artist's Guild Handbook of Pricing & Ethical Guidelines, by Graphic Artist's Guild, ©1994, 240 pp., ISBN: 0-932102-08-5, $24.95. North Light Books, 1507 Dana Ave., Cincinnati, OH 45207. (800) 289-0963; (513) 531-4082 (fax). This classic reference provides the latest information on graphics-business pricing and ethical standards, including market data in nearly every discipline of the visual communications industry. Details on copyright, taxes, and the impact of computers is also featured.

How to Make Your Design Business Profitable, by Joyce Stewart, ©1992, 136 pp., ISBN: 0-89134-391-1, $21.95. North Light Books, 1507 Dana Ave., Cincinnati, OH 45207. (800) 289-0963; (513) 531-4082 (fax). A graphic designer's guide to watching and increasing the bottom line profit. Includes helpful checklists and personal profiles.

 Purchasing for Owners of Small Plants, $0.50. U.S. Small Business Administration, SBA Publications, PO Box 30, Denver, CO 80201-0030. (800) 827-5722; (202) 205-6665. This pamphlet provides an outline of an effective purchasing program. It also contains a bibliography for further sources of information on the subject.

 Simple Break-Even Analysis for Small Stores, $1.00. U.S. Small Business Administration, SBA Publications, PO Box 30, Denver, CO 80201-0030. (800) 827-5722; (202) 205-6665. Directed at small store owners/managers, this booklet enables you to make better sales and cost decisions.

 Sound Cash Management and Borrowing, $0.50. U.S. Small Business Association, SBA Publications, PO Box 30, Denver, CO 80201-0030. (800) 827-5722; (202) 205-6665. This pamphlet describes ways in which small business managers can avoid a financial crises through proper use of cash flow management and budgeting strategies.

 The Small Business Survival Guide, by Robert E. Fleury, ©1994, 256 pp., ISBN: 0-942061-12-8, $17.95. Sourcebooks, PO Box 372, Naperville, IL 60566. (800) SBS-8866; (708) 961-3900. A guide to managing cash, profits, and taxes in your business. Includes tips on simplifying your recordkeeping, managing cash flow, understanding accounting and tax cycles, and more.

 The Small Business Survival Kit: 134 Troubleshooting Tips for Success, by John Ventura, ©1994, 272 pp., ISBN: 0-79310-608-7, $19.95. Dearborn Trade, 520 N. Dearborn St., Chicago, IL 60610-4354. (800) 245-2665; (312) 836-4400; (312) 836-1021 (fax). John Ventura, a certified bankruptcy attorney, presents successful tactics for limiting liability, protecting assets, and controlling cash flow. He also examines ways in which entrepreneurs can minimize the emotional stresses of tough times in business.

Understanding and Managing Financial Information, by Michael M. Coltman, ©1993, 232 pp., ISBN: 0-88908-297-9, $9.95. Self-Counsel Press, Inc., 1704 N. State St., Bellingham, WA 98225. (800) 663-3007; (206) 676-4530; (206) 676-4549 (fax). This book explains in plain English how business finance really works. It includes information about balancing books, understanding income statements, and establishing internal financial controls. Readers also learn valuable skills in areas such as setting fiscal objectives and getting more out of financial reports.

Budgeting

 Basic Budgets for Profit Planning, $1.00. U.S. Small Business Administration, SBA Publications, PO Box 30, Denver, CO 80201-0030. (800) 827-5722; (202) 205-6665. This booklet helps you put together a comprehensive budgeting system to monitor and assess your financial operations.

 Budgeting Basics and Beyond, by Jae K. Shim & Joel G. Siegel, ©1994, ISBN: 0-13-312232-8, $19.95. Prentice Hall, Career & Personal Development, Paramount Publishing, 200 Old Tappan Rd., Old Tappan, NJ 07675. (800) 922-0579; (800) 445-6991 (fax). This budgeting primer is designed for the nonfinancial business-person. It explains what budgets are, how they work, how to prepare and present them, and how to monitor actual results against budget figures.

 Budgeting for a Small Business: A Primer for Entrepreneurs, by Terry Dickey, ©1992, 200 pp., ISBN: 1-56052-171-6, $15.95. Crisp Publications, 1200 Hamilton Ct., Menlo Park, CA 94025. (415) 323-6100; (415) 323-5800 (fax). This book teaches the skills necessary for cost-effective analysis of business budgets. It provides many examples, checklists, and worksheets to help readers improve their own budgeting skills.

 Budgeting in a Small Service Firm, $.050. U.S. Small Business Administration, SBA Publications, PO Box 30, Denver, CO 80201-0030. (800) 827-5722; (202) 205-6665. This pamphlet teaches you how to set up and maintain sound financial records and use journals, ledgers, and charts to increase profits.

How to Develop and Administer a Budget Seminar, 1 day, $199.00. Fred Pryor Seminars, 2000 Shawnee Mission Pkwy., Shawnee Mission, KS 66205. (800) 938-6330; (913) 722-8580 (fax). This seminar teaches strategies and techniques on how to make budgeting a reliable and powerful management tool.

Cash Flow and Collections

Cash Flow Letter Book for the Small Business, by Thomas Morton, ©1993, 194 pp., ISBN: 0-471-58079-1, $69.95. John Wiley & Sons, Inc., 605 Third Ave., New York, NY 10158-0012. (800) CALL-WILEY; (212) 850-6000; (212) 850-8641 (fax). This book is geared toward maintaining and promoting better cash flow for the small business. It contains over 200 letters and provides a step-by-step method to assist business owners in achieving a steady cash flow.

Cash Flow Problem Solver, by Bryan E. Milling, ©1994, 304 pp., ISBN: 0942061-27-6, $19.95. Sourcebooks, PO Box 372, Naperville, IL 60566. (800) SBS-8866; (708) 961-3900. Presents common problems and practical solutions for managing cash flow and other financial matters in your business.

Cashflow, Credit and Collection, by Basil P. Mavrovitis, ©1994, 400 pp., ISBN: 1-55738-522-X, $32.50. Probus Publishing, Inc., 1925 N. Clyburn Ave. #401, Chicago, IL 60614. (800) PROBUS-1; (312) 868-6250 (fax). A hands-on manual featuring tips, trends, and tactics for improving your balance sheet.

Collect Those Debts!, by Timothy R. Paulsen, ©1992, 128 pp., ISBN: 0-88908-541-2, $8.95. Self-Counsel Press, Inc., 1704 N. State St., Bellingham, WA 98225. (800) 663-3007; (206) 676-4530; (206) 676-4549 (fax). This how-to book provides tips and techniques to make debt collection easier and more effective.

Collection Techniques for a Small Business, by Gini G. Scott & John J. Harrison, ©1994, 320 pp., ISBN: 1-55571-171-5, $19.95. Oasis Press, 300 N. Valley Dr., Grants Pass, OR 97526. (800) 228-2275; (503) 479-9464; (503) 476-1479 (fax). Designed especially for the small business owner, this book offers tips, examples, and advice on: establishing a business credit policy; tracking accounts and debts; communicating with debtors by phone, letter or in person; using lawyers, collection agencies, and courts; and more.

Extending Credit and Collecting Cash, by Lynn Harrison, ©1993, 175 pp., ISBN: 1-56052-168-6, $15.95. Crisp Publications, 1200 Hamilton Ct., Menlo Park, CA 94025. (415) 323-6100; (415) 323-5800 (fax). This book provides its readers with helpful advice for developing an effective collection program and offers tips for dealing with slow payers and legally volatile situations.

 Getting Paid in Full, by W. Kelsea Wilber, ©1994, 156 pp., ISBN: 0-942061-68-3, $8.95. Sourcebooks, PO Box 372, Naperville, IL 60566. (800) SBS-8866; (708) 961-3900. A guide on how to establish a successful credit policy in your business, including how to set up a new account, what to do about nonpayment of services, how to locate missing customers, and more.

 The Cash-Flow Control Guide, by David H. Bangs, Jr., ©1994, 88 pp., ISBN: 0-936894-02-4, $14.95. Upstart Publishing Co., Inc., 12 Portland St., Dover, NH 03820. (800) 235-8866; (603) 749-5071; (603) 742-9121 (fax). This book uses real-life examples to illustrate the importance and effectiveness of cash-flow planning, one of the largest challenges facing small businesses.

 Understanding Cash Flow, $1.00. U.S. Small Business Administration, SBA Publications, PO Box 30, Denver, CO 80201-0030. (800) 827-5722; (202) 205-6665. This booklet teaches the small business manager how to monitor the flow of cash through the budget and thus plan for future requirements.

Funding

 A Venture Capital Primer for Small Business, $0.50. U.S. Small Business Administration, SBA Publications, PO Box 30, Denver, CO 80201-0030. (800) 827-5722; (202) 205-6665. This pamphlet helps you learn which venture capital resources are available to you and teaches you how to develop a proposal regarding their acquisition.

  ABC's of Borrowing, $1.00. U.S. Small Business Administration, SBA Publications, PO Box 30, Denver, CO 80201-0030. (800) 827-5722; (202) 205-6665. This booklet, one of the SBA's best-sellers, teaches you what to expect when borrowing money for your small business and provides tips regarding the qualities which lenders look for most.

ACCION International, 130 Prospect St., Cambridge, MA 02139. (617) 492-4930; (617) 876-9509 (fax). This private, nonprofit organization provides the tools of economic self-sufficiency— small loans and business training—to the self-employed poor in the United States and Latin America. Innovative programs and its high success rate in nurturing small business ventures has made the organization a recognized leader in the microenterprise arena. ACCION focuses on education and microlending, and recently established additional U.S. affiliate centers in Albuquerque, Chicago, New York City, San Antonio, and San Diego.

 Directory of U.S. Microenterprise Programs, ©1994, 326 pp., ISBN: 0-89843-152-2, $12.00 (postpaid). Aspen Institute, PO Box 222, Queenstown, MD 21658. (410) 820-5326. Compiled by the Self-Employment Learning Project of the Aspen Institute, this directory profiles nearly 200 microenterprise development programs in operation throughout the United States. It provides information on each program's orientation, geographic area served, target population, typical client profile, loan statistics, technical and educational assistance offered, and brief descriptions of future development strategies. Full contact information is also given. (The $12.00 price of the book includes shipping costs.)

 Finding Money for Your Small Business: The One-Stop Guide to Raising All the Money You Will Need, by Max Fallek, ©1994, 208 pp., ISBN: 0-79310-422-X, $19.95. Upstart Publishing Co., Inc., 12 Portland St., Dover, NH 03820. (800) 235-8866; (603) 749-5071; (603) 742-9121 (fax). This book, written by the founder of the American Institute of Small Business, explores every potential avenue for raising money for your small business.

 Free Money for Small Businesses and Entrepreneurs, by Laurie Blum, ©1992, 304 pp., ISBN: 0-471-58122-4, $14.95. John Wiley & Sons, Inc., 605 Third Ave., New York, NY 10158-0012. (800) CALL-WILEY; (212) 850-6000. More than 600 sources of "free money" to help entrepreneurs tap into billions of dollars of available capital, from start-up funds to research grants.

Getting a Business Loan: Your Step-By-Step Guide, by Orlando J. Antonini, ©1993, 175 pp., ISBN: 1-56052-164-3, $15.95. Crisp Publications, 1200 Hamilton Ct., Menlo Park, CA 94025. (415) 323-6100; (415) 323-5800 (fax). Clearly written for any layperson, this book explains the details involved with getting a loan for your business. It covers what lenders look for, why your assets may become a liability, and what to do if you are denied the loan.

 Guerrilla Financing, by Jay Conrad Levinson & Bruce Jan Blechman, ©1992, 320 pp., ISBN: 0-395-52264-1, $10.95. Houghton Mifflin Company, Wayside Rd., Burlington, MA 01803. (800) 225-3362. A sourcebook for finance in the 1990s, this book describes in detail traditional and alternative sources of funding for small- and medium-sized businesses.

 How to Get a Loan or Line of Credit for Your Business, by Bryan Milling, ©1994, 152 pp., ISBN: 0-942061-43-8, $8.95. Sourcebooks, PO Box 372, Naperville, IL 60566. (800) SBS-8866; (708) 961-3900. Written by a banker, this book shows you how to apply for a bank loan, the criteria banks look for in approving your loan, and an explanation of the different types of loans available. Includes step-by-step financial forms to guide you through the process.

Microloans, Maximum Impact

A new category of funding has sprung up in the past few years: microloans, or loans ranging from a few hundred to a few thousand dollars. While small in dollar amount, these funds can have a big impact on fledgling solo businesses. Several nonprofit agencies have launched successful microenterprise programs in developing nations and U.S. urban areas. Similarly, the U.S. Small Business Administration (SBA) recently launched a nationwide microloan program through participating nonprofit organizations and banks that is open to the self-employed. SBA microloans range from $100 to $25,000 (averaging $10,000) and must be paid back within six years. Use the resources listed here and contact your SBA office (listed in Government Resources*) for details.*

Income Opportunities, by Stephen Wagner, Ed., monthly, $9.97/yr. IO Publications, Inc., 1500 Broadway, New York, NY 10036-4015. (212) 642-0600; (212) 302-8269 (fax). This magazine focuses on a wide variety of money-making opportunities for entrepreneurs and small business owners.

 National Association of Small Business Investment Companies, Jeanette D. Smith, 1199 N. Fairfax St., Ste. 200, Alexandria, VA 22314-1437. (703) 683-1601; (703) 683-1605 (fax). More than 300 companies who are licensed under the Small Business Investment Act of 1958 belong to this association. They publish a monthly newsletter and host an annual meeting in the fall.

 Raising Capital: How to Finance Your Business, 90 min., $99.00. Inc. Business Resources, 350 N. Pennsylvania Ave., PO Box 1365, Wilkes-Barre, PA 13703-1365. (800) 468-0800 x4760; (717) 822-8899. In this video, key financial issues are discussed, including attracting money in the 1990s, developing a strong relationship with a bank, improving collection procedures, increasing cash flow, and reducing expenses.

 Raising Capital: How to Write a Financing Proposal, by Lawrence Flanagan, ©1994, 230 pp., ISBN: 1-55571-305-X, $19.95. Oasis Press, 300 N. Valley Dr., Grants Pass, OR 97526. (800) 228-2275; (503) 479-9464; (503) 476-1479 (fax). Professional tips and detailed examples on how to write and present a winning loan proposal.

 SBA Loans, by Patrick D. O'Hara, ©1994, 304 pp., ISBN: 0-471-30331-3, $19.95. John Wiley & Sons, Inc., 605 Third Ave., New York, NY 10158-0012. (800) CALL-WILEY; (212) 850-6000. Step-by-step guidance on how to apply for an SBA loan, including business plan guidelines, loan and grant programs, and loan terms and requirements.

 Start Up Money, by Jennifer Lindsay, ©1989, 256 pp., ISBN: 0-471-50031-3, $17.95. John Wiley & Sons, Inc., 605 Third Ave., New York, NY 10158-0012. (800) CALL-WILEY; (212) 850-6000. This book presents a wide range of traditional and nontraditional techniques for raising money for your small business start-up.

The Complete Small Business Loan Kit, by the Consumer Law Foundation, ©1989, 192 pp., ISBN: 1-55850-996-8, $12.95. Bob Adams, Inc., 260 Center St., Holbrook, MA 02343. (800) 872-5627; (617) 767-8100; (800) 872-5628 (fax). This book shows how to assemble and prepare the needed information to get loans from both private and public sources. It also features completed sample forms from the loan department of the U.S. Small Business Administration (SBA).

 The Money Connection: Where & How to Apply for Business Loans, by Lawrence Flanagan, ©1994, 177 pp., ISBN: 1-55571-307-6, $24.95. Oasis Press, 300 N. Valley Dr., Grants Pass, OR 97526. (800) 228-2275; (503) 479-9464; (503) 476-1479 (fax). A comprehensive listing of funding sources, including the latest federal state, county, and community loan, investment and assistance programs. Hundreds of nationally recognized business loan and venture capital firms are also listed.

Pricing

 A Pricing Checklist for Small Retailers, $1.00. U.S. Small Business Administration, SBA Publications, PO Box 30, Denver, CO 80201-0030. (800) 827-5722; (202) 205-6665. This booklet provides a checklist to help small business owners apply pricing strategies which can lead to business profits.

 Pricing Your Products and Services Profitably, $1.00. U.S. Small Business Administration, SBA Publications, PO Box 30, Denver, CO 80201-0030. (202) 205-6665. This booklet shows you how to price your products for profitability and offers tips on pricing techniques and when to use them.

 Profit Costing and Pricing for Manufacturers, $1.00. U.S. Small Business Administration, SBA Publications, PO Box 30, Denver, CO 80201-0030. (800) 827-5722; (202) 205-6665. This booklet discloses the latest methods available to help you price your products profitably.

Pricing for Profit

Establishing pricing for your product or service can be a delicate balance between what the market will bear and what your business needs to be profitable. Many new entrepreneurs base their prices on what others charge, or on guesstimates of what seems appropriate. A more financially sound approach is to determine your target income for the year as well as what total costs are incurred in creating your product or service (including items such as overhead, labor, materials, and marketing). With these figures in hand, you can build a more realistic pricing structure. Adjustments to account for market demand and competition may occur—but you'll have a strong financial basis on which to make your decisions.

Setting the Right Price for Your Design and Illustration, by Barbara Ganim, ©1994, 160 pp., ISBN: 1-55870-569-8, $24.99. Betterway Books, 1507 Dana Avenue, Cincinnati, OH 45207. (800) 289-0963; (513) 531-4082 (fax). This book helps designers establish pricing through a series of more than 30 interactive worksheets. It also covers how to prepare proposals, assemble a portfolio, make presentations, negotiate with difficult clients, stay competitive, and get paid.

The Pricing Advisor Newsletter, by Eric Mitchell, Publisher, monthly, $195.00/yr. The Pricing Advisor, Inc., 3277 Roswell Rd. Ste. 620, Atlanta, GA 30305. (404) 509-9933; (404) 509-1963 (fax). This monthly newsletter focuses on pricing strategies and policies. Publisher Eric Mitchell also conducts workshops and conferences on the subject. Several how-to workbooks are available.

Franchises

Buying a franchise gives a new small business owner a jump-start on launching a business, since the franchise fee generally covers the concept, marketing materials, and management assistance from the main office. Most franchises are "larger" small businesses that require facilities and staffs far beyond the scope of a solo effort. Many independent entrepreneurs investigate franchises, however, as a way to stay in touch with new business ideas and current trends. Often a franchise concept can be modified to a smaller scale or personalized to suit the interests and goals of a solo business owner.

 American Franchisee Association (AFA), Pamela Smith, 53 W. Jackson Blvd., Ste. 205, Chicago, IL 60604. (800) 334-4AFA; (312) 431-0545. AFA is a national trade association representing more than 13,000 outlets in 27 different industry areas. The group's aim is to represent and educate franchisees, and to protect and enhance the economic investment franchisees have made in their businesses. Members receive a quarterly publication, referrals to legal and business services, and discounts on business-related products and services. AFA also provides consulting services to individuals considering purchasing a franchise. Membership is $35/year.

 Business Opportunities Journal, Gina Petrone, Ed., monthly, $30.00/yr. Business Service Corporation, PO Box 990, Olalla, WA 98359. (800) 254-6570; (206) 857-7444; (206) 857-3720 (fax). This magazine covers business, real estate, and franchise opportunities.

 Buying Your First Franchise, by Rebecca Luhn, ©1994, 175 pp., ISBN: 1-56052-190-2, $15.95. Crisp Publications, 1200 Hamilton Ct., Menlo Park, CA 94025. (415) 323-6100; (415) 323-5800 (fax). This book helps first-time buyers make decisions about which franchise to buy, how to finance it, and how to make it succeed.

Entrepreneur's Guide to Franchise & Business Opportunities, Rieva Lesonsky, Ed., annually, $3.95. Entrepreneur Media, Inc., 2392 Morse Avenue, Irvine, CA 92714. (714) 261-2325. This annual report provides a comprehensive listing of franchise, business, and investment opportunities.

 Evaluating Franchise Opportunities, $1.00. U.S. Small Business Administration, SBA Publications, PO Box 30, Denver, CO 80201-0030. (800) 827-5722; (202) 205-6665. This booklet helps individuals determine if a franchise is the business opportunity right for them.

 Franchise Opportunities, ©1993, 320 pp., ISBN: 0-8069-8619-0, $12.95. Sterling Publishing Co., Inc., 387 Park Ave. South, New York, NY 10016-8810. (800) 367-9692; (212) 532-7160; (800) 542-7567 (fax). Every type of franchise is covered in this book: retail, food, vending machines, lodging, and more. Also includes general information on franchising, and details on operations, financing, and management.

 Franchising in the U.S., by Michael M. Coltman, ©1988, 160 pp., ISBN: 0-88908-923-X, $6.95. Self-Counsel Press, Inc., 1704 N. State St., Bellingham, WA 98225. (800) 663-3007; (206) 676-4530; (206) 676-4549 (fax). This book is full of advice about the pros and cons of franchise ownership. It provides the reader with a questionnaire to help determine which kinds of franchises might coincide with his or her interests. A sample franchise contract is included.

 Small Business Franchises Made Simple, by W. Lasher & C. Hausman, ©1994, ISBN: 0-385-42552-X, $12.00. Doubleday & Co. Inc., 1540 Broadway, New York, NY 10036. (800) 223-6834; (212) 354-6500. This book teaches readers how to establish a franchise, including legal information, financial concerns and practical tips.

 The 50 Best Low-Investment, High-Profit Franchises, by Robert L. Perry, ©1994, 325 pp., ISBN: 0-13-300393-0, $12.95. Prentice Hall, Career & Personal Development, Paramount Publishing, 200 Old Tappan Rd., Old Tappan, NJ 07675. (800) 922-0579; (800) 445-6991 (fax). A new edition of a classic best-seller that highlights 50 of the best franchises that can be started for as little as $2,000. It describes each franchise in detail, including start-up costs, hidden costs, requirements, franchise support packages, and more.

The Complete Franchise Book, by Dennis L. Foster, ©1994, 336 pp., ISBN: 1-55958-316-9, $14.95. Prima Publishing, PO Box 1260, Rocklin, CA 95677-1260. (916) 632-7400; (916) 632-7668 (fax). Everything you need to know about buying or starting your own franchise, including negotiating the contract, choosing the opportunity, and understanding your legal obligations.

 The Info Franchise Newsletter, Edward L. Dixon, Jr., Ed., monthly, $96.00/yr. Info Press, Inc., 728 Center St., PO Box 550, Lewiston, NY 14092-0550. (716) 754-4669. This newsletter is directed at those who are or wish to be involved in the world of franchising.

 Women in Franchising (WIF), Pamela Smith, 53 W. Jackson Blvd., #205, Chicago, IL 60604. (800) 222-4943; (312) 431-1467. WIF, a 100% woman-owned firm, educates and trains women and minorities about franchise business ownership. WIF offers pre-franchise management training for women and minorities, diversity training for franchisor organizations, and consulting services for prospective buyers of franchised businesses as well as prospective franchisors.

General Business Information

See also Choosing a Business; Starting a Business

This section of the WORKING SOLO SOURCEBOOK features resources that present a general overview of small business, ranging from start-up issues to advice on managing daily operations. While the subject matter may overlap in some of these materials, each presents the unique viewpoint of the author, often reflecting years of real-life experience. Many of these resources also can serve as a jumping-off point for a more in-depth study of a particular subject, based on the references found in their bibliographies and resource sections.

 American Dreams, by Kenneth Morris, ©1991, 224 pp., ISBN: 0-8109-3656-9, $35.00. Harry N. Abrams, Inc., 100 Fifth Ave., New York, NY 10011-6999. (212) 206-7715; (212) 645-8437 (fax). This book shares the stories of successful business owners and examines the history behind the American dream of self-sufficiency.

 Audio-Tech Business Book Summaries, Inc., Audio Tech Business Book Summaries, Inc., 117 W. Harrison Bldg. Ste. A-461, Chicago, IL 60605. (800) 776-1910; (312) 345-1910; (312) 345-1913 (fax). This company offers a wide variety of business book summaries on tape. Each title is selected and summarized so that listeners can capture the key points and ideas of each book.

 Barbara Brabec's Self-Employment Survival Letter, bimonthly, $29.00/yr. Barbara Brabec Productions, PO Box 2137, Naperville, IL 60567-2137. (708) 717-4188. This useful newsletter, formerly called the *National Home Business Report,* is directed at the small business owner or entrepreneur and covers issues such as marketing, advertising, management, and new resources. A sample issue is $5.00.

Bootstrappin' Entrepreneur, Kimberly Stanséll, Ed., quarterly, ISSN: 1063-3561, $30.00/yr. Research Done Right, 8726 S. Sepulveda Blvd., Ste. B261-WS, Los Angeles, CA 90045-4082. (310) 568-9861. This quarterly publication, subtitled "The Newsletter for Individuals with Great Ideas and a Little Bit of Cash," is filled with articles on low-cost marketing strategies, business-building tips and ideas, nationwide networking contacts, free products and services, and more. A sample issue is $8.00.

 Building a Profitable Business, by Greg Straughn & Charles Chickadel, ©1992, 320 pp., ISBN: 0-55850-272-6, $15.95. Bob Adams, Inc., 260 Center St., Holbrook, MA 02343. (800) 872-5627; (617) 767-8100; (800) 872-5628 (fax). Provides a general business overview of the challenges and opportunities in launching and running a small business.

 Business Careers and Lifestyles Series, RMI Media Productions, Inc., 2807 W. 47th Street, Shawnee Mission, KS 66205. (800) 745-5480; (913) 262-3974; (913) 362-6910 (fax). This series of 56 half-hour videos features host Dick Goldberg interviewing a variety of successful business people.

 Business Ideas & Shortcuts, Peter Joseph, Ed., monthly, $69.00/yr. Editorial Board, IBIS, PO Box 4082, Irvine, CA 92716-4082. (714) 552-8494. This publication is loaded with tips, advice, profit-raising shortcuts, and business opportunities.

 Country Bound! Trade Your Business Suit Blues for Blue Jean Dreams, by Marilyn and Tom Ross, ©1992, 430 pp., ISBN: 0-918880-30-0, $19.95. Communication Creativity, PO Box 909, 425 Cedar St., Buena Vista, CO 81211. (800) 331-8355; (719) 395-8659. A hands-on guide for individuals who want to move to rural areas and establish their own business. Includes hundreds of ideas and strategies for creating a profitable enterprise as well as checklists, quizzes, charts, and maps to guide you. Also available on audio for $59.95.

 Country Bound! Connection, Marilyn and Tom Ross, Eds., quarterly, $49.00/yr. Communication Creativity, PO Box 909, 425 Cedar St., Buena Vista, CO 81211. (800) 331-8355; (719) 395-8659. This quarterly newsletter is filled with country trends, career ideas, entrepreneurial marketing strategies, real estate bargain tips, and more.

Entrepreneur, Rieva Lesonsky, Ed., monthly, $19.97/yr. Entrepreneur Magazine, 2392 Morse Ave., Irvine, CA 92714. (800) 421-2300. This monthly publication is filled with practical and inspiring articles on every aspect of entrepreneurship.

 Entrepreneurship: Creativity at Work, by Harvard Business Review, ©1984, 140 pp., ISBN: 0-87584-285-2, $19.95. Harvard Business School Press, Operations Dept., Harvard Business School Publishing Division, Boston, MA 02163. (800) 545-7685; (617) 495-6192. A collection of articles from the *Harvard Business Review* on entrepreneurial topics, including start-up financing, business plans, strategy, people management, and the role of entrepreneurship in the national economy.

 Going Freelance: A Guide for Professionals, by Robert Laurance, ©1988, 218 pp., ISBN: 0-471-63255-4, $14.95. John Wiley & Sons, 605 Third Ave., New York, NY 10158-0012. (800) CALL-WILEY; (212) 850-6000. This book provides an overview of what it takes to be a successful freelancer, including determining whether you have the qualifications, how to set up and manage your business, and how to win and keep customers. A reference section features listings on associations, organizations, and publications.

 How to Build a Successful One-Person Business, by Veltisezar B. Bautista, ©1994, 320 pp., ISBN: 0-931613-09-4, $23.95. Bookhaus, 28091 Hickory Dr., PO Box 3277, Farmington Hills, MI 48333-3277. (313) 489-8460; (313) 778-5688 (fax). This comprehensive book is designed to guide readers through the many stages of running a one-person business, using common-sense management strategies and practical techniques.

 How to Run a Small Business, by J.K. Lasser Institute Staff, ©1993, ISBN: 0-07-036576-8, $27.95. McGraw-Hill, 10 Union Square E., New York, NY 10003. (800) 822-8158; (212) 353-5300. This classic helps readers choose the right business and suggests many ways to improve profits, avoid worry, and save time and money. Includes chapters on wholesale, manufacturing, and mail order.

How to Think Like an Entrepreneur, by Michael Shane, ©1994, 137 pp., ISBN: 0-9640346-0-3, $9.95. Brett Publishing, 1120 Avenue of the Americas, New York, NY 10036. (800) 469-2844. Insights and practical advice on running a business from a seasoned entrepreneur who founded five multimillion-dollar businesses. Covers: things to consider before you start a business; the value of information; how to make decisions; and mastering the three fundamental areas of business—marketing, management and money.

 In Business for Yourself, by Bruce Williams with Warren Sloat, ©1991, 267 pp., ISBN: 0-8128-4011-9, $19.95. Scarbrough House, Madison Books, 4720 Boston Way, Lanham, MD 20706. (301) 459-3366; (301) 459-2118 (fax). Radio talk-show host Bruce Williams gives his unique perspective on starting your own business. Includes details on start-up money and expansion capital; finding advice and assistance from bankers, lawyers, accountants, family, and friends; and advice on the practical operations of keeping a fledgling enterprise growing.

 Inc., George Gendron, Ed., monthly, ISSN: 0162-8968, $12.00/yr. Inc., 38 Commercial Wharf, Boston, MA 02110. (800) 234-0999; (617) 248-8000. This magazine, subtitled "The Magazine for Growing Companies," focuses on "larger" small businesses but consistently offers information useful for solo professionals.

 Journal of Small Business Management, Frederick C. Scherr, Ed., quarterly, $30.00/yr. West Virginia Bureau of Business Research, Box 6025, Morgantown, WV 26506-6025. (304) 293-7534. This quarterly publication features articles, essays, and editorials on small business and entrepreneurship.

 Keyboard Connection, Nancy Malvin, Ed., quarterly, $30.00/yr. PO Box 338-WSS, Glen Carbon, IL 62034-0338. (618) 667-8002 (fax). This quarterly newsletter is designed for individuals who run secretarial and office support service businesses in the U.S. and Canada. Each 12-page issue is full of practical ideas on how to get and keep customers, increase income, and work more efficiently and effectively. A sample issue is $4.00.

Kiplinger's Working for Yourself: Full-time, Part-Time, Anytime, by Joseph Anthony, ©1992, 328 pp., ISBN: 0-938721-23-2, $14.95. Kiplinger Books & Tapes, 1729 H Street NW, Washington, DC 20006. (800) 462-6420; (202) 887-6431. This informative guide covers the full spectrum of self-employment, including consulting, turning a hobby into a part-time business, franchising or buying an existing business, as well as advice on marketing, finances, customers, and more. Includes worksheets and checklists.

 Make it Happen!, C.E. Colwell, Ed., monthly, $25.00/yr. Action Marketing, Inc., 3747 NE Sandy Blvd., Portland, OR 97232. (503) 287-8321. This publication offers advice and how-to tips on business communications and marketing, networking, time management and more. Free in the Portland metro area.

 Making a Living Without a Job, by Barbara J. Winter, ©1993, 260 pp., ISBN: 0-553-37165-7, $10.95. Bantam Books, Inc., 1540 Broadway, New York, NY 10036. (800) 323-9872; (212) 354-6500. An inspiring book for those thinking about self-employment. It covers how to discover your talents, the overlooked link between self-esteem and self-employment, ways to develop multiple income sources, and more. Also includes exercises, checklists, and self-tests.

 McGraw-Hill 36-Hour Course in Entrepreneurship, by James W. Halloran, ©1994, 406 pp., ISBN: 0-07-0258-77-5, $16.95. McGraw-Hill, Inc., 11 W. 19th St., New York, NY 10011. (800) 822-8158. This step-by-step guide walks the reader through the many phases of entrepreneurship, from self-assessment, spotting lucrative trends, and start-up funding to staffing and expansion. In true academic tradition, a final exam is included in the back of the book.

 Mind Your Own Business!, by La Verne Ludden, Ed.D & Bonnie Maitlen, Ed.D, ©1994, 213 pp., ISBN: 1-56370-083-2, $9.95. JIST Works, Inc., 720 North Park Ave., Indianapolis, IN 46202-3431. (800) 648-5478; (317) 264-3720; (800) 547-8329 (fax). Written by two successful entrepreneurs, this book covers the basics of starting a new business or becoming self-employed. Includes questionnaires, assessment forms, worksheets, and checklists.

My Own Boss, quarterly, $12.00/yr. CAE Consultants, Inc., 41 Travers Ave., Yonkers, NY 10705. (914) 963-3695; (914) 963-3695 (fax). This is a trade publication that targets the professional who has or is considering beginning their own business.

 Nation's Business, Robert T. Gray, Ed., monthly, $22.00/yr. Nation's Business, 1615 H. St. NW, Washington, DC 20062-2000. (800) 638-6582; (202) 463-5650 (editorial). This magazine, published by the U.S. Chamber of Commerce, contains information of interest to anyone in the world of business. Each issue contains articles, news, and editorials on a wide range of important business topics.

 On Your Own, by Carol S. Lewis & Harry L. Helms, ©1994, 209 pp., ISBN: 1-879707-13-2, $14.95. HighText Publication, Inc., 125 North Acacia Ave., Ste. 110, Solana Beach, CA 92075. (800) 247-6553; (619) 793-4141; (619) 793-1955 (fax). This book details how to make the transition from corporate employee to successful independent contractor, including how to contact prospective clients, presenting your proposal, establishing fees, and keeping it all legal.

 Running a One-Person Business, by Claude Whitmyer, Salli Rasberry & Michael Phillips, ©1994, 224 pp., ISBN: 0-89815-598-3, $14.00. Ten Speed Press, PO Box 7123, Berkeley, CA 94707. (800) 841-BOOK; (510) 845-8414; (510) 524-1052 (fax). This book, aimed at those already in business or just considering the possibility, provides an overview of growing a business as an independent entrepreneur.

 Small Business Bulletin, Gina Roberts, Ed., bimonthly, Small Business Service Bureau, 554 Main St., PO Box 15014, Worcester, MA 01615-0014. (508) 756-3513; (508) 791-4709 (fax). This publication covers issues such as management assistance, benefits and services for the small business owner, as well as tax and retirement planning.

 Small Business Gazette, Jim Donovan, Pub., monthly, $18.00/yr. Bovan Associates, PO Box 1147, Buckingham, PA 18912. (215) 794-3826; (215) 794-3827 (fax). This monthly newspaper features news and informative articles targeted to small businesses and solo entrepreneurs. Distributed in the New York City and Philadelphia metro areas, it is available by subscription nationwide.

Small Business Opportunities, Susan Rakowski, Ed., bimonthly, $9.97/yr. Harris Publications, Inc., 1115 Broadway, 8th fl., New York, NY 10010. (212) 807-7110; (212) 627-4678 (fax). This how-to magazine is designed for budding entrepreneurs and small business owners.

 Small Business Reports: For Decision Makers in America's Small and Midsize Companies, Abby Livingston, Ed., monthly, $98.00/yr. American Management Association (AMA), Small Business Reports, PO Box 53140, Boulder, CO 80322-3140. (800) 234-1094; (303) 447-9330. This magazine, published by the AMA, contains a variety of information for the small-to-midsize business manager and entrepreneur.

 Sticks...For People Who Are Serious About Moving to the Country, Lisa Angowski, Ed., bimonthly, $36.00/yr. Moose Mountain Press, RR 1, Box 1234, Grafton, NH 03240. (603) 523-7877. This newsletter is directed at urban dwellers who are interested in moving to the country.

 Succeeding in Small Business, by Jane Applegate, ©1992, $12.00. Dutton, 120 Woodbine St., Bergenfield, NJ 07621. (800) 253-6476. Applegate, a nationally syndicated small business columnist, presents the answers to the 101 toughest problems small business owners are likely to face.

 Success, Scott DeGarmo, Ed., 10x/yr., ISSN: 0745-2489, $19.97/yr. Success Magazine Company, PO Box 3038, Harlan, IA 51537-3038. (800) 234-7324 (subscriptions). This magazine, subtitled "The Magazine for Today's Entrepreneurial Mind," has been tracking the American entrepreneurial spirit for nearly 100 years. Each issue features a variety of inspirational and informative articles along with real-life stories of entrepreneurial challenges and success.

 Success Essentials, $149.95. SkillPath, Inc., 6900 Squibb Rd., PO Box 2768, Mission, KS 66201-2768. (800) 873-7545; (913) 677-3200; (913) 362-4241 (fax). Compiled and published by the American Management Association, this 20-cassette library is filled with information related to every aspect of a small business.

The Accidental Entrepreneur, bimonthly, $24.00/yr. Dixie Darr, 3421 Alcott St., Denver, CO 80211. (303) 433-0345. This newsletter offers information, inspiration, tips, resources, and practical guidance to individuals making the transition from employee to being self-employed. Send a self-addressed stamped envelope for a sample issue.

 The Best of SkillPath, $49.95. SkillPath, Inc., 6900 Squibb Rd., PO Box 2768, Mission, KS 66201-2768. (800) 873-7545; (913) 677-3200; (913) 362-4241 (fax). Highlights of SkillPath's most effective seminars on audiotape. Six cassettes (60 minutes each) include: How to Manage Projects; How to Provide Excellent Customer Service; How to Supervise People; Managing Multiple Projects; Powerful Proofreading and Editing Skills; and Reading Essentials.

 The Business of Being an Artist, by Daniel Grant, ©1991, 224 pp., ISBN: 0-9607118-5-6, $16.95. Allworth Press, 10 E. 23rd St., New York, NY 10010. (800) 247-6553; (212) 777-8395. This honest and helpful guide addresses issues faced by visual artists, including how to find a dealer, make contracts, sell work, obtain grants and commissions, promote your work, and more.

 The Business Owner, Thomas J. Martin, Ed., bimonthly, $88.00/yr. The Business Owner, 383 S. Broadway, Hicksville, NY 11801. (516) 681-2111. This magazine, aimed at the small business owner, provides detailed information regarding specific topics of interest to the readership. For example, an entire issue may be devoted to retirement planning, or buying and selling a business.

Calling All Advisors

One of the most valuable skills any entrepreneur can develop is knowing how to locate expert help. Some business owners assemble advisory boards, either formally or on a casual basis. Others keep professionals "on call" to guide them through specific twists and turns along the business journey.

Remember, even the most experienced business leaders rely on outside help. In addition to getting superb advice, you'll send a message to people you admire—and they'll be glad you asked.

The Creative Glow: How to Be More Original, Inspired and Productive in Your Work, by Marcia Yukin, Ph.D. Ed., bimonthly, $49.00/yr. Creative Ways, PO Box 1310, Boston, MA 02117. (617) 266-1613; (617) 438-7830 (fax). This idea-packed newsletter brings fresh perspectives on accessing and expressing your creativity.

 The E-Myth, by Michael E. Gerber, ©1990, 164 pp., ISBN: 0-88730-472-9, $14.00. HarperBusiness, 10 E. 53rd St., New York, NY 10022-5299. (800) 982-4377; (212) 207-7000; (800) 822-4090 (fax). Gerber addresses the "myth" of entrepreneurship and why so many American businesses fail—particularly how being skilled in one's work is critically different from knowing how to run a business—and offers solutions and advice for success.

 The Entrepreneur's Relocation Guide, by Kimberly Stanséll, 32 pp., $7.95. Research Done Right, 8726 S. Sepulveda Blvd., Ste. B261-WS, Los Angeles, CA 90045-4082. (310) 568-9861. This guide provides a six-step plan for successfully relocating your business. It contains money-saving research tips, a profile of entrepreneur relocators, a directory of small business assistance agencies, and a collection of unique relocation services.

 The Entrepreneur's Roadmap to Business Success, by Lyle R. Maul & Dianne C. Mayfield, ©1992, 288 pp., ISBN: 0-929382-60-9, $14.95. Saxton's River Publications, PO Box 1609, Alexandria, VA 22313. (800) 729-9124. In a straightforward, easy-to-read style, this book leads the reader on the journey to entrepreneurial success. The authors point out the pitfalls and opportunities that likely will be encountered along the way and offer practical advice based on their own business experience.

 The Free-Lancer's Hand-Book, by Judy E. Pickens, ©1981, 135 pp., ISBN: 0-13-330688-7, $4.95. Prentice-Hall, Inc., 113 Sylvan Ave., Englewood Cliffs, NJ 07632. (800) 922-0579; (201) 592-2281. This book presents an overview of freelancing, including details on approaching prospective clients, managing your workload, handling finances, and building a freelance business.

 The Small Business Bible, by Paul Resnick, ©1994, 230 pp., ISBN: 0-471-62985-5, $19.95. John Wiley & Sons, Inc., 605 Third Ave., New York, NY 10158-0012. (800) CALL-WILEY; (212) 850-6000; (212) 850-8641 (fax). This book provides answers to many of the most frequently asked questions about small business.

The Ultimate No B.S. Business Success Package, by Dan Kennedy, ©1994, ISBN: 0-88908-839-X, $14.95. Self-Counsel Press, Inc., 1704 N. State St., Bellingham, WA 98225. (800) 663-3007; (206) 676-4530; (206) 676-4549 (fax). This two-cassette package is a companion to Kennedy's book (see listing below), and features the author and a cast of characters acting out real-life business situations with humor, energy, and drama.

 The Ultimate No B.S., No Holds Barred, Kick Butt, and Make Tons of Money Business Success Book, by Dan Kennedy, ©1993, 168 pp., ISBN: 0-88908-278-2, $8.95. Self-Counsel Press, Inc., 1704 N. State St., Bellingham, WA 98225. (800) 663-3007; (206) 676-4530; (206) 676-4549 (fax). Written in a lighthearted and spirited style, this book presents some challenging and innovative ideas about being an entrepreneur.

 The Upright Ostrich, Peggy Poor, Ed., 10x/yr., $25.00/yr. Order of the Upright Ostrich, 2824 N. Stowell Ave., Milwaukee, WI 53211-3774. (414) 332-5075. This publication supports independent farmers and small businesses.

 TOWERS Club USA Newsletter, Jerry Buchanan, Ed., monthly, $195.00/yr. TOWERS Club, USA, Inc., 9107 NW 11th Avenue, PO Box 2038, Vancouver, WA 98668-9958. (206) 574-3084. Marketing advice, tips and techniques, mail order information, and inspiration for the home-based entrepreneur.

 When Friday Isn't Payday, by Randy W. Kirk, ©1993, 352 pp., ISBN: 0-446-39398-3, $12.99. Warner Books, Inc., 1271 Avenue of the Americas, New York, NY 10019. (800) 222-6747. Targeted to businesses with less than 10 people, this book offers insights into the many details of launching a business and keeping it running. Strong sections on financial management and collections.

 Winning Ways, Barbara J. Winter, Ed., bimonthly, $29.00/yr. Winning Ways, PO Box 39412, Minneapolis, MN 55439. This upbeat bimonthly newsletter—its subtitle is "the unabashedly positive newsletter for self-bossers"—mixes inspiration with information. It emphasizes personal development as well as how-to business details to help independent entrepreneurs find balance and personal fulfillment in their lives. A sample issue is $4.00.

Working Alone, by Murray Felsher, ©1994, 208 pp., ISBN: 0-425-15824-1, $10.00. Berkeley Publishing Group, 200 Madison Ave., New York, NY 10016. (212) 951-8800; (212) 213-6706 (fax). This book presents insights and practical advice on working independently. Its 67 chapters offer bite-size nuggets of practical advice based on the author's experience as a self-employed consultant.

 Working Solo Newsletter, Terri Lonier, Ed., quarterly, $24.00. Portico Press, PO Box 190, New Paltz, NY 12561-0190. (800) 222-SOLO (orders only); (914) 255-7165; (914) 255-2116 (fax). This quarterly newsletter keeps solo entrepreneurs up to date on news, marketing, legal and tax issues, new products and services, resources, and other opportunities affecting the self-employed community. Readers of the book WORKING SOLO can receive a free trial subscription by returning the bound-in postcard in the back of that book. A sample issue is $4.00.

 Working Solo: The Real Guide to Freedom & Financial Success with Your Own Business, by Terri Lonier, ©1994, 400 pp., ISBN: 1-883282-40-3, $14.95. Portico Press, PO Box 190, New Paltz, NY 12561-0190. (800) 222-SOLO (orders only); (914) 255-7165; (914) 255-2116 (fax). This best-seller is the companion volume to the WORKING SOLO SOURCEBOOK. Chosen by *Inc.* magazine as the #1 book for independent entrepreneurs, this guide presents a detailed road map to solo success. In an easy-to-read style, it shows how to: choose the solo business perfect for you; get money for your business without going to a bank; develop cost-effective marketing; join forces with other independents; hire associates on your own terms; painless manage bookkeeping, taxes, and insurance; and design your business so it stays fresh, exciting, and profitable. A bonus Solo Business Directory features more than 1,000 solo business opportunities. Readers also receive a free trial subscription to the WORKING SOLO Newsletter (see above). Ordering details in the back of this volume.

 Working Solo Online, Apple Computer, Inc., 1 Infinite Loop, Cupertino, CA 65014. (408) 996-1010. This online forum for independent entrepreneurs on Apple Computer's eWorld electronic network features host Terri Lonier, co-host Fred Showker, and assistant Barrie Selack. Subscribers can exchange news and ideas, download valuable information and software, and network with other solo professionals. Details in listing on page 81.

Government Resources

See also Patents, Trademarks and Copyrights; Taxes

The U.S. Government offers a wealth of information to small business owners—but the challenge is figuring out how to find it. The listings gathered in this section provide you a shortcut through the bureaucratic maze. The primary source for small business information is the U.S. Small Business Administration (SBA), which has branch offices in every state. Other government agencies also furnish small business assistance on programs they sponsor. The cardinal rule in dealing with the government: have patience and be persistent. There are resources to assist small businesses of every type and size—and we've already paid for them with our tax dollars!

General Information

 Business America: The Magazine of International Trade, Douglas F. Carroll, Ed., monthly, $32.00. U.S. Department of Commerce, International Trade Administration, Government Printing Office, Superintendent of Documents, Mail Stop: SSOM, Washington, DC 20401. (800) 872-8723 (Trade Information Center). This magazine, published by the U.S. Department of Commerce, contains articles regarding international trade issues, import/export information, and U.S. Government involvement with international business.

 Doing Business with the U.S. Government, by Herman Holtz, ©1994, 352 pp., ISBN: 1-55958-320-7, $24.95. Prima Publishing, PO Box 1260, Rocklin, CA 95677-1260. (916) 632-7400; (916) 632-7668 (fax). How to sell your goods and services into the $200 billion federal market.

Free Help From Uncle Sam to Help You Start or Expand Your Own Business, by William Alarid, ©1994, 300 pp., ISBN: 0-940673-54-1, $14.95. John Baptiste, Puma Publishing, 1670 Coral Drive, Santa Maria, CA 93454. (800) 255-5730, ext. 100; (805) 925-3216; (805) 925-2656 (fax). Offers advice and information regarding free government help for small businesses and entrepreneurs. It includes a listing of over 100 government agencies which purchase from small businesses, and programs which offer financial assistance.

 Free Money from the Federal Government for Small Businesses and Entrepreneurs, by Laurie Blum, ©1993, 400 pp., ISBN: 0-471-59943-3, $14.95. John Wiley & Sons, Inc., 605 Third Ave., New York, NY 10158-0012. (800) CALL-WILEY; (212) 850-6000; (212) 850-8641 (fax). This book tells entrepreneurs how to tap into the many sources of government funding to help launch or expand a small business.

 How to Access the Government's Electronic Bulletin Boards, by Bruce Maxwell, ©1994, 350 pp., ISBN: 1-56802-000-7, $19.95. Congressional Quarterly Books, 1414 22nd St. NW, Washington, DC 20037. (800) 638-1710; (202) 822-1475; (202) 887-6706 (fax). This book contains detailed descriptions of nearly 200 computer bulletin board systems (BBSs) operated by federal government agencies and departments that the public can access for free. The BBSs offer everything from White House documents to Census data to procurement notices.

 Small Business Advocate, monthly, Free. U.S. Small Business Administration, Office of Advocacy, Mail Code 3114, 409 3rd St. SW, Washington, DC 20416. (202) 205-6531; (202) 205-6928 (fax). This publication deals with legislative and regulatory issues which pertain to small business, and also includes economic research based on government studies.

 Small Business in the American Economy, ©1988, 214 pp., ISBN: 0-16-004557-6, $6.50. U.S. Small Business Administration, New Orders, Superintendent of Documents, PO Box 371954, Pittsburgh, PA 15250-7954. (202) 783-3238; (202) 512-2250 (fax). This volume summarizes detailed business research funded by the SBA, and provides in-depth information on employee training in small firms, small manufacturing businesses, growth patterns of women-owned businesses, minority entrepreneurship, and more.

Tapping the Government Grapevine: The User-Friendly Guide to U.S. Government Information Sources, by Judith Schiek Robinson, ©1993, 240 pp., ISBN: 0-89774-712-7, $34.50. Oryx Press, 4041 N. Central Ave., Ste. 700, Phoenix, AZ 85012-3397. (800) 279-6799; (602) 265-2651; (800) 279-4663 (fax). This book shows effective searching techniques to quickly find research and information materials from the U.S. government. Includes details on searching in a variety of media and sources, including print, microfiche, databases, CD-ROMs, agencies, research labs, collections, National Archives, Library of Congress, and more.

 The State of Small Business: A Report of the President, ©1993, 458 pp., ISBN: 0-16-036008-0, $16.00. U.S. Small Business Administration, New Orders, Superintendent of Documents, PO Box 371954, Pittsburgh, PA 15250-7954. (202) 783-3238; (202) 512-2250 (fax). Published annually by the SBA, this book is a comprehensive reference source for small business topics, including information and statistics on small business in the economy, jobs, new businesses, growth industries, government procurement from minorities and women, financing, and more.

Help from a Wise Uncle

When it comes to starting or expanding your business, the U.S. government can be a great source of low-cost information. The Small Business Administration (SBA) sponsors Small Business Development Centers (SBDCs) in every state, often at universities. These centers offer "one-stop" assistance to entrepreneurs, including counseling, training, and technical assistance.

Another SBA program is SCORE, the Service Corps of Retired Executives. This 13,000-member volunteer organization matches seasoned business owners with entrepreneurs seeking expert advice on small business matters.

To tap into these resources, check the listings in this chapter or consult the blue (government) pages of your telephone directory. You're only a phone call away from an expert who could make a big difference in your business success.

The States and Small Business, ©1993, 462 pp., ISBN: 0-16-041654-X, $21.00. U.S. Small Business Administration, New Orders, Superintendent of Documents, PO Box 371954, Pittsburgh, PA 15250-7954. (202) 783-3238; (202) 512-2250 (fax). This book lists over 1,000 state programs that will help you find the financial resources you need and discusses the ways in which state legislation may affect your business. In addition it lists the locations where you can seek advice about state legal requirements.

Federal Information Centers

Federal Information Centers serve as a referral service for individuals seeking information about government programs or agencies. By dialing one of the toll-free numbers listed below, you are connected with prerecorded voice mail options that lead you to information, or you can speak with an information specialist who can direct you to the correct source for your request. The center operates from 9am-8pm Eastern Time. If your metropolitan area is not listed or the number for your area is not in effect, try calling (301) 722-9098.

Alabama
Birmingham, Mobile
(800) 366-2998

Alaska
Anchorage
(800) 729-8003

Arizona
Phoenix
(800) 359-3997

Arkansas
Little Rock
(800) 366-2998

California
Los Angeles, San Diego,
San Francisco, Santa Ana
(800) 726-4995

California
Sacramento (only)
(916) 973-1695

Colorado
Colorado Springs, Denver,
Pueblo
(800) 359-3997

Connecticut
Hartford, New Haven
(800) 347-1997

Florida
Ft. Lauderdale, Jacksonville,
Miami, Orlando,
St. Petersburg, Tampa,
W. Palm Beach
(800) 347-1997

Federal Information Centers *(continued)*

Georgia
Atlanta
(800) 347-1997

Hawaii
Honolulu
(800) 733-5996

Illinois
Chicago
(800) 366-2998

Indiana
Gary
(800) 366-2998

Indiana
Indianapolis
(800) 347-1997

Iowa
All areas
(800) 735-8004

Kansas
All areas
(800) 735-8004

Kentucky
Louisville
(800) 347-1997

Louisiana
New Orleans
(800) 347-366-2998

Maryland
Baltimore
(800) 347-1997

Massachusetts
Boston
(800) 347-1997

Michigan
Detroit, Grand Rapids
(800) 347-1997

Minnesota
Minneapolis
(800) 366-2998

Missouri
St. Louis
(800) 366-2998

Missouri
All areas except St. Louis
(800) 735-8004

Nebraska
Omaha
(800) 366-2998

Nebraska
All areas except Omaha
(800) 735-8004

New Jersey
Newark, Trenton
(800) 347-1997

New Mexico
Albuquerque
(800) 359-3997

New York
Albany, Buffalo, New York,
Rochester, Syracuse
(800) 347-1997

North Carolina
Charlotte
(800) 347-1997

Federal Information Centers *(continued)*

Ohio
Akron, Cincinnati,
Cleveland, Columbus,
Dayton, Toledo
(800) 347-1997

Oklahoma
Oklahoma City, Tulsa
(800) 366-2998

Oregon
Portland
(800) 746-4995

Pennsylvania
Philadelphia, Pittsburgh
(800) 347-1997

Rhode Island
Providence
(800) 347-1997

Tennessee
Chattanooga
(800) 347-1997

Tennessee
Memphis, Nashville
(800) 366-2998

Texas
Austin, Dallas, Ft. Worth,
Houston, San Antonio
(800) 366-2998

Utah
Salt Lake City
(800) 359-3997

Virginia
Norfolk, Richmond,
Roanoke
(800) 347-1997

Washington
Seattle, Tacoma
(800) 726-4995

Wisconsin
Milwaukee
(800) 366-2998

 Government Hotline Numbers

**Bureau of Economic
Analysis**
1401 K Street NW
Washington, DC 20230
(202) 523-0777
(Public Information Office)

Bureau of the Census
Washington, DC 20233
(301) 763-4051
(Public Information Office)
(301) 763-5820
(Data User Services)

**Consumer Product Safety
Commission Hotline**
(800) 638-2772

Department of Labor
200 Constitution Ave. NW
Washington, DC 20210
(202) 219-9154
(Small Business Specialist)

**Dept. of Commerce,
Library Reference Desk**
(202) 482-2161

Government Hotline Numbers *(continued)*

Federal Communications Commission (FCC)
1919 M St. NW
Washington, DC 20554
(202) 632-5050

Federal Trade Commission (FTC)
Pennsylvania Ave. &
6th St. NW
Washington, DC 20580
(202) 326-2258

Government Contracts for Small Business
Dept. of Labor
200 Constitution Ave. NW
Rm. C2318
Washington, DC 20210
(202) 523-9148

House Committee on Small Business
2361 Rayburn House Office Bldg.
Washington, DC 20515
(202) 225-5821

International Trade Administration
14th St. &
Constitution Ave. NW
Washington, DC 20230
(202) 377-3808
(202) 482-5487
(Publications)

Interstate Commerce Commission
12th St. &
Constitution Ave. NW
Washington, DC 20423
(202) 927-5350

Library of Congress
101 Independence Ave. SE
Washington, DC 20540
(202) 707-5000

Minority Business Development Agency
14th St. &
Constitution Ave. NW
Washington, DC 20230
(202) 482-2366
(Bus. Development Div.)

Occupational Safety & Health Administration (OSHA)
200 Constitution Ave. NW
Washington, DC 20210
(202) 523-8148

Office of Business Liaison
14th St. &
Constitution Ave. NW
Washington, DC 20230
(202) 482-3176

Senate Committee on Small Business
Russell Senate Office Bldg.
Ste. 428A
Washington, DC 20510
(202) 224-5175

Government Hotline Numbers *(continued)*

Social Security Hotline
(800) 772-1213

The White House
1600 Pennsylvania Ave. NW
Washington, DC 20500
(202) 456-1414

**U.S. Postal Service/
General Information**
(202) 268-2284

**U.S. Postal Service/
Publications**
(202) 268-2178

U.S. Small Business Administration (SBA)

Since it was founded in 1953, the SBA has helped millions of Americans
build successful businesses. The agency offers a full range of information
and support programs, on national, statewide, and local levels (see also
the sidebar on p. 137).

 SBA Answer Desk, U.S. Small Business Administration, 409 3rd St.
SW, Washington, DC 20416. (800) U-ASK-SBA; (202) 205-6740. A
call to this toll-free number gives you access to prerecorded information about SBA programs and can provide details on where to
go for further information.

 SBA Hotline Answer Book, by Gustav Berle, ©1991, 288 pp.,
ISBN: 0-471-54297-0, $14.95. John Wiley & Sons, Inc., 605 Third
Ave., New York, NY 10158-0012. (800) CALL-WILEY; (212) 850-
6000; (212) 850-8641 (fax). The 200 most frequently asked
questions about starting a business, as answered by the U.S. Small
Business Administration.

 SBA Online, U.S. Small Business Administration, 409 3rd St. SW,
Washington, DC 20416. (800) 697-4636; (900) 463-4636. The SBA
has established an electronic computer network to provide information on its programs and services via computer modem. The
toll-free number offers access to information on SBA services,
loans, business programs, and information from other government agencies. Through a low-cost 900 line users can access
e-mail and gateway functions to the Environmental Protection
Agency, the Department of Commerce, and the Census Bureau
bulletin board services. The first minute of connect time is free; 30
cents for the second minute; 10 cents for each additional minute.
Telecommunications settings are 8 data bits, 1 stop bit, no parity.

SBA Regional Offices

SBA Region 1
155 Federal St., 9th fl.
Boston, MA 02110
(617) 451-2030
(617) 565-8695 (fax)
Connecticut, Maine,
Massachusetts, Vermont,
New Hampshire, and
Rhode Island

SBA Region 2
26 Federal Plaza, Rm. 31-08
New York, NY 10278
(212) 264-1450
(212) 264-0900 (fax)
New Jersey, New York,
Puerto Rico and the
Virgin Islands

SBA Region 3
475 Allendale Rd., Ste. 201
King of Prussia, PA 19406
(215) 962-3700
(215) 962-3743 (fax)
Delaware, the District of
Columbia, Maryland,
Pennsylvania, Virginia, and
West Virginia

SBA Region 4
1375 Peachtree St. NE
Rm. 502
Atlanta, GA 30367-8102
(404) 347-2797
(404) 347-2355 (fax)
Alabama, Florida, Georgia,
Kentucky, Mississippi,
Tennessee, North Carolina,
and South Carolina

SBA Region 5
300 S. Riverside Plaza
Rm. 1975 S
Chicago, IL 60606-6611
(312) 353-5000
(312) 353-3426 (fax)
Illinois, Indiana, Michigan,
Minnesota, Ohio, and
Wisconsin

SBA Region 6
8625 King George Dr.
Bldg. C
Dallas, TX 75235-3391
(214) 767-7633
(214) 767-7870 (fax)
Arkansas, Louisiana,
New Mexico, Oklahoma,
and Texas

SBA Region 7
Federal Office Bldg.
911 Walnut St., 13th fl.
Kansas City, MO 64106
(816) 426-3608
(816) 426-5559 (fax)
Iowa, Kansas, Missouri,
and Nebraska

SBA Region 8
999 18th St., Ste. 701
Denver, CO 80202
(303) 294-7186
(303) 294-7153 (fax)
Colorado, Montana,
Utah, North Dakota,
South Dakota, and
Wyoming

SBA Regional Offices *(continued)*

SBA Region 9
71 Stevenson St.
San Francisco, CA 94105
(415) 744-6402
(415) 744-6435 (fax)
American Samoa, Arizona,
California, Guam, Hawaii,
Nevada, and Trust Territory
of the Pacific Islands

SBA Region 10
2615 4th Ave., Rm. 440
Seattle, WA 98121
(206) 553-5676
(206) 553-4155 (fax)
Alaska, Idaho, Oregon, and
Washington

 SBA Statewide Offices

Alabama
2121 8th Ave. N, Ste. 200
Birmingham, AL 35203
(205) 731-1344
(205) 731-1404 (fax)

Alaska
Federal Bldg. Annex
222 W. 8th Ave., Rm. 67
Anchorage, AK 99513-7559
(907) 271-4022
(907) 271-4545 (fax)

Arizona
2828 N. Central Ave.
Ste. 800
Phoenix, AZ 85004-1025
(602) 640-2316
(602) 640-2360 (fax)

Arizona
300 W. Congress St.
Rm. 7-H
Tucson, AZ 85701-1319
(602) 670-4759
(602) 670-4763 (fax)

Arkansas
2120 Riverfront Dr., Ste. 100
Little Rock, AR 72202
(501) 740-5278
(501) 324-5199 (fax)

California
2719 N. Air Fresno Dr.
Ste. 107
Fresno, CA 93727-1547
(209) 487-5189
(209) 487-5636 (fax)

California
330 N. Brand Blvd.
Ste. 1200
Glendale, CA 91203-2304
(213) 894-2956
(213) 894-5665 (fax)

California
660 J. St., Ste. 215
Sacramento, CA 95814
(916) 551-1426
(916) 551-1439 (fax)

California
Federal Bldg.
880 Front St., Ste. 4-S-29
San Diego, CA 92188
(619) 557-7252
(619) 557-5894 (fax)

California
211 Main St., 4th fl.
San Francisco, CA 94105
(415) 744-6820
(415) 744-6812 (fax)

California
901 W. Civic Center Dr.
Ste. 160
Santa Ana, CA 92703-2352
(714) 836-2494
(714) 836-2528 (fax)

California
6477 Telephone Dr., Ste. 10
Ventura, CA 93003-4459
(805) 642-1866
(805) 642-9538 (fax)

Colorado
721 19th St., Rm. 426
Denver, CO 80202-2599
(303) 844-3984
(303) 844-6468 (fax)

Connecticut
330 Main St., 2nd fl.
Hartford, CT 06106
(203) 240-4700
(203) 240-4659 (fax)

District of Columbia
1110 Vermont Ave. NW Ste. 900
Washington, DC 20036
(202) 606-4000
(202) 606-4225 (fax)

Delaware
920 N. King St., Rm. 412
Wilmington, DE 19801
(302) 573-6295
(302) 573-6060 (fax)

Florida
1320 S. Dixie Hwy., Ste. 501
Coral Gables, FL 33146
(305) 536-5521
(305) 536-5058 (fax)

Florida
7825 Baymeadows Way
Ste. 100-B
Jacksonville, FL 32256-7504
(904) 443-1900
(904) 443-1980 (fax)

Florida
501 E. Polk St., Rm. 104
Tampa, FL 33602-3945
(813) 228-2594
(813) 228-2111 (fax)

Florida
5601 Corporate Way
Ste. 402
West Palm Beach, FL 33407
(407) 689-3922

SBA Statewide Offices *(continued)*

Georgia
1720 Peachtree Rd. NW
Ste. 600
Atlanta, GA 30309
(404) 347-4749
(404) 347-4745 (fax)

Georgia
Federal Bldg.
52 N. Main St., Rm. 225
Statesboro, GA 30458
(912) 489-8719

Hawaii
300 Ala Moana Blvd.
Rm. 2213
Honolulu, HI 96850-4981
(808) 541-2990
(808) 541-2976 (fax)

Idaho
1020 Main St., Ste. 290
Boise, ID 83702-5745
(208) 334-1696
(208) 334-9353 (fax)

Illinois
500 W. Madison, Ste. 1250
Chicago, IL 60661-2511
(312) 353-4258
(312) 886-5108 (fax)

Illinois
511 W. Capitol St., Ste. 302
Springfield, IL 62704
(217) 492-4416
(217) 492-4867 (fax)

Indiana
Federal Bldg., Ste. 100
429 N. Pennsylvania St.
Indianapolis, IN 46204
(317) 226-7272
(317) 226-7259 (fax)

Iowa
373 Collins Rd. NE
Rm. 100
Cedar Rapids, IA 52402
(319) 393-8630
(319) 393-7585 (fax)

Iowa
210 Walnut St., Rm. 749
Des Moines, IA 50309
(515) 284-4422
(515) 284-4572 (fax)

Kansas
100 E. English St., Ste. 510
Wichita, KS 67202
(316) 269-6273
(316) 269-6499 (fax)

Kentucky
600 Dr. Martin L. King Jr. Pl.
Rm. 188
Louisville, KY 40202
(502) 582-5971
(502) 582-5009 (fax)

Louisiana
Ford-Fisk Bldg.
1661 Canal St., Ste. 2000
New Orleans, LA 70112
(504) 589-6685
(504) 589-2339 (fax)

Louisiana
500 Fannin St., Rm. 8A-08
Shreveport, LA 71101
(318) 676-3196
(318) 676-3214 (fax)

Maine
Federal Bldg.
40 Western Ave., Rm. 512
Augusta, ME 04330
(207) 622-8378
(207) 622-8277 (fax)

Maryland
10 S. Howard St., Rm. 608
Baltimore, MD 21202
(410) 962-4392
(410) 962-1805 (fax)

Massachusetts
10 Causeway St., Rm. 265
Boston, MA 02222-1093
(617) 565-5590
(617) 565-5598 (fax)

Massachusetts
Federal Bldg. & Courthouse
Rm. 212, 1550 Main St.
Springfield, MA 01103
(413) 785-0268
(413) 785-0267 (fax)

Michigan
515 McNamara Bldg.
477 Michigan Ave.
Detroit, MI 48226
(313) 226-6075
(313) 226-4769 (fax)

Michigan
300 S. Front St.
Marquette, MI 49885
(906) 225-1108
(906) 225-1109 (fax)

Minnesota
100 N. 6th St.
610-C Butler Sq.
Minneapolis, MN 55403
(612) 370-2324
(612) 370-2303 (fax)

Mississippi
1 Hancock Plaza, Ste. 1001
Gulfport, MS 39501-7758
(601) 863-4449
(601) 864-0179 (fax)

Mississippi
101 W. Capitol St., Ste. 400
Jackson, MS 39201
(601) 965-4378
(601) 965-4294 (fax)

Missouri
323 W. 8th St., Ste. 501
Kansas City, MO 64105
(816) 374-6708
(816) 374-6759 (fax)

Missouri
815 Olive St., Rm. 242
St. Louis, MO 63101
(314) 539-6600
(314) 539-3785 (fax)

SBA Statewide Offices *(continued)*

Missouri
620 S. Glenstone St.
Ste. 110
Springfield, MO 65802-3200
(417) 864-7670
(417) 864-4108 (fax)

Montana
301 S. Park, Rm. 528
Federal Office Bldg.
Drawer 10054
Helena, MT 59626
(406) 449-5381
(406) 449-5474 (fax)

Nebraska
11145 Mill Valley Rd.
Omaha, NE 68154
(402) 221-4691
(402) 221-3680 (fax)

Nevada
301 E. Stewart St., Rm. 301
Las Vegas, NV 89125-2527
(702) 388-6611
(702) 388-6469 (fax)

Nevada
50 S. Virginia St., Rm. 238
Reno, NV 89505-3216
(702) 784-5268

New Hampshire
143 N. Main St., Ste. 202
Concord, NH 03302-1257
(603) 225-1400
(603) 225-1409 (fax)

New Jersey
2600 Mt. Ephraim Ave.
Camden, NJ 08104
(609) 757-5183
(609) 757-5335 (fax)

New Jersey
Military Park Bldg.
60 Park Pl., 4th fl.
Newark, NJ 07102
(201) 645-2434
(201) 645-6265 (fax)

New Mexico
625 Silver Ave. SW, Ste. 320
Albuquerque, NM 87102
(505) 766-1870
(505) 766-1057 (fax)

New York
Leo O'Brien Bldg., Rm. 815,
Clinton & Pearl Streets
Albany, NY 12207
(518) 472-6300
(518) 472-7138 (fax)

New York
111 W. Huron St., Rm. 1311
Buffalo, NY 14202
(716) 846-4301
(716) 846-4418 (fax)

New York
333 E. Water St., 4th fl.
Elmira, NY 14901
(607) 734-8130
(607) 733-4656 (fax)

New York
35 Pinelawn Rd., Rm. 102E
Melville, NY 11747
(516) 454-0750
(516) 454-0769 (fax)

New York
26 Federal Plaza, Rm. 3100
New York, NY 10278
(212) 264-2454
(212) 264-4963 (fax)

New York
Federal Bldg., Rm. 410
100 State St.
Rochester, NY 14614
(716) 263-6700
(716) 263-3146 (fax)

New York
Federal Bldg., Rm. 1071
100 S. Clinton St.
Syracuse, NY 13260
(315) 423-5383
(315) 423-5370 (fax)

North Carolina
200 N. College St.
Ste. A2015
Charlotte, NC 28202-2137
(704) 344-6563
(704) 344-6769 (fax)

North Dakota
Federal Office Bldg.
Rm. 218, 657 2nd Ave. N.
Fargo, ND 58108-3086
(701) 239-5131
(701) 239-5645 (fax)

Ohio
525 Vine St., Ste. 870
Cincinnati, OH 45202
(513) 684-2814
(513) 684-3251 (fax)

Ohio
1111 Superior Ave., Ste. 630
Cleveland, OH 44144-2507
(216) 522-4180
(216) 522-2038 (fax)

Ohio
2 Nationwide Plaza
Ste. 1400
Columbus, OH 43215-2592
(614) 469-6860
(614) 469-2391 (fax)

Oklahoma
200 NW 5th St.
Ste. 670
Oklahoma City, OK 73102
(405) 231-4301
(405) 231-4876 (fax)

Oregon
222 SW Columbia St.
Ste. 500
Portland, OR 97201-6605
(503) 326-2682
(503) 326-2808 (fax)

Pennsylvania
100 Chestnut St., Rm. 309
Harrisburg, PA 17101
(717) 782-3840
(717) 782-4839 (fax)

SBA Statewide Offices *(continued)*

Pennsylvania
475 Allendale Rd., Ste. 201
King of Prussia, PA 19406
(215) 962-3804
(215) 962-3795 (fax)

Pennsylvania
960 Penn Ave., 5th fl.
Pittsburgh, PA 15222
(412) 644-2780
(412) 644-5446 (fax)

Pennsylvania
Penn Plaza
20 N. Pennsylvania Ave.
Rm. 2327
Wilkes-Barre, PA 18702
(717) 826-6497
(717) 826-6287 (fax)

Puerto Rico
Federico Degatau Fed. Bldg.
Rm. 691
Carlos Chardon Ave.
Hato Rey, PR 00918-1729
(809) 766-5572
(809) 766-5309 (fax)

Rhode Island
380 Westminster Mall
5th fl.
Providence, RI 02903
(401) 528-4561
(401) 528-4539 (fax)

South Carolina
1835 Assembly St., Rm. 358
Columbia, SC 29201
(803) 765-5376
(803) 765-5962 (fax)

South Dakota
Security Bldg., Ste. 101
101 S. Main Ave.
Sioux Falls, SD 57102-0527
(605) 330-4231
(605) 330-4215 (fax)

Tennessee
50 Vantage Way, Ste. 201
Nashville, TN 37228-1500
(615) 736-5881
(615) 736-7232 (fax)

Texas
Federal Bldg., Rm. 520
300 E. 8th St.
Austin, TX 78701
(512) 482-5288
(512) 482-5290 (fax)

Texas
606 N. Carancahua
Ste. 1200
Corpus Christi, TX 78476
(512) 888-3331
(512) 888-3418 (fax)

Texas
10737 Gateway W.
Ste. 320
El Paso, TX 79935
(915) 540-5676
(915) 540-5636 (fax)

Texas
4300 Amon Carter Blvd.
Ste. 114
Fort Worth, TX 76155
(817) 885-6500
(817) 885-6516 (fax)

Texas
222 E. Van Buren St.
Ste. 500
Harlingen, TX 78550
(512) 427-8533
(210) 427-8537 (fax)

Texas
9301 Southwest Freeway
Ste. 550
Houston, TX 77074-1591
(713) 773-6500
(713) 773-6550 (fax)

Texas
Regency Plaza
1611 Tenth St., Ste. 200
Lubbock, TX 79401
(806) 743-7462
(806) 743-7487 (fax)

Texas
505 E. Travis, Rm. 103
Marshall, TX 75670
(903) 935-5257
(903) 935-5258 (fax)

Texas
7400 Blanco Rd., Ste. 200
San Antonio, TX 78216
(210) 229-4535
(210) 229-4556 (fax)

Texas
819 Taylor St., Rm. 8A-27
Fort Worth, TX 76102
(817) 334-3777

Utah
W. F. Bennett Federal Bldg.
125 S. State St., Rm. 2237
Salt Lake City, UT 84138
(801) 524-5804
(801) 524-4160 (fax)

Vermont
87 State St., Rm. 205
Montpelier, VT 05602
(802) 828-4422
(802) 828-4485 (fax)

Virgin Islands
4200 United Shopping
Plaza, Ste. 7, Christiansted
St. Croix, VI 00820-4487
(809) 778-5380
(809) 778-1102 (fax)

Virgin Islands
Veterans Drive, Rm. 210
St. Thomas, VI 00802
(809) 774-8530
(809) 776-2312 (fax)

Virginia
Federal Bldg., Rm. 3015
400 N. 8th St.
Richmond, VA 23240
(804) 771-2400
(804) 771-8018 (fax)

Washington
915 Second Ave., Rm. 1792
Seattle, WA 98174-1088
(206) 220-6520
(206) 220-6570 (fax)

SBA Statewide Offices *(continued)*

Washington
W. 601 First Ave.
Spokane, WA 99204
(509) 353-2800
(509) 353-2829 (fax)

West Virginia
550 Eagan St., Rm. 309
Charleston, WV 25301
(304) 347-5220
(304) 347-5350 (fax)

West Virginia
168 W. Main St., 5th fl.
Clarksburg, WV 26301
(304) 623-5631
(304) 623-0023 (fax)

Wisconsin
212 E. Washington Ave.
Rm. 213
Madison, WI 53703
(608) 264-5261
(608) 264-5541 (fax)

Wisconsin
Henry S. Reuss Federal Pl.
310 W. Wisconsin Ave.
Ste. 400
Milwaukee, WI 53203
(414) 297-3941
(414) 297-1377 (fax)

Wyoming
Federal Bldg., Rm. 4001
100 E. B St.
Casper, WY 82602-2839
(307) 261-5761
(307) 261-5499 (fax)

Growth and Expansion

See also Managing Your Business

After the rush of start-up passes, and a business survives its first few months or years, a new challenge sets in—how to continue a course of stable growth and possible expansion. For solo entrepreneurs, this phase can be particularly difficult, as individuals learn about pacing and endurance and how to keep a business fresh and on track toward personal and professional goals. If you're facing this development stage in your business, let the following resources guide you in charting your next level of growth. If you're a newly formed solo business, keep this list close at hand—the years pass, and growth can happen much more quickly than you think.

 Business Alliances Guide, by Robert P. Lynch, $29.95. John Wiley & Sons, Inc., 605 Third Ave., New York, NY 10158-0012. (800) CALL-WILEY; (212) 850-6000; (212) 850-8641 (fax). This book presents practical and strategic plans for expanding a business by forging alliances with other companies. Includes assessment checklists and tips on what to look for in creating lasting win-win partnerships

 Creating Your Future: Personal Strategic Planning for Professionals, by George L. Morrisey, ©1992, 216 pp., ISBN: 1-881052-06-0, $15.95. Berrett-Koehler Publishers, Inc., 155 Montgomery St., San Francisco, CA 94104. (800) 929-2929; (415) 288-0260; (415) 362-2512 (fax). This book explores the notion of establishing a pattern for growth on a personal level. It offers valuable tools for creating a strategic plan for personal, career, business, and financial objectives. Includes interactive worksheets, checklists, and charts.

Entrepreneurial Growth Strategies, by Lawrence W. Tuller, ©1994, 300 pp., ISBN: 1-55850-353-6, $10.95. Bob Adams, Inc., 260 Center St., Holbrook, MA 02343. (800) 872-5627; (617) 767-8100; (800) 872-5628 (fax). Reveals a wide range of creative ideas an owner can implement immediately to maintain steady and safe growth.

 Growing Pains, by Eric G. Flamholtz, ©1990, 445 pp., ISBN: 1-55542-272-1, $31.95. Jossey-Bass Publishers, 350 Sansome St., San Francisco, CA 94104-1310. (415) 433-1767; (415) 433-0499 (fax). This book explores the seven predictable stages of entrepreneurial growth, from start-up enterprise to mature organization. It identifies the steps needed to ensure continued success and offers practical guidance for implementing professional management systems and strategies.

 Kiplinger's Guide to Small Business Growth, ©1993, 35 min., ISBN: 0-945800-11-8, $29.95. Kiplinger Books & Tapes, 1729 H Street NW, Washington, DC 20006. (800) 462-6420; (202) 887-6431. This video and guidebook set features interviews with small business owners that highlight the challenges facing entrepreneurs as they grow their businesses. Topics include: financing, tax management, getting the most from accountants and lawyers, and hiring the best employees. The 64-page guidebook includes detailed worksheets.

Double Vision

Seasoned entrepreneurs know that building a successful business requires keeping a dual focus on daily actions and long-term goals. Day-to-day office operations, ongoing marketing, and financial management are crucial activities that must be mastered and sustained if a business is to survive the challenges of its early years. At the same time, business owners must never lose sight of three- and five-year targets, so that energies are directed properly. By maintaining that double vision, entrepreneurs can build today's achievements into future success.

Managing by the Numbers: Financial Essentials for the Growing Business, by David H. Bangs, Jr., ©1994, 160 pp., ISBN: 0-936894-26-1, $19.95. Upstart Publishing Co., Inc., 12 Portland St., Dover, NH 03820. (800) 235-8866; (603) 749-5071; (603) 742-9121 (fax). This book simplifies the task of financial management for a growing enterprise. It provides straightforward techniques for getting the maximum return on your business with the minimum amount of complicated details.

 Success is the Quality of Your Journey, by Jennifer James, Ph.D., ©1986, 136 pp., ISBN: 0-937858-66-8, $7.95. Newmarket Press, 18 East 48th St., New York, NY 10017. (800) 733-3000; (212) 832-3575. Personal and philosophical insights, blended with warmth and wit, on the nature of success—and the path along the way.

 Successful Business Expansion, by Philip Orsino, ©1994, 256 pp., ISBN: 0-471-08624-X, $17.95. John Wiley & Sons, Inc., 605 Third Ave., New York, NY 10158-0012. (800) CALL-WILEY; (212) 850-6000. A blueprint for business growth without limiting risk, as presented by a successful entrepreneur who has been through the process. Covers strategies and techniques for financing, expanding current markets, developing new markets, exporting, merging, and more.

 Surviving the Start-Up Years in Your Own Business, by Joyce S. Marder, ©1991, 172 pp., ISBN: 1-55870-200-8, $7.95. Betterway Books, 1507 Dana Avenue, Cincinnati, OH 45207. (800) 289-0963; (513) 531-4082 (fax). Discusses managing money, marketing a business successfully, handling employees, defining success, the problems of too rapid business growth, and more.

 Take Off: Charting a New Course to Business Growth, National Education Center for Women in Business (NECWB), Seton Hill College, Seton Hill Dr., Greensburg, PA 15601-1599. (800) NECWB-4-U; (412) 830-4625; (412) 834-7131 (fax). This three-day program is designed exclusively for established women business owners who want to reach the next level of business growth. Sponsored by the NECWB at a rural resort one hour east of Pittsburgh. Program cost: $650; NECWB members: $595. Accommodations additional.

The Entrepreneur's Guide to Going Public, by James B. Arkebauer with Ron Schultz, ©1994, 310 pp., ISBN: 0-936894-58-X, $19.95. Upstart Publishing Co., Inc., 12 Portland St., Dover, NH 03820. (800) 235-8866; (603) 749-5071; (603) 742-9121 (fax). When it's time to take your company public with an initial public offering (IPO), this book can give you an in-depth look at the pros and cons of the decision, costs, legal issues, rules and regulations, and other details of the process.

 The Entrepreneur's Guide to Growing Up, by Edna Sheedy, ©1993, 136 pp., ISBN: 0-88908-549-8, $8.95. Self-Counsel Press, Inc., 1704 N. State St., Bellingham, WA 98225. (800) 663-3007; (206) 676-4530; (206) 676-4549 (fax). This book is directed at business owners who have passed the start-up period and reached that awkward stage of growth. The book speaks clearly about the changes necessary to ensure a smooth and profitable transition.

 The Entrepreneurial Experience, by Gibb W. Dyer, Jr., ©1992, 288 pp., ISBN: 1-55542-417-1, $28.95. Jossey-Bass Publishers, 350 Sansome St., San Francisco, CA 94104-1310. (415) 433-1767; (415) 433-0499 (fax). In-depth interviews and case studies examine the emotional side of business, offering strategies entrepreneurs can use to cope with the stress and isolation they may feel. Also uncovers the dilemmas entrepreneurs confront at each stage of growth of their businesses.

Home-Based Businesses

*See also Choosing a Business; General Business Information;
Managing a Business; Starting a Business*

Not all solo businesses operate from home, although many home-based enterprises are run by independent entrepreneurs. Working from home presents a unique set of challenges often not shared by offices located elsewhere. Issues such as professional image, children, time management, and zoning can be of particular concern to home-based entrepreneurs trying to establish a thriving business. While many of the resources featured in this chapter offer general advice, all have a particular focus on entrepreneurs who have chosen the "10-second commute" and work from home.

 101 Home Office Success Secrets, by Lisa Kanarek, ©1994, 160 pp., ISBN: 1-56414-130-6, $8.95. Career Press, 180 Fifth Ave., PO Box 34, Hawthorne, NJ 07507. (800) CAREER-1; (201) 427-2037 (fax). Insider tips on operating a home-based business from successful home-office professionals.

 American Association of Home-Based Businesses, Beverley Williams, PO Box 10023, Rockville, MD 20849. (301) 963-9153; (202) 310-3130; (301) 963-7042 (fax). This nonprofit association provides a network of and for home-based businesses through local chapters around the country. Members receive discounts on books and magazines, information sheets, and local networking support, including legislative and zoning advocacy. Dues are established by local chapters. Send a self-addressed stamped envelope for an informational brochure.

Association of Home Businesses (AHB), Linda Engebretsen, 423 SW Fourth Ave., Portland, OR 97204. (503) 223-1493; (503) 223-1454 (fax). AHB's purpose is to assist home-based businesses by providing business and technical information that is current and practical; promoting professional standards and a professional image; providing advocacy and appropriate group services; and offering forums for socializing and networking.

 Earning Power in the Home, Patricia Galbraith, Ed., bimonthly, $10.00/yr. Earning Power in the Home, PO Box 368, Weatherford, TX 76086. (817) 594-4415. This newsletter targets individuals who are interested in running a home-based business, and has a special column for individuals with disabilities.

 Extra Income, bimonthly, $11.95/yr. Business Concepts, Inc., PO Box 22957, Santa Barbara, CA 93121. (805) 569-1363; (805) 569-0861 (fax). This publication is full of ideas for people interested in starting home-based businesses.

 Home Business, Big Business, by Mel Cook, ©1992, 270 pp., ISBN: 0-02-008165-0, $12.00. Macmillan Publishing Co., 201 West 103rd St., Indianapolis, IN 42690. (800) 428-5331; (317) 581-3500. This overview of setting up a successful home-based business includes profiles of 38 innovative entrepreneurs. A reference section includes details on firms that sell products and services through home-based businesses, companies that regularly use homeworkers, and popular franchise opportunities.

 Home Business Institute (HBI), David Hanania, President, PO Box 301, White Plains, NY 10605-0301. (914) 946-6600. This membership organization of more than 40,000 home-based businesses provides a wide range of benefits, including: a newsletter and bulletin published five times/year; discounts on phone services, office supplies, insurance, travel, and prescription drugs; attendance at HBI conferences; and more. Dues are $49.00/year.

 Home Business Made Easy, by David Hanania, ©1992, 233 pp., ISBN: 1-55571-164-2, $14.95. Oasis Press, 300 N. Valley Dr., Grants Pass, OR 97526. (800) 228-2275; (503) 479-9464; (503) 476-1479 (fax). This book shows how to select and start a business that fits your interests, lifestyle, and pocketbook. The author walks the reader through 153 different full- or part-time businesses and shows current home-based workers how to expand.

Home Business Prospects, Michael B. Wilke, Ed., bimonthly, $24.00/yr. Pride Publishing, 126 School Dr., Sierra Vista, AZ 85635. (602) 458-2260. This publication is directed toward individuals involved in computer-based home businesses.

 Home Business Report, Rick Kerner, Ed., monthly, $24.00/yr. The Kerner Group, Inc., 3231 Forks St., Easton, PA 18042. (800) 972-6664; (215) 559-8553 (fax). This monthly newsletter focuses on strategies for running a successful home-based business. Includes real-life success stories, reports on the latest trends in marketing, discussions on issues facing home businesses, and more.

 Home Office & Business Opportunities Association of California, Debra Schacher, 92 Corporate Park, Ste. C-250, Irvine, CA 92714. (714) 261-9474; (714) 757-4626 (fax). This nonprofit statewide organization provides information on home-office topics and lobbies legislators to broaden laws regulating home-based businesses. Membership is $67/year for operators of home businesses; newsletter subscription is $15.

 Home Office Computing, Bernadette Grey, Ed., monthly, $19.97/yr. Home Office Computing, PO Box 2511, Boulder, CO 80302. (800) 288-7812. While this magazine is aimed primarily at the computer-oriented, home-based entrepreneur, it contains a wealth of valuable articles, tips, research, and small business information in every issue.

 Home Office Opportunities, Diane Wolverton, Ed., bimonthly, $18.00/yr. Deneb Publishing, PO Box 780, Lyman, WY 82937. (307) 786-4513. This magazine is directed toward the home-based business owner and contains articles about marketing, advertising, employee management, financial decisions, nurturing of the entrepreneurial spirit, and networking with other home-based business owners.

 Home Workers Association, Francine DiFillippo, 7235 Saddle Creek Circle, Sarasota, FL 34241-9543. (813) 925-1909; (813) 923-3597 (fax). This association of 2,300 individuals provides job referrals to members and assists workers at home no matter whether the business is traditional cottage handcrafts or high-tech services. They have produced several workbooks for business and marketing planning, and also offer team and project management assistance for solo entrepreneurs.

Homebased Businesses, by Beverly Neuer Feldman, Ed. D, ©1982, 242 pp., ISBN: 0-449-21810-4, $4.99. Ballantine Books, 201 East 50th St., New York, NY 10022. (800) 733-3000; (212) 751-2600. A step-by-step guide to setting up a home-based business, including hundreds of ideas for potential businesses. An extensive resource section features books and organizations related to specific businsss and industries.

 Homebased Businesswomen's Network, Sandra M. King, PO Box 681, Newburyport, MA 01950. (508) 462-2063. The goal of this association is to promote a positive image of women with home-based businesses and to provide opportunities for the exchange of resources, information, and support. The group meets monthly and publishes a newsletter 10 times/year. Annual dues are $40.

 Homemade Money, by Barbara Brabec, ©1994, 400 pp., ISBN: 1-55870-328-4, $23.95 (postpaid). Barbara Brabec Productions, PO Box 2137, Naperville, OH 60567-2137. (708) 717-4188. Brabec's classic has been revised and updated in its fifth edition, and still remains one of the most comprehensive guides and sourcebooks on how to select, start, manage, market, and multiply the profits of a business at home. Available direct from the author (postage included in price).

 How to Run Your Own Home Business, by Coralee Smith Kern & Tammara Hoffman Wolfgram, 160 pp., ISBN: 0-8442-6666-3, $9.95. National Textbook Company, 4255 W. Touhy Ave., Lincolnwood, IL 60646-1975. (800) 323-4900; (708) 679-5500; (708) 679-2494 (fax). A guide to establishing a successful home-based business, including evaluating the pros and cons, planning, financing, and more. Includes a discussion of trends likely to affect home-based businesses.

 How to Succeed in a Home Business, 70 min., $39.95. Inc. Business Resources, 350 N. Pennsylvania Ave., PO Box 1365, Wilkes-Barre, PA 13703-1365. (800) 468-0800 x4760; (717) 822-8899. In this video, viewers can see and hear how five successful entrepreneurs got started in their home-based businesses. Learn how to get your home and family ready, tips on insurance, zoning, permits, how to minimize taxes, and the pros and cons of home businesses.

Income Plus, Donna Ruffini, Ed., monthly, $15.89/yr. Opportunity Associates, 73 Spring St., Ste. 303, New York, NY 10012. (212) 925-3180; (212) 925-3612 (fax). This magazine is directed specifically toward home-based workers and small business owners.

 Making Money with Your Computer at Home, by Paul & Sarah Edwards, ©1993, 304 pp., ISBN: 0-87477-736-4, $12.95. Putnam Publishing Group, 200 Madison Ave., New York, NY 10016. (800) 631-8571; (212) 951-8400. Features details on 75 computer-based businesses, including full-time and part-time options. Questions and checklists help you assess which business is right for you.

 Marketing for the Home-Based Business, by Jeffery P. Davidson, ©1993, 204 pp., ISBN: 1-55850-945-3, $9.95. Bob Adams, Inc., 260 Center St., Holbrook, MA 02343. (800) 872-5627; (617) 767-8100; (800) 872-5628 (fax). This book offers an exclusive focus on marketing effectively from home.

 Million Dollar Home-Based Businesses, by Sunny & Kim Baker, ©1993, 228 pp., ISBN: 1-55850-246-9, $9.95. Bob Adams, Inc., 260 Center St., Holbrook, MA 02343. (800) 872-5627; (617) 767-8100; (800) 872-5628 (fax). Real-life stories of entrepreneurs who found the formula for home-based success.

 Mind Your Own Business at Home, Coralee Smith Kern, Ed., bimonthly, $30.00/yr. Coralee Smith Kern Publishing, Box 14850, Chicago, IL 60614. (312) 472-8116. Covers a broad view of issues pertinent to home-based businesses including zoning, marketing, financing, legal, and tax issues.

 National Association for the Cottage Industry, Coralee Smith Kern, Box 14850, Chicago, IL 60614. (312) 472-8116. This association involves more than 16,000 individuals who work in home-based businesses. The organization monitors public policy issues of home-based business, such as zoning, tax laws and labor laws, and sponsors trade shows and seminars. Members receive the quarterly *Cottage Connection* newsletter. Membership is $45/year.

National Home-Based Business Conference, Marcia Stuckey, PO Box 81, Grafton, NE 68365. (402) 282-7349; (402) 282-7351 (fax). The goal of this annual conference is to provide opportunities for those working in the home-based business arena to network and be made aware of changes in research, legislation, products, and services. It is held the first weekend in May in Lincoln, Nebraska.

 National Telecommuting and Telework Association, Larry Barrett, 1650 Tysons Blvd., Ste. 200, McLean, VA 22102. (703) 506-3295; (703) 506-3266 (fax). This trade association serves as a spokesperson to advocate a "telecommuting friendly" policy environment and to champion telecommuting as a productive workplace alternative.

 Nebraska Home-Based Business Association, Marcia Stuckey, PO Box 81, Grafton, NE 68365. (402) 282-7349; (402) 282-7351 (fax). This association's mission is to encourage education and enhance opportunities for home-based businesses in Nebraska. Membership is $36/year and is open to individuals or organizations nationwide. Members receive a newsletter, networking support, discounts on educational programs, and can take part in the National Home-Based Business Conference held in Lincoln, Nebraska each spring (see separate listing).

 Sisters in Business (SIB), Joyce Berry, Founder/President, 1107 Fair Oaks Ave., Ste. 165, South Pasadena, CA 91030. (213) 485-4256; (818) 797-8223; (818) 441-3159 (fax). SIB is a home-based networking system whose main objective is to share business ideas on professional and personal growth, and provide a community support team for current and future home-based businesses. They offer an educational program on "How to Start a Home-Based Business" that emphasizes women-owned and minority-owned start-ups.

 Start and Run a Profitable Home-Based Business, by Edna Sheedy, ©1990, 152 pp., ISBN: 0-88908-877-2, $12.95. Self-Counsel Press, Inc., 1704 N. State St., Bellingham, WA 98225. (800) 663-3007; (206) 676-4530; (206) 676-4549 (fax). This book provides an overview of practical information for readers interested in starting a home-based business.

The Business Plan for Home-Based Business, $1.00. U.S. Small Business Administration, SBA Publications, PO Box 30, Denver, CO 80201-0030. (800) 827-5722; (202) 205-6665. This booklet offers a comprehensive approach to writing a business plan for a home-based business.

 The Complete Work-At-Home Companion, by Herman Holtz, ©1994, 368 pp., ISBN: 1-55958-347-9, $14.95. Prima Publishing, PO Box 1260, Rocklin, CA 95677-1260. (916) 632-7400; (916) 632-7668 (fax). Advice for home-based entrepreneurs on setting up the ideal office as well as getting the most mileage from computer hardware and software.

 The Home Business Bible, by David R. Eyler, ©1994, 288 pp., ISBN: 0-471-59577-2, $17.95. John Wiley & Sons, Inc., 605 Third Ave., New York, NY 10158-0012. (800) CALL-WILEY; (212) 850-6000. Details on terms, topics, and problems confronted in a home-based business, listed in a simple A-to-Z format. Includes checklists, forms, letters, worksheets, and real-life stories. Also available as a book/disk set for $55.00.

 The Home Office & Small Business Answer Book, by Janet Attard, ©1993, 512 pp., ISBN: 0-8050-2565-0, $19.95. Henry Holt & Company, Inc., 115 W. 18th St., New York, NY 10011. (800) 488-5233; (212) 886-9200. A comprehensive compilation of answers to frequently asked small business questions gathered from the author's experiences as the host of online computer business forums.

Emphasis on Business

To combat the perception of not being on par with their counterparts in high-priced office suites, savvy home-based entrepreneurs use a variety of measures to underscore their professionalism. Voice mail systems can create the impression of a much larger firm. Laser-printed correspondence on quality letterhead presents a polished look in print. Keeping regular hours and answering calls with a business name also reveal your seriousness, contributing to a successful business image.

The Home-Based Entrepreneur: The Complete Guide to Working at Home, by Linda Pinson & Jerry Jinnett, ©1994, 192 pp., ISBN: 0-936894-46-6, $19.95. Upstart Publishing Co., Inc., 12 Portland St., Dover, NH 03820. (800) 235-8866; (603) 749-5071; (603) 742-9121 (fax). This book covers all the issues of starting a home-based business by two respected business owners and consultants.

The Joy of Working From Home, by Jeff Berner, ©1994, 240 pp., ISBN: 1-881052-46-X, $12.95. Berrett-Koehler Publishers, Inc., 155 Montgomery St., San Francisco, CA 94104. (800) 929-2929; (415) 288-0260; (415) 362-2512 (fax). In a tone both pragmatic and inspiring, this book shows the current or prospective home-based worker how to set up an efficient and successful business. It focuses on the nuts-and-bolts details of daily operations as well as the importance of striking a healthy balance between business and personal life.

The Work-At-Home Sourcebook, by Lynie Arden, ©1994, 300 pp., ISBN: 0-911781-11-0, $16.95. Live Oak Publications, 1515 23rd St., PO Box 2193, Boulder, CO 80306. (800) 634-9024; (303) 447-1087. This book features detailed listings of more than 1,000 companies who use home-based workers in a wide variety of markets and industries. It also includes case studies and answers to frequently asked questions regarding home-based opportunities.

Working From Home, Allan Cohen, Ed., monthly, $60.00/yr. Working From Home, PO Box 1722, Hallandale, FL 33008. (800) 283-3008. This newsletter focuses on home-based independent consultants, entrepreneurs, and small business owners. The firm also produces directories and seminars.

Working From Home, by Paul & Sarah Edwards, ©1994, 550 pp., ISBN: 0-87477-764-X, $15.95. Putnam Publishing Group, 200 Madison Ave., New York, NY 10016. (800) 631-8571; (212) 951-8400. The fourth edition of this classic presents a comprehensive overview of starting a home-based business, from deciding what business is right for you to marketing, managing, and expanding your venture.

Working From Home Forum, CompuServe Information Service, 5000 Arlington Center Blvd., PO Box 20212, Columbus, OH 43220. (800) 848-8199; (614) 457-8600; (614) 457-0348. This online forum, hosted by co-authors Paul & Sarah Edwards, provides an electronic link between individuals who work from home. Subscribers can find news, do research, and exchange ideas with home-based business owners from around the world.

 Your Home Business Can Make Dollars and Sense, by Jo Frohbeiter-Meuller, ©1990, 290 pp., ISBN: 0-8019-7995-1, $16.95. Chilton Book Company, One Chilton Way, Radnor, PA 19089. (800) 695-1214; (610) 964-4745 (fax). A nuts-and-bolts approach to starting and operating a business out of your home. Also explains how to take advantage of the many tax breaks available to home business owners.

Insurance

I nsurance brings the peace of mind of knowing that what you value is protected. For solo business owners, these concerns usually focus on health care, business property, and liability issues. Since sick days are a luxury of those who work for someone else, savvy solo entrepreneurs know that health insurance is a central part of smart business planning. Protecting property from theft and personal assets from legal conflicts are other common concerns for solo entrepreneurs. The resources in this section will help you determine your insurance needs and show you how to make wise buying decisions.

 Business Continuation Planning, $1.00. U.S. Small Business Administration, SBA Publications, PO Box 30, Denver, CO 80201-0030. (800) 827-5722; (202) 205-6665. This booklet discusses the life insurance needs of a small business owner and how important business life insurance is when planning for the future of any enterprise.

 Curtailing Crime—Inside and Out, $2.00. U.S. Small Business Administration, SBA Publications, PO Box 30, Denver, CO 80201-0030. (800) 827-5722; (202) 205-6665. This booklet discusses crime prevention and includes measures to guard against theft, bad check passing, burglary, and employee dishonesty.

 Health Insurance for the Self-Employed, by Lenore Janecek, ©1993, 160 pp., ISBN: 1-879903-11-3, $15.95. Allworth Press, 10 E. 23rd St., New York, NY 10010. (800) 247-6553; (212) 777-8395. This book provides do-it-yourself advice from an expert for artists, consultants, entrepreneurs, and other self-employed individuals who need to find adequate, affordable health insurance. Covers health insurance options, including dental, disability, life insurance, long-term care, Medicare/Medicaid, and retirement planning.

How to Buy the Right Insurance at the Right Price, by Bailard, Biehl, & Kaiser, Inc., ©1989, 250 pp., ISBN: 1-55623-146-6, $15.00. Irwin Professional Publishing, Inc., 1333 Burr Ridge Pkwy., Burr Ridge, IL 60521. (800) 634-3961; (708) 789-4000. This book provides insights into the many insurance options available to small business owners. It teaches readers how to classify their risks and provide for their own needs in order to choose the appropriate policy.

 Insurance Information Institute, 110 William St., New York, NY 10038. (800) 942-4242 (helpline); (212) 669-9200; (212) 732-1916 (fax). The mission of the Insurance Information Institute is to improve public understanding of insurance—what it does and how it works. The association serves as a primary source of information, analysis, and referral concerning insurance for the media, governments, universities, and the public. It publishes a range of books and pamphlets on insurance matters. In conjunction with the American Council of Life Insurance and the Health Insurance Association of America, it sponsors the National Insurance Consumer Helpline (see separate listing below).

 National Insurance Consumer Hotline (NICH), (800) 942-4242. This toll-free telephone advice and referral resource is co-sponsored by the Health Insurance Association of America, the American Council of Life Insurance, and the Insurance Information Institute. NICH personnel, who have undergone training in auto, homeowners', and health and life insurance, answer questions and provide callers with brochures and additional assistance to help them solve insurance problems.

Group Savings

In addition to terrific networking opportunities, many professional associations offer solo entrepreneurs access to group health and business insurance. Because they represent a large number of members, organizations can negotiate better rates and coverage. Individuals should shop carefully and make a comparison of premiums, deductibles, and coverage based on similar situations. Also check out the ease and speed of claim payments.

Quotesmith Corporation, 50 N. Brockaway, Palatine, IL 60067. (800) 556-9393; (708) 358-9542 (fax). For $15.00 this company will generate a price comparison report reviewing 350 leading insurance companies based on your business needs.

 Small Business Risk Management Guide, $1.00. U.S. Small Business Administration, SBA Publications, PO Box 30, Denver, CO 80201-0030. (800) 827-5722; (202) 205-6665. This booklet helps you strengthen your insurance program by identifying, minimizing, and eliminating unnecessary risks.

 The Buyer's Guide to Business Insurance, by Don Bury & Larry Heischman, ©1994, 200 pp., ISBN: 1-55571-162-6, $19.95. Oasis Press, 300 N. Valley Dr., Grants Pass, OR 97526. (800) 228-2275; (503) 479-9464; (503) 476-1479 (fax). Straightforward advice on shopping for insurance, understanding types of coverage, comparing proposals, and premium rates. Includes worksheets to assist in analyzing risk.

 Wilkinson Benefit Consultants, Inc., 100 West Rd., Ste. 300, Towson, MD 21204. (800) 296-3030 (hotline); (410) 832-7503. This firm will conduct a 24-point analysis of your insurance needs, run it through their extensive database of insurance companies and HMOs, and provide you with a report of the 10 best plans for your consideration. Pricing is a flat fee based on the size of your company and number of employees.

International Business

In today's global economy, an increasing number of solo entrepreneurs are extending their reach across national borders to operate international businesses. Some launch import/export firms, while others expand their American products or services to new markets in different lands and languages. Another approach is to forge collaborative partnerships for marketing and distribution. The following resources can guide you through the myriad rules and regulations that accompany international business, as well as the cultural subtleties of doing business in other lands. Let them inspire you to explore how your solo business might expand to a global scale.

 Building an Import/Export Business, by Kenneth D. Weiss, ©1991, 272 pp., ISBN: 0-471-53627-X, $16.95. John Wiley & Sons, Inc., 605 Third Ave., New York, NY 10158-0012. (800) CALL-WILEY; (212) 850-6000; (212) 850-8641 (fax). This book provides the technical details on how to start and run an import/export business, including choosing a product and market, preparing a business plan, and staying on top of the legislation and customs regulations that govern international trade.

 Doing Business in Latin America and the Caribbean, by Lawrence W. Tuller, ©1993, 300 pp., ISBN: 0-8144-5035-0, $32.95. AMACOM Books, PO Box 1026, Saranac Lake, NY 12983. (800) 262-9699; (518) 891-3653 (fax). A guide to business dealings in Mexico, the U.S. Virgin Islands, Puerto Rico, Central America and South America.

Doing Business In Mexico, by Jay Jessup & Maggie Jessup, ©1994, 288 pp., ISBN: 1-55958-570-6, $14.95. Prima Publishing, PO Box 1260, Rocklin, CA 95677-1260. (916) 632-7400; (916) 632-7668 (fax). A step-by-step guide, with checklists, from business consultants specializing in Mexico. Includes information on exporting, importing, investing, and manufacturing as well as opportunities for environmental products and forecasts for emerging industries.

Export Now: A Guide for Small Business, by Richard L. Leeza, ©1993, 240 pp., ISBN: 1-55571-167-7, $19.95. Oasis Press, 300 N. Valley Dr., Grants Pass, OR 97526. (800) 228-2275; (503) 479-9464; (503) 476-1479 (fax). This book describes the current world of export, then articulates specific requirements for export licensing, preparation of documents, payment methods, packaging, and shipping. Also offers advice on evaluating foreign representatives, planning international marketing strategies, and more.

Export/Import, by Joseph A. Zodl, ©1992, 160 pp., ISBN: 1-55870-252-0, $12.95. Betterway Books, 1507 Dana Avenue, Cincinnati, OH 45207. (800) 289-0963; (513) 531-4082 (fax). Details on what you and your company need to know to compete in world markets, including definitions of terms and vocabulary.

Export/Import Procedures and Documentation, by Thomas E. Johnson, ©1994, 393 pp., ISBN: 0-8144-0237-2, $65.00. AMACOM Books, PO Box 1026, Saranac Lake, NY 12983. (800) 262-9699; (518) 891-3653 (fax). Step-by-step instructions and more than 100 sample documents lead the reader through every area of importing and exporting, including shipping, insurance, banks, currency exchange, contracts, customs, transportation, and more.

Exporter's Guide to Federal Resources for Small Businesses, ©1992, 122 pp., ISBN: 0-16-030231-5, $4.75. U.S. Small Business Administration, New Orders, Superintendent of Documents, PO Box 371954, Pittsburgh, PA 15250-7954. (202) 783-3238; (202) 512-2250 (fax). This one-volume guide is designed to inform business owners/entrepreneurs of the major federal programs that can help them export their products or services. It includes names and phone numbers of key personnel at each agency and an annotated bibliography of selected international trade publications.

Exporting From the United States, by U.S. Department of Commerce, ©1994, 176 pp., ISBN: 1-55958-328-2, $14.95. Prima Publishing, PO Box 1260, Rocklin, CA 95677-1260. (916) 632-7400; (916) 632-7668 (fax). Details on exporting products from the U.S., including information on export strategy, market research, distribution, contracts, and regulations.

 Exporting, Importing, and Beyond, by Lawrence W. Tuller, ©1994, 300 pp., ISBN: 1-55850-464-8, $10.95. Bob Adams, Inc., 260 Center St., Holbrook, MA 02343. (800) 872-5627; (617) 767-8100; (800) 872-5628 (fax). This volume demystifies the jargon and clarifies the financial and legal aspects of how to set up a small business exporting program.

 How to Be an Importer and Pay for Your World Travel, by Mary Green & Stanley Gilmar, ©1993, 160 pp., ISBN: 0-89815-501-0, $8.95. Ten Speed Press, PO Box 7123, Berkeley, CA 94707. (800) 841-BOOK; (510) 845-8414; (510) 524-1052 (fax). A revised edition of a classic guide to launching an import business.

 Importing Into the United States, by U.S. Department of Commerce, ©1994, 96 pp., ISBN: 1-55958-177-8, $12.95. Prima Publishing, PO Box 1260, Rocklin, CA 95677-1260. (916) 632-7400; (916) 632-7668 (fax). Detailed information on bringing products into the United States.

 International Business Culture Series, by Peggy Kenna & Sondra Lacy, ©1994, 64 pp., $7.95/each. National Textbook Company, 4255 W. Touhy Ave., Lincolnwood, IL 60646-1975. (800) 323-4900; (708) 679-5500; (708) 679-2494 (fax). This series of books features practical, pocket-sized guides to doing business in Japan, Mexico, France, Taiwan, China, and Germany. Features advice and details on cultural differences, and how to interact, solve problems, and reach decisions in each of the different countries.

Kiss, Box, or Shake Hands, by Terri Morrison, Wayne A. Conaway, & George A. Borden, Ph.D., ©1994, 400 pp., ISBN: 1-55850-444-3, $17.95. Bob Adams, Inc., 260 Center St., Holbrook, MA 02343. (800) 872-5627; (617) 767-8100; (800) 872-5628 (fax). A guide to doing business in 60 countries, including insights on business customs, negotiating techniques, entertaining, behavioral styles, social customs, gift giving, and more.

Market Overseas with U.S. Government Help, $1.00. U.S. Small Business Administration, SBA Publications, PO Box 30, Denver, CO 80201-0030. (800) 827-5722; (202) 205-6665. This booklet introduces programs available to help small businesses break into the international market and the world of exporting.

 Professional International Network Society (PINS), Pat Poole Newsome, Executive Director, 280 Blacks Mill Valley, Dawsonville, GA 30534. (800) 850-2611; (706) 216-2611; (706) 216-2720 (fax). PINS is a nonprofit organization established to encourage the cultivation of new and challenging ways to meet the needs of an international and multicultural society for tomorrow's professionals. Annual meetings are held in the spring.

 The Complete Guide to Doing Business in Mexico, by Anita Winsor, ©1994, 336 pp., ISBN: 0-8144-0211-9, $29.95. AMACOM Books, PO Box 1026, Saranac Lake, NY 12983. (800) 262-9699; (518) 891-3653 (fax). This book features essential economic, cultural, and political information for successful business operations in Mexico. Includes a detailed 70-page directory of key business and government contacts.

Beyond the Border

While some solo businesses are intentionally launched as international enterprises, a great number expand beyond the border in unexpected ways. Products that gain popularity in the United States are sent to customers' friends and families abroad, and that leads to a request for international distribution. Or a regular customer is transferred abroad, misses your product, and places an order. Your subsequent shipment introduces your business to a wide new market. Or you discover a product you'd like to import while on a vacation trip.

Although international dealings can bring certain complications, many solo entrepreneurs have discovered the benefits outweigh potential pitfalls. Explore and see if international operations might work for your business. The world grows smaller by the day.

Trade Information Center Hotline, U.S. Department of Commerce, (800) USA-TRADE. A telephone call to this toll-free hotline will put you in touch with government trade specialists.

Worldwide Business Tours for Women, National Education Center for Women in Business (NECWB), Seton Hill College, Seton Hill Dr., Greensburg, PA 15601-1599. (800) NECWB-4-U; (412) 830-4625; (412) 834-7131 (fax). These international business tours are sponsored by the National Education Center for Women in Business (NECWB). Limited to 20 participants, each trip introduces women business owners to international trade by exploring markets in specific countries, where they can visit retail and industrial areas, and network with local entrepreneurs. Tours are led by American businesspersons acquainted with business practices and customs in the destination country. Among the countries and cities visited are Australia, India, Indonesia, Italy, Mexico, and Moscow. Fees vary by country, and trips average about a week in length.

Legal Information

See also Patents, Trademarks, and Copyrights

While the intricacies of the law are best handled by legal professionals, solo entrepreneurs are wise to keep abreast of legal issues for two important reasons: control and costs. An informed business owner has a greater chance of anticipating potential legal trouble—and avoiding it. If you're involved in a legal situation, you can retain control and save money by accessing resources in this section as a prelude to seeking professional help. The preparation will enable you to ask better questions, explore alternatives, and reduce the time spent in your lawyer's office.

 How to Find the Right Lawyer, by Alice Griffin, ©1994, 32 pp., ISBN: 0-9636341-1-9, $5.95, postpaid. The Cakewalk Press, PO Box 1536-WS, New York, NY 10276. (212) 673-7133. This booklet gives inside information about locating and hiring the best lawyer for any legal problem. In addition to telling readers how to locate excellent professional legal help, it shows how to interview and negotiate with lawyers, check up on prospective lawyers, and handle fee disputes.

 How to Start Your Own Business: Small Business Law, by Ralph Warner with Joanne Greene, ©1993, 60 min., ISBN: 0-87337-210-7, $14.95. Nolo Press, 950 Parker St., Berkeley, CA 94710. (800) 955-4775; (510) 549-1976; (800) 645-0895 (fax). This 60-minute tape covers the most-asked legal questions facing the small business owner, including how to protect the business name, partnership or corporation, legal pitfalls in renting a space, employees and taxes, and more.

 Inc. Yourself, by Judith H. McQuown, ©1993, 288 pp., ISBN: 0-88730-611-X, $12.00. HarperCollins International, 10 E. 53rd St., New York, NY 10022-5299. (800) 982-4377; (212) 207-7641; (800) 822-4090 (fax). Guidelines on setting up your own business, including advice on whether to establish it as a corporation.

Keeping Track, by Anne E. Krause, ©1991, 112 pp., ISBN: 0-88908-931-0, $14.95. Self-Counsel Press, Inc., 1704 N. State St., Bellingham, WA 98225. (800) 663-3007; (206) 676-4530; (206) 676-4549 (fax). This book is designed to help you organize your legal, business, and personal records either by yourself, or with the additional help of a professional planner, so you can plot legal and investment strategies and plan your estate.

 Legal Guide for the Visual Artist, by Tad Crawford, ©1994, 256 pp., ISBN: 0-927629-11-9, $19.95. Allworth Press, 10 E. 23rd St., New York, NY 10010. (800) 247-6553; (212) 777-8395. An updated edition of a classic reference on the legal issues facing visual artists which includes information on important new areas such as digital technologies and multimedia. Covers copyrights, contracts, taxes, estate planning, grants, and more.

 Legal Handbook for Small Business, by Marc J. Lane, ©1989, 272 pp., ISBN: 0-81445951-X, $19.95. AMACOM Books, PO Box 1026, Saranac Lake, NY 12983. (800) 262-9699; (518) 891-3653 (fax). This book contains a wealth of easy-to-understand, accessible legal information regarding the most frequently raised questions in small business.

 Nolo's Partnership Maker, by Anthony Mancuso & Michael Radtke, ©1993, ISBN: 0-87337-165-8, $129.95. Nolo Press, 950 Parker St., Berkeley, CA 94710. (800) 955-4775; (510) 549-1976; (800) 645-0895 (fax). This software prepares a partnership agreement that is valid in any state, includes online legal help screens, glossary, tutorial and 256-page manual. Available in DOS format only.

 S Corporations: A Comprehensive Analysis, by Federal Tax Workshops, Inc., Center for Video Education, PO Box 635, North White Plains, NY 10603. (800) 621-0043; (914) 428-0180 (fax). In this self-study video prepared by Federal Tax Workshops, you can discover the key opportunities and pitfalls of establishing your business as a Subchapter S corporation. Covers the basics of S Corporation election, operation, distributions, and liquidations, as well as the details on computing taxes and year-round planning.

Selecting the Legal Structure for Your Business, $1.00. U.S. Small Business Administration, SBA Publications, PO Box 30, Denver, CO 80201-0030. (800) 827-5722; (202) 205-6665. This booklet discusses the various legal structures available for small businesses and helps identify the advantages and disadvantages of each.

 Standard Legal Forms and Agreements for Small Businesses, by Steve Sanderson, ed., ©1990, 208 pp., ISBN: 0-88908-925-6, $14.95. Self-Counsel Press, Inc., 1704 N. State St., Bellingham, WA 98225. (800) 663-3007; (206) 676-4530; (206) 676-4549 (fax). A wide selection of commonly used business agreements and indispensable legal forms, all in a large-format book with a lay-flat binding.

 The Artist as a Self-Employed Person, by Robert Jack Hoerner, Shelba D. Meek, Jean M. Cullen, Andréa L. Caruso, & C. Corcos, ©1993, 230 pp., $20.00, postpaid. New Organization for the Visual Arts (NOVA), 4614 Prospect Ave., Ste. 410, Cleveland, OH 44103. (216) 431-7500. This workbook, co-published by NOVA and the Cleveland, Ohio chapter of the Volunteer Lawyers for the Arts, contains information on visual artists' rights, intellectual property issues, contracts, taxes, estate planning, and other legal matters affecting creative professionals. Two other workbooks are also available in the series.

 The Complete Book of Small Business Legal Forms, by Daniel Sitarz, ©1991, 248 pp., ISBN: 0-935755-03-9, $17.95. Nova Publishing Company, 4882 Kellogg Circle, Boulder, CO 80303. (303) 443-7745; (303) 545-9901 (fax). This book contains the copy-ready masters for almost all the general business forms you might need to operate a small business.

 The Law in (Plain English) for Small Businesses, by Leonard D. DuBoff, ©1991, 240 pp., ISBN: 0-471-53616-4, $14.95. John Wiley & Sons, Inc., 605 Third Ave., New York, NY 10158-0012. (800) CALL-WILEY; (212) 850-6000; (212) 850-8641 (fax). This book explains—in plain, simple English—the complex legal issues involved in all aspects of starting and running a small business.

The Legal Guide for Starting and Running a Small Business, by Fred S. Steingold, ©1992, 400 pp., ISBN: 0-87337-174-7, $19.95. Nolo Press, 950 Parker St., Berkeley, CA 94710. (800) 955-4775; (510) 549-1976; (800) 645-0895 (fax). A clearly written guide to legal matters covering what every business owner needs to know to establish and run a small business.

The Legal Guide for Starting and Running a Small Business, by Fred S. Steingold, ©1994, ISBN: 0-87337-273-5, $24.95. Nolo Press, 950 Parker St., Berkeley, CA 94710. (800) 955-4775; (510) 549-1976; (800) 645-0895 (fax). A disk-based version of the legal guide of the same name. Includes a 10-page users' guide. Available in Windows format only.

The Partnership Book: How to Write a Partnership Agreement, by Dennis Clifford & Ralph Warner, ©1993, 368 pp., ISBN: 0-87337-141-0, $24.95. Nolo Press, 950 Parker St., Berkeley, CA 94710. (800) 955-4775; (510) 549-1976; (800) 645-0895 (fax). This book explains the legal and practical issues involved in forming a partnership, and offers clear step-by-step guidance for creating a strong agreement.

The Software Developer's Complete Legal Companion, by Thorne D. Harris III, ©1994, 304 pp., ISBN: 1-55958-502-1, $39.95. Prima Publishing, PO Box 1260, Rocklin, CA 95677-1260. (916) 632-7400; (916) 632-7668 (fax). This book provides practical information for the software designer regarding legal agreements, use permits, and copyrights. Includes a disk containing templates for legal forms.

Managing Your Business

See also Employees; Office Design and Operation; Project Management;
Time Management

I t's a common entrepreneurial trait that the challenges of start-up can be accomplished with relative ease—it's the daily management issues that trip us up and create the most problems! For solo entrepreneurs, the issues of running a successful business often center on managing ourselves and others. The resources in this section provide advice on how to get the most out of your own abilities and how to create productive relationships with those who work with you. In addition, you'll find materials to help you develop leadership and negotiating skills, as well as resources filled with management insights from longtime entrepreneurs.

General Management Resources

 301 Great Management Ideas, by Sara P. Noble, Ed., ©1991, 306 pp., ISBN: 0-9626146-4-5, $12.95. Inc. Publishing, 38 Commercial Wharf, Boston, MA 02110. (800) 468-0800 x4760; (617) 248-8000. A collection of 301 innovative management ideas gathered from small companies and the pages of *Inc.* magazine.

 American Management Association (AMA), 135 W. 50th St., New York, NY 10020. (800) 262-6969; (212) 586-8100; (212) 903-8186 (fax). The AMA provides educational forums worldwide where members and their colleagues learn practical business skills. The organization publishes a monthly magazine as well as videos, books, and self-study courses that enable individuals to learn beyond the classroom. (Several AMA training programs and publications can be found elsewhere in this volume.) An annual meeting is held in April.

Assertiveness Training for Professionals, by Helga Rhode, 4 hrs., $59.95. CareerTrack, 3085 Center Green Dr., Boulder, CO 80301-5408. (800) 334-1018; (800) 832-9489 (fax). Step-by-step techniques presented by psychologist Helga Rhode to help individuals behave in a more confident, more effective manner. Also on video (2 vol., 3.5 hrs.) for $149.95.

 Avoiding Mistakes in Your New Business, by David Karlson, ©1994, 175 pp., ISBN: 1-56052-173-2, $15.95. Crisp Publications, 1200 Hamilton Ct., Menlo Park, CA 94025. (415) 323-6100; (415) 323-5800 (fax). Directed at the new business owner, this book discusses the various pitfalls involved in running a business and teaches readers how to avoid them.

 Be an Even Better Manager, by Michael Armstrong, ©1990, 400 pp., ISBN: 0-88908-874-8, $9.95. Self-Counsel Press, Inc., 1704 N. State St., Bellingham, WA 98225. (800) 663-3007; (206) 676-4530; (206) 676-4549 (fax). This practical book aims at making you the best manager you can possibly be. Techniques and tips are listed alphabetically to make your learning experience more efficient.

 Be the Boss, by Sandi Wilson, ©1985, 262 pp., ISBN: 0-380-89634-6, $5.95. Avon Books, 1350 Avenue of the Americas, New York, NY 10019. (800) 238-0658; (800) 6633-1607 (in TN); (212) 261-6800. Practical insights on the day-to-day details of making a service business work, mixed with humor and wit from the owner of a small advertising agency.

 Be the Boss II: Running a Successful Service Business, by Sandi Wilson, ©1993, 248 pp., ISBN: 0-380-76614-0, $4.99. Avon Books, 1350 Avenue of the Americas, New York, NY 10019. (800) 238-0658; (800) 6633-1607 (in TN); (212) 261-6800. More entertaining success secrets, updated for the world of the 1990s.

 Beating the Odds: 10 Smart Steps to Small Business Success, by Scott A. Clark, ©1992, 283 pp., ISBN: 0-8144-7811-5, $15.95. AMACOM Books, PO Box 1026, Saranac Lake, NY 12983. (800) 262-9699; (518) 891-3653 (fax). A popular-selling guide to funding and running your business, broken down into key areas most entrepreneurs find challenging.

Boardroom Reports, Martin Edelston, Ed., semimonthly, $49.00/yr. 330 W. 42 St., New York, NY 10036. (800) 274-5611. This information-packed newsletter contains concise bits of business news, tips, and techniques gathered from leading books and consultants to help you manage your business more efficiently.

 Bottom Line/Personal, Martin Edelston, Ed., semimonthly, ISSN: 0274-4805, $49.00/yr. Boardroom Reports, 330 W. 42 St., New York, NY 10036. (800) 274-5611. Like its cousin publication, *Boardroom Reports* (see separate listing above), this newsletter is filled with capsule summaries of information and resources to help you manage your time, energy, and money more effectively.

 Business Mastery, by Cherie Sohnen-Moe, ©1991, 246 pp., ISBN: 0-9321265-3-5, $19.95. Sohnen-Moe Associates, 3906 W. Ina Rd. #200-348, Tucson, AZ 85741. (800) 786-4774; (602) 743-3877. Written by a successful business consultant and healing arts practitioner, this book is filled with examples, exercises, and forms for creating a successful business, as well as information that balances practical skills with a humanistic approach. Shows how to increase your success by using proven techniques that integrate your values into your business.

What's It Worth?

In the early stages of their businesses, most solo entrepreneurs wear many hats—accountant, receptionist, marketing manager, new product development engineer, maintenance staff, and more. While exhausting, it's actually good training in understanding the complex needs of a business.

As your firm matures, however, it may be wiser to pass off some duties to freelance associates or assistants. If your specialized skills can generate greater income than the amount you would pay an assistant to do administrative tasks, you're losing money. By freeing up your time, you increase your ability to attract and serve higher-paying clients—and take your business to its next level of growth.

Business Partnering for Continuous Improvement, by Charles C. Poirier & William F. Houser, ©1994, 260 pp., ISBN: 1-881052-39-7, $19.95. Berrett-Koehler Publishers, Inc., 155 Montgomery St., San Francisco, CA 94104. (800) 929-2929; (415) 288-0260; (415) 362-2512 (fax). This book shows how to forge enduring alliances among employees, suppliers, and customers by focusing on building long-term partnerships.

 Center for Entrepreneurial Management (CEM), Joseph Mancuso, Executive Director, 180 Varick St., New York, NY 10014. (212) 633-0060; (212) 633-0063 (fax). Under the leadership of one of the nation's most respected entrepreneurs, CEM has built a vital network of more than 3,000 entrepreneurs, and publishes a monthly newsletter entitled *Entrepreneurial Management.* Annual dues are $96.00 and include a subscription to *Inc.* and *Success* magazines as well as the CEM newsletter.

 Fail-Safe Small Businesses, by Ron Tepper, ©1994, 256 pp., ISBN: 0-471-01437-0, $14.95. John Wiley & Sons, Inc., 605 Third Ave., New York, NY 10158-0012. (800) CALL-WILEY; (212) 850-6000; (212) 850-8641 (fax). Based on a detailed review of more than a dozen highly profitable small businesses, this book shows the winning characteristics of a failure-proof business. Includes sample direct mail pieces, press releases, client letters, and examples of successful business ventures.

 How to Avoid 101 Small Business Mistakes, Myths, & Misconceptions, by Gary L. Schine, ©1991, 124 pp., ISBN: 0-913969-30-2, $19.95. The Consultant Press, Ltd., 163 Amsterdam Ave., Ste. 201, New York, NY 10023. (212) 838-8640; (212) 873-7065 (fax). Straightforward advice on common mistakes that small business owners make—from start-up to managing time, employees, and finances as well as sales and marketing.

 How to Grow a Profitable Business, by Frank Cooper, ©1993, 263 pp., ISBN: 0-917219-01-5, $29.95. World Professional Publishing Company, PO Box 3206, Everett, WA 98203-1206. (800) 359-3719; (206) 348-5533; (206) 353-0503 (fax). Insights from a professional speaker and small business owner on the "street smarts" needed to succeed as an entrepreneur, ranging from establishing a sharp business focus to time management, customer relations, sales, and staying motivated.

IMCOR, 60 Guernsey Ave., Stamford, CT 06901. (800) 468-3746; (203) 975-8000; (203) 975-8199 (fax). This nationwide company operates five regional offices in major cities throughout the United States. They provide top-level, project-oriented executives to satisfy temporary management assignments in all functions and across all industries. Solo entrepreneurs may want to use IMCOR's professionals to guide them in a specific aspect of managing their businesses. Other independents may be interested in becoming part of their talent pool.

 International Council for Small Business (ICSB), Jefferson Smurfit Ctr. for Entrepreneurial Studies, St. Louis University, 3674 Lindell Blvd., St. Louis, MO 63108. (314) 658-3896; (314) 658-3874 (fax). The ICSB is a nonprofit organization devoted to continuing management education for entrepreneurs and small business. Members receive the *Journal of Small Business Management* and the quarterly ICSB *Bulletin*. International meetings are held annually. Membership is $60/year for individuals.

 I-Power, by Martin Edelston & Marion Buhagiar, 223 pp., Boardroom Classics, PO Box 11401, Des Moines, IA 50336-1401. (800) 274-5611. A leading entrepreneur shares management tips that cover every aspect of business success, including: ideas, ingenuity, invention, incentive, individuals, inquisitiveness, innovation, inspiration, intelligence, imagination, improvement, and more.

 I-Power Seminars, $75.00. Boardroom, Inc., 330 W. 42 St., New York, NY 10036. (212) 613-5282. This three-hour seminar for businesses of all types and sizes is based on principles found in the best-selling book of the same name. Seminars are held in New York City and around the country.

 In Business, Jerome Goldstein, Ed., bimonthly, $23.00/yr. J.G. Press, 419 Stale Avenue, Emmaus, PA 18049. (215) 967-4135. This magazine focuses on small business management and environmental entrepreneurship.

 Inventory Management, $0.50. U.S. Small Business Administration, SBA Publications, PO Box 30, Denver, CO 80201-0030. (800) 827-5722; (202) 205-6665. This booklet discusses the purpose of inventory management, types of inventories, recordkeeping, and the role of forecasting.

Locating or Relocating Your Business, $1.00. U.S. Small Business Administration, SBA Publications, PO Box 30, Denver, CO 80201-0030. (800) 827-5722; (202) 205-6665. This booklet focuses on the elements involved in changing the location of your business, such as the company's market, the potential work force, transportation options, and raw materials availability.

 Making It On Your Own, by Paul & Sarah Edwards, ©1991, 250 pp., ISBN: 0-87477-636-8, $11.95. Putnam Publishing Group, 200 Madison Ave., New York, NY 10016. (800) 631-8571; (212) 951-8400. A guide to surviving and thriving the ups and downs of being your own boss, including details on mastering confidence, motivation, and self-discipline.

 Operating a Really Small Business, by Betty Bivins, ©1993, 150 pp., ISBN: 1-56052-169-4, $15.95. Crisp Publications, 1200 Hamilton Ct., Menlo Park, CA 94025. (415) 323-6100; (415) 323-5800 (fax). This book teaches the owners of very small businesses important management and marketing strategies designed especially for their needs.

 Small Business Resource, Small Business Partnership, American Express Corp., PO Box 53788, Phoenix, AZ 85072-3788. (602) 954-1000; (602) 492-7891 (fax). This free monthly publication provides information to help small business owners manage their companies better.

 Successful Self-Management, by Paul R. Timm, 80 pp., ISBN: 0-931961-26-2, $8.95. Crisp Publications, 1200 Hamilton Ct., Menlo Park, CA 94025. (415) 323-6100; (415) 323-5800 (fax). Learn an effective, psychologically sound way of improving personal productivity. Also available as a video/audiotape program for $95.00.

 Techniques for Problem Solving, $1.00. U.S. Small Business Administration, SBA Publications, PO Box 30, Denver, CO 80201-0030. (800) 827-5722; (202) 205-6665. This booklet instructs the small business owner in the process of problem identification and effective problem solving.

The Designer's Commonsense Business Book, by Barbara Ganim, 192 pp., ISBN: 0-8442-3376-5, $29.95. National Textbook Company, 4255 W. Touhy Ave., Lincolnwood, IL 60646-1975. (800) 323-4900; (708) 679-5500; (708) 679-2494 (fax). How to transform your freelance design career into a stable and financially rewarding business. Includes ready-to-use forms and checklists.

 The Entrepreneur & Small Business Problem Solver, by William A. Cohen, ©1990, 565 pp., ISBN: 0-471-50124-7, $29.95. John Wiley & Sons, Inc., 605 Third Ave., New York, NY 10158-0012. (800) CALL-WILEY; (212) 850-6000; (212) 850-8641 (fax). An encyclopedic guide covering all aspects of running a small business, including legal, financial, marketing, sales, publicity, and business-planning matters.

 Top Performance, by Zig Ziglar & Jim Savage, $59.95. Nightingale Conant, 7300 N. Lehigh Ave., Niles, IL 60714. (800) 525-9000 (orders); (800) 323-3938; (708) 647-7145 (fax). In these six tapes, Zig Ziglar teaches the qualities of good leadership and management, and how to develop excellence in yourself and others.

 Winning Management Strategies for the Real World, by Tom Peters & Robert Townsend, $69.95. Nightingale Conant, 7300 N. Lehigh Ave., Niles, IL 60714. (800) 525-9000 (orders); (800) 323-3938; (708) 647-7145 (fax). Robert Townsend, the executive who revolutionized American Express, joins Tom Peters to discuss the many business strategies that can be useful for getting things done faster, better, and more profitably. Six audio tapes.

Negotiating Skills

 Getting to Yes, by Roger Fisher & William Ury, © 1981, 162 pp., ISBN: 0-1400-6534-2, $5.95. Penguin Group, 120 Woodbine St., Bergenfield, NJ 07621. (800) 253-6476. This classic on negotiating is based on studies and conferences conducted by the Harvard Negotiation Project, a group that deals continually with all levels of conflict resolution from domestic to business to international disputes. It focuses on win/win negotiations and how to achieve mutually acceptable agreements. Also available on audiotape.

Guide to Everyday Negotiating, by Roger Dawson, 45 min., $59.95. Nightingale Conant, 7300 N. Lehigh Ave., Niles, IL 60714. (800) 525-9000 (orders); (800) 323-3938; (708) 647-7145 (fax). This video seminar presents the fundamentals as well as the finer points of negotiation to help ensure positive agreements in every sort of conflict.

 Negotiate Like the Pros, by John Patrick Dolan, ©1992, 168 pp., ISBN: 0-399-51775-8, $9.95. Perigee Books, Putnam Publishing Group, 200 Madison Ave., New York, NY 10016. (800) 631-8571; (212) 951-8400. A master negotiator shares his professional secrets on improving everyday negotiating skills, including: how to counteract pressure tactics; which strategies put you in the strongest bargaining position; how to avoid surprises and adjust your approach; and what to do when negotiations reach an impasse. Also available in a two-volume video set or a six-tape audio series from CareerTrack (800) 334-1018.

 The Secrets of Power Negotiating, by Roger Dawson, $59.95. Nightingale Conant, 7300 N. Lehigh Ave., Niles, IL 60714. (800) 525-9000 (orders); (800) 323-3938; (708) 647-7145 (fax). Learn the principles, techniques, and tactics of negotiating, including the five key facts and three stages of all negotiations. Includes six audiotapes, flash cards, and a workbook.

Marketing

*See also Advertising; Communication Skills; Direct Marketing;
Promotion and Public Relations; Sales*

Marketing is a broad concept that includes any activity your firm undertakes to successfully communicate your business message to a target audience. For solo entrepreneurs who frequently face tight budgets, marketing also becomes an exercise in creativity—discovering new ways to generate memorable materials or programs inexpensively that motivate customers to buy. The resources in this section lead you through the steps of creating a marketing plan and budget and provide examples and inspiration for innovative, effective marketing approaches. Even if your solo business is very different from one that's featured, the marketing fundamentals often translate easily. By keeping an open mind and studying a wide variety of marketing techniques, you'll be able to glean many new ideas to adapt to your specific solo enterprise.

 101 Big Ideas for Promoting a Business on a Small Budget, by Barbara Lambesis, ©1989, 97 pp., ISBN: 0-9624798-0-2, $9.95. Marketing Methods Press, 2811 N. 7th Ave., Phoenix, AZ 85007. (800) 745-5047. This book provides innovative marketing and promotional plans that independent business owners can implement with limited resources. Covering everything from sales calls to skywriting, it shows how to let potential customers learn about your goods and services.

 123 Great Marketing Ideas to Grow Your Business, by Barbara J. Leff, ©1994, 24 pp., The Marketing Menu, Dept. WSS, 70 W. Burton, Ste. 1804, Chicago, IL 60610. (312) 604-1620; (312) 951-5172 (fax). This easy-to-read booklet offers a jump-start for brainstorming marketing ideas. Covers topics such as marketing research, image, business cards, public speaking, advertising, conventions and trade shows, and more.

American Marketing Association (AMA), Barbara Waldorf, 250 S. Wacker Dr., Ste. 200, Chicago, IL 60606. (312) 648-0536; (312) 831-2764; (312) 993-7542 (fax). Nearly 50,000 individuals are members of this national association that promotes education and professional development in the field of marketing. Dues are $145/year (introductory), $25/year (student).

 American Wholesale Marketers Association, David E. Strachan, 1128 16th St. NW, Washington, DC 20036-4802. (800) 467-0559; (202) 463-2124. This association promotes interests in wholesale confectionery marketing through legislative activity at both national and state levels. Membership includes 1,200 individuals and 2,500 companies. Semiannual meetings are held, and five publications are produced. Dues range from $125–1,350/year.

 Association for Innovative Marketing, Alan Rosenspan, 34 Summit Ave., Sharon, MA 02067. (617) 784-1747. This association, comprised of advertising and marketing professionals, is dedicated to discovering and sharing the latest innovations in marketing. They also refer freelancers in advertising and direct mail, and publish a quarterly newsletter.

 Association of Retail Marketing Services (ARMS), Gerri Hopkins, 3 Caro Ct., Red Bank, NJ 07701-2315. (908) 842-5070; (908) 219-1938 (fax). ARMS represents suppliers of incentive services to retailers and direct marketers in all industries. It holds a Retail Promotion Show in Chicago each January, in which exhibitors offer varied retail promotions. A monthly newsletter is produced and an annual meeting is in January. Membership is $300/year.

 Beyond Maximarketing, by Stan Rapp & Thomas L. Collins, ©1993, ISBN: 0-07-051343-0, $21.95. McGraw-Hill, Inc., 11 W. 19th St., New York, NY 10011. (800) 822-8158. This third book in a trilogy presents ideas about innovative marketing in the 1990s, when "caring and daring" will be key tools for success.

 Big Ideas for Small Service Businesses, by Marilyn and Tom Ross, ©1993, 276 pp., ISBN: 0-918880-16-5, $15.95. Communication Creativity, PO Box 909, 425 Cedar St., Buena Vista, CO 81211. (800) 331-8355; (719) 395-8659. How to successfully advertise, publicize, and maximize your business or professional practice. Filled with hundreds of innovative marketing strategies for any type of service business.

Business Generator, by Paul & Sarah Edwards, 75 min., $99.00. Here's How, PO Box 5091, Santa Monica, CA 90409. (310) 396-1892 (fax). This video/workbook package is an interactive tool that helps you assess your personal marketing style and create a "five-star" marketing plan based on your style inventory. Includes a copy of the Edwards' book *Getting Business to Come to You.*

 Cash Copy, by Jeffrey Lant, ©1992, 480 pp., ISBN: 0-940374-23-4, $38.50. JLA Publications, PO Box 38-2767, Cambridge, MA 02238. (617) 547-6372; (617) 547-0061 (fax). A comprehensive guide to creating client-centered marketing copy that gets people to buy your product or service.

 Do-It-Yourself Marketing, by David Ramacitti, ©1994, 192 pp., ISBN: 0-8144-7800-X, $18.95. AMACOM Books, PO Box 1026, Saranac Lake, NY 12983. (800) 262-9699; (518) 891-3653 (fax). An overview of all the basics to position and market your services professionally. Includes a sample marketing plan, glossary, and action segments after each chapter.

 Endless Referrals, by Bob Burg, ©1993, ISBN: 0-07-008942-6, $14.95. McGraw-Hill, Inc., 11 W. 19th St., New York, NY 10011. (800) 822-8158. How to build a solid gold network of dependable business contacts—quickly, efficiently, and at remarkably low cost.

 Environmental Marketing Imperative, by Bob Frause & Julie A. Colebour, ©1994, 275 pp., ISBN: 1-55738-538-6, $35.00. Probus Publishing, Inc., 1925 N. Clyburn Ave. #401, Chicago, IL 60614. (800) PROBUS-1; (312) 868-6250 (fax). Strategies for transforming environmental commitment into a competitive advantage.

 Event & Entertainment Marketing, by Barry Avrich & Len Gill, ©1994, 300 pp., ISBN: 1-55738-573-4, $32.50. Probus Publishing, Inc., 1925 N. Clyburn Ave. #401, Chicago, IL 60614. (800) PROBUS-1; (312) 868-6250 (fax). A comprehensive guide for corporate event sponsors and entertainment entrepreneurs.

 Getting Business to Come to You, by Paul & Sarah Edwards with Laura Clampitt Douglas, ©1991, 262 pp., ISBN: 0-87477-629-5, $11.95. Putnam Publishing Group, 200 Madison Ave., New York, NY 10016. (800) 631-8571; (212) 951-8400. Creative ideas and strategies for generating cost-effective PR and promotion for your business.

Getting Business to Come to You, by Paul & Sarah Edwards, 4 hrs., $59.00. Here's How, PO Box 5091, Santa Monica, CA 90409. (310) 396-1892 (fax). This six-cassette audiotape series presents a condensation of the Edwards' book on innovative ideas for generating cost-effective marketing and PR for your business.

 Getting New Clients, by Dick Connor & Jeff Davidson, ©1993, 300 pp., ISBN: 0-471-55528-2, $29.95. John Wiley & Sons, Inc., 605 Third Ave., New York, NY 10158-0012. (800) CALL-WILEY; (212) 850-6000. This book presents a wide range of strategies and techniques for building a client base, including prospecting, creating referrals, cultivating long-term customers, and more.

 Guerrilla Marketing, by Jay Conrad Levinson, ©1993, 316 pp., ISBN: 0-395-64496-8, $11.95. Houghton Mifflin Company, Wayside Rd., Burlington, MA 01803. (800) 225-3362. Levinson's classic on guerrilla marketing defines the strategies and offers hundreds of low-cost, high-impact ideas for making big profits from your small business.

 Guerrilla Marketing Attack, by Jay Conrad Levinson, ©1989, 194 pp., ISBN: 0-395-47693-3, $7.95. Houghton Mifflin Company, Wayside Rd., Burlington, MA 01803. (800) 225-3362. An expanded look at strategies, tactics, and weapons for the devoted guerrilla marketer.

 Guerrilla Marketing Excellence, by Jay Conrad Levinson, ©1993, 207 pp., ISBN: 0-395-60844-9, $9.95. Houghton Mifflin Company, Wayside Rd., Burlington, MA 01803. (800) 225-3362. Levinson offers 50 basic truths about guerrilla marketing, including his wisdom for gaining customer mind-share, employing guerrilla gimmicks, and using marketing combinations to increase your business profits.

 Guerrilla Marketing Handbook, by Jay Levinson & Seth Godin, ©1994, 304 pp., ISBN: 0-395-70013-2, $14.95. Houghton Mifflin Company, Wayside Rd., Burlington, MA 01803. (800) 225-3362. A compelling combination of advice on developing an effective marketing campaign accompanied by a detailed compilation of more than 100 specific marketing tools. Includes anecdotes, contact names, addresses, graphics, rules of thumb, and more.

That's Guerrilla, Not Gorilla

Guerrillas are fiercely independent fighters who are committed to a cause and use every possible method and tool to win. If you think that sounds a lot like a solo entrepreneur, you've captured the essence of guerrilla marketing. As swift-footed commandos who live by their wits and imagination, guerrilla marketers concentrate on the buyer's perspective and deliver customer-centered products and services. On the marketing battlefield, being focused and nimble brings a powerful competitive advantage.

 Guerrilla Marketing Newsletter, by Jay Conrad Levinson, bimonthly, $49.00/yr. Guerrilla Marketing International, Box 1336, Mill Valley, CA 94942. (800) 748-6444; (415) 381-8361. This bimonthly newsletter keeps you up to date on the latest guerrilla marketing information, including practical advice, research, upcoming trends, and brand-new marketing techniques. In true guerrilla style, it comes with a money-back guarantee.

 Guerrilla Marketing Weapons, by Jay Conrad Levinson, ©1990, 258 pp., ISBN: 0-452-26519-3, $9.95. Penguin Books, 120 Woodbine St., Bergenfield, NJ 07621. (800) 253-6476. One hundred specific guerrilla marketing weapons that provide practical, cost-effective ways to market your business.

 How to Get Clients, by Jeff Slutsky, ©1992, 256 pp., ISBN: 0-446-39315-0, $10.99. Warner Books, Inc., 1271 Avenue of the Americas, New York, NY 10019. (800) 222-6747. A spunky, informative survival manual for entrepreneurs that helps them attract clients, increase their billings, and overcome the competition.

 How to Really Create a Successful Marketing Plan, by David E. Gumpert, ©1994, 238 pp., ISBN: 1-880394-11-1, $15.95. Inc. Business Resources, 350 N. Pennsylvania Ave., PO Box 1365, Wilkes-Barre, PA 13703-1365. (800) 468-0800 x4760; (717) 822-8899. This book helps readers create their own marketing plan by taking them step-by-step through the process, using real-life examples of successful companies and innovative start-ups.

How to Write a Successful Marketing Plan, by Roman G. Hiebing, Jr. & Scott W. Cooper, 362 pp., ISBN: 0-8442-3197-5, $79.95. National Textbook Company, 4255 W. Touhy Ave., Lincolnwood, IL 60646-1975. (800) 323-4900; (708) 679-5500; (708) 679-2494 (fax). Everything you need to know to develop a "real world" marketing plan presented in a comprehensive, step-by-step guide. Includes worksheets, flowcharts, and outlines.

 Marketing Boot Camp, by Arnold Sanow & J. Daniel McComas, ©1994, 172 pp., ISBN: 0-8403-9301-6, $24.95. Kendall/Hunt Publishing Company, 4050 Westmark Dr., PO Box 1840, Dubuque, IA 52004-1840. (800) 228-0810; (703) 237-1907. This book presents 85 profit-packed tools, techniques, and strategies to help boost your marketing power. It shows ways to think like a marketer, and how to create a relationship-building system to consistently connect with customers so they keep coming back.

 Marketing Checklist for Small Retailers, $1.00. U.S. Small Business Administration, SBA Publications, PO Box 30, Denver, CO 80201-0030. (800) 827-5722; (202) 205-6665. This booklet contains a checklist designed specifically for the small retailer, and includes topics such as customer analysis, buying, pricing, promotion, and other factors affecting retail sales.

 Marketing for Small Business: An Overview, $1.00. U.S. Small Business Administration, SBA Publications, PO Box 30, Denver, CO 80201-0030. (800) 827-5722; (202) 205-6665. This booklet contains an overview of effective marketing processes and an extensive bibliography.

 Marketing Magic, by Don Debelack, ©1994, 300 pp., ISBN: 1-55850-351-X, $10.95. Bob Adams, Inc., 260 Center St., Holbrook, MA 02343. (800) 872-5627; (617) 767-8100; (800) 872-5628 (fax). Action-oriented ideas any business needs in order to locate, develop, and maintain the company's customer base—its most valuable asset.

 Marketing News, Thomas Caruso, Ed., biweekly, $50.00/yr. American Marketing Association (AMA), 250 S. Wacker Dr., Ste. 200, Chicago, IL 60606-5819. (312) 648-0586; (312) 993-7540 (fax). This trade magazine reports on the marketing profession and includes the proceedings of the AMA. Members can subscribe for $25.00/year.

Marketing on a Shoestring, by Jeff Davidson, ©1994, 266 pp., ISBN: 0-471-31094-8, $14.95. John Wiley & Sons, Inc., 605 Third Ave., New York, NY 10158-0012. (800) CALL-WILEY; (212) 850-6000; (212) 850-8641 (fax). This book offers cost-conscious entrepreneurs techniques and strategies for stretching scarce marketing dollars. It provides effective, low-cost marketing ideas that can be put to work immediately in any business.

 Marketing Research Association, Helane Weston, 2189 Silas Deane Hwy., Ste. 5, Rocky Hill, CT 06067. (203) 257-4008; (203) 257-3990 (fax). More than 2,300 individuals and companies involved in the design, administration, or analysis of market research studies belong to this association. The organization has produced several publications on research services, training those in the area of data collection, and promoting marketing and opinion research to consumers. A monthly publication and annual research service directory are produced. Semiannual meetings are held in June and October. Membership is $159/year.

 Marketing Strategies for a Small Business, by Richard F. Gerson, ©1992, 306 pp., ISBN: 1-56052-180-5, $15.95. Crisp Publications, 1200 Hamilton Ct., Menlo Park, CA 94025. (415) 323-6100; (415) 323-5800 (fax). This book gives advice to small business owners who need to get the most out of a small marketing budget.

 Marketing: Winning Customers with a Workable Plan, $30.00. U.S. Small Business Administration, SBA Publications, PO Box 30, Denver, CO 80201-0030. (800) 827-5722; (202) 205-6665. This video offers a step-by-step approach on how to write the best possible marketing plan for your business. A workbook is included to help you use this information to meet your marketing goals.

 Marketing with Newsletters, by Elaine Floyd, ©1994, 230 pp., ISBN: 0-9630222-0-2, $24.95. EF Communications, 6614 Pernod Ave., St. Louis, MO 63139-2149. (800) 264-6305 (orders only); (314) 647-6788; (314) 647-1609 (fax). Newsletters can be powerful marketing tools, and in this book newsletter guru Elaine Floyd shares her insights on how to write and design newsletters that inspire people to buy more, faster. Includes hundreds of tips on how to save money, find other people to write for you, target prospects, and create time-saving shortcuts.

Marketing Without a Marketing Budget, by Craig S. Rice, ©1989, 320 pp., ISBN: 1-55850-986-0, $9.95. Bob Adams, Inc., 260 Center St., Holbrook, MA 02343. (800) 872-5627; (617) 767-8100; (800) 872-5628 (fax). Award-winning business writer and former executive Craig Rice shares examples and strategies of how small companies can compete without a Fortune 500 marketing budget.

 Marketing Without Money, by Nicholas Bade, ©1994, 160 pp., ISBN: 0-8442-3335-8, $19.95. National Textbook Company, 4255 W. Touhy Ave., Lincolnwood, IL 60646-1975. (800) 323-4900; (708) 679-5500; (708) 679-2494 (fax). A collection of 175 inexpensive and offbeat ways to stretch a limited marketing budget.

 Marketing Your Product, by Donald G. Cyr & Douglas A. Gray, ©1994, 144 pp., ISBN: 0-88908-768-7, $12.95. Self-Counsel Press, Inc., 1704 N. State St., Bellingham, WA 98225. (800) 663-3007; (206) 676-4530; (206) 676-4549 (fax). This planning guide covers marketing essentials and teaches how to build a niche for your product. Also includes section on how to use demographics and psychographics to better understand your customers.

 Marketing Your Service Business, by Jean Withers & Carol Viperman, ©1992, 160 pp., ISBN: 0-88908-530-7, $12.95. Self-Counsel Press, Inc., 1704 N. State St., Bellingham, WA 98225. (800) 663-3007; (206) 676-4530; (206) 676-4549 (fax). Detailed information, worksheets, and case studies to help the service business owner market their business more effectively.

 Money Making Marketing, by Jeffrey Lant, ©1993, 285 pp., $39.50. JLA Publications, PO Box 38-2767, Cambridge, MA 02238. (617) 547-6372; (617) 547-0061 (fax). How to find the people who need what you're selling and make sure they buy it. Covers how to handle marketing research, generating a steady stream of qualified prospects, writing client-centered marketing, getting free publicity, telephone sales, and more. Also available on audiotape (18 hrs.) for $125.00; 40-minute video (VHS or Beta) for $29.95.

 Newsletter on Newsletters, Howard Penn Hudson, Ed., semi-monthly, ISSN: 0028-9507, $120.00/yr. The Newsletter Clearinghouse, 44 W. Market St., PO Box 311, Rhinebeck, NY 12572. (914) 876-2081; (914) 876-2561 (fax). The premier publication reporting on all aspects of the newsletter world—editing, graphics, management, promotion, newsletter reviews, and surveys.

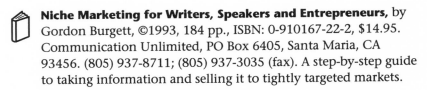

Niche Marketing for Writers, Speakers and Entrepreneurs, by Gordon Burgett, ©1993, 184 pp., ISBN: 0-910167-22-2, $14.95. Communication Unlimited, PO Box 6405, Santa Maria, CA 93456. (805) 937-8711; (805) 937-3035 (fax). A step-by-step guide to taking information and selling it to tightly targeted markets.

Positioning: The Battle for Your Mind, by Al Ries & Jack Trout, ©1987, 224 pp., ISBN: 0-446-34794-9, $5.50. Warner Books, Inc., 1271 Avenue of the Americas, New York, NY 10019. (800) 222-6747. This marketing classic shows the crucial importance of creating a unique identity for your business so that it can be seen and heard in the overcrowded marketplace.

Power Marketing for Small Business, by Jody Horner, ©1993, 300 pp., ISBN: 1-55571-166-9, $19.95. Oasis Press, 300 N. Valley Dr., Grants Pass, OR 97526. (800) 228-2275; (503) 479-9464; (503) 476-1479 (fax). A wealth of how-to marketing information, including the essentials of marketing and sales strategies, customer database marketing, advertising, public relations, budgeting, and follow-up marketing systems. Includes 37 worksheets and sample marketing plan. Also available on audiotape (2 hrs.) for $49.95.

Rain Making, by Ford Harding, ©1994, 240 pp., ISBN: 1-55850-420-6, $12.95. Bob Adams, Inc., 260 Center St., Holbrook, MA 02343. (800) 872-5627; (617) 767-8100; (800) 872-5628 (fax). A books that shows professionals the best way to win new clients, including personal networking, speaking engagements, writing articles, and more.

Strategic Database Marketing, by Arthur M. Hughes, ©1994, 300 pp., ISBN: 1-55738-551-3, $35.00. Probus Publishing, Inc., 1925 N. Clyburn Ave. #401, Chicago, IL 60614. (800) PROBUS-1; (312) 868-6250 (fax). A master plan for starting and managing a profitable, customer-based marketing program.

Strategic Database Marketing, by Robert R. Jackson & Paul Want, ©1994, 256 pp., ISBN: 0-8442-3232-7, $39.95. National Textbook Company, 4255 W. Touhy Ave., Lincolnwood, IL 60646-1975. (800) 323-4900; (708) 679-5500; (708) 679-2494 (fax). A practical, hands-on guide to setting up a database marketing program written in easy-to-understand, nontechnical language. Includes real-world case studies and examples.

Think Backwards

Effective marketing campaigns begin with thinking about the end first. What is your desired goal? How can that be achieved? What must happen in the customers' minds for it to occur?

The answers to these questions will help you create worthwhile marketing strategies, many of which may be easy and inexpensive to implement. By thinking through each phase of the customer interaction in reverse, you can create realistic and potent marketing plans.

Don't be seduced by glitzy, four-color marketing materials. Producing them is no guarantee of sales—or profits! Instead, focus on communicating the benefits of your product or service.

 Target Marketing for the Small Business, by Linda Pinson & Jerry Jinnett, ©1994, 176 pp., ISBN: 0-936894-51-2, $19.95. Upstart Publishing Co., Inc., 12 Portland St., Dover, NH 03820. (800) 235-8866; (603) 749-5071; (603) 742-9121 (fax). This book helps take the mystery out the marketing process and is helpful for entrepreneurs with varying degrees of marketing experience.

 Targeting Transitions, by Paula Mergenhagen DeWitt, ©1994, 250 pp., ISBN: 0-936889-30-6, $29.95. Probus Publishing, Inc., 1925 N. Clyburn Ave. #401, Chicago, IL 60614. (800) PROBUS-1; (312) 868-6250 (fax). This book examines consumer businesses that have successfully positioned products and services to serve market niches of consumers experiencing life changes.

 Ten-Minute Marketing, by Patricia M. Brenna, ©1994, ISBN: 1-883678-50-1, $39.95. Devine Multi-Media Publishing, Inc., 346 Chester St., St. Paul, MN 55107. (612) 699-5436; (612) 221-9722 (fax). This multimedia package on marketing includes a 110-page book, a 25-minute video, a 45-minute audiotape, worksheets, a filing system, and software. It teaches small business owners how to set aside 10 minutes each day to focus on marketing and increase visibility, sales, and profits. Program software is available for Windows-based computers only.

The 22 Immutable Laws of Marketing, by Al Ries & Jack Trout, ©1993, 143 pp., ISBN: 0-88730-666-7, $12.00. HarperBusiness, 10 E. 53rd St., New York, NY 10022-5299. (800) 982-4377; (212) 207-7000; (212) 822-4090 (fax). In this wry, insightful book, two world-renowned marketing consultants present 22 innovative laws for achieving marketing success. They explore why certain marketing campaigns flourished while others often failed, and offer their own ideas on what would have worked better. Also available on a 90-minute audiotape for $11.00.

The Art of Self Promotion, by Ilise Benun, Ed., quarterly, ISSN: 1068-9753, $25.00/yr. CMM, PO Box 23, Hoboken, NJ 07030-0023. (201) 653-0783; (201) 222-2494 (fax). This quarterly newsletter offers a nuts-and-bolts approach to manageable marketing, providing readers with ideas and resources that fit into busy lives and limited budgets. Each issue has a theme, such as "Cutting Through Clutter," "Taking the Cold Out of Calling," or "The Non-Brochure Brochure." A sample issues is $2.00.

The "I'm Too Busy To Read" Marketing Report Service, monthly, $95.00. Win-Win Marketing, 662 Crestview Dr., San Jose, CA 95117. (800) 292-8625; (408) 247-0122; (408) 249-5754 (fax). This monthly service offers in-depth reports on single topics that range from eight to 20 pages in length. It gathers and condenses material from key sources into quickly readable reports. Covers marketing topics such as cost-cutting techniques, customer surveys, telemarketing, business cards, brochures, and more.

The Market Planning Guide: Creating a Plan to Successfully Market Your Business, Products or Service, by David H. Bangs, Jr., ©1994, 164 pp., ISBN: 0-936894-03-2, $19.95. Upstart Publishing Co., Inc., 12 Portland St., Dover, NH 03820. (800) 235-8866; (603) 749-5071; (603) 742-9121 (fax). This book teaches how to create an effective marketing plan that is matched to the goals and resources of your own business.

Word-of-Mouth Marketing, by Jerry R. Wilson, ©1994, 256 pp., ISBN: 0-471-00858-3, $14.95. John Wiley & Sons, Inc., 605 Third Ave., New York, NY 10158-0012. (800) CALL-WILEY; (212) 850-6000; (212) 850-8641 (fax). How to harness the power of word-of-mouth marketing and use it as a valuable marketing tool to launch new products or services, control disasters, and attract profitable new customers.

Minority-Owned Businesses

Entrepreneurial opportunities for minorities are booming as the business world discovers that quality providers of products and services come in every shape, size, and color. The resources featured in this section highlight the unique concerns that minorities face in starting and managing their small businesses. Publications can keep you up to date on recent legislation, funding opportunities, or other business issues. Minority-focused associations can be powerful networks for exchanging ideas, sharing experiences, providing leads for new business, and offering mutual support.

 American Association of Black Women Entrepreneurs (BWE), Brenda Alford, PO Box 13858, Silver Spring, MD 20911-3858. (301) 585-8051. Founded in 1982, this national nonprofit membership organization is designed to increase the success rate of companies owned and operated by African-American women engaged in business ventures geared toward the government and major corporate markets. Annual membership is $100.00 for business owners, plus a one-time $25.00 application fee.

 Association of Black Women Entrepreneurs (ABWE), D. Ratcliffe, PO Box 4936, Los Angeles, CA 90049. (213) 624-8639. This association is geared toward female minorities. Membership includes ABWE's bimonthly newsletter that features resource information along with trends and business tips. Membership also includes two free newsletter ads.

 Better Business, by John F. Robinson, Ed., semiannual, $12.00/yr. National Minority Business Council, Inc., 235 E. 42nd St., New York, NY 10017. (212) 573-2385. This publication covers issues that affect minorities and minority-owned businesses.

Hispanic Business, by Jesus Chavarria, Ed., monthly, $18.00/yr. Hispanic Business, Inc., 360 S. Hope Avenue, Ste. 300C, Santa Barbara, CA 93105. (800) 334-8152 (subscriptions); (805) 682-5843. Directed at Hispanic entrepreneurs, this magazine looks at issues of concern to minority-owned businesses such as finance, education, advertising, and ongoing management issues.

 Minorities and Women in Business, by John D., bimonthly, $15.00/yr. Minorities and Women in Business, PO Drawer 210, Burlington, NC 27216. (919) 229-1462. This magazine covers issues and topics of interest to minorities and women in the business world. Once a year it publishes an issue entitled "Women Who Make a Difference" honoring outstanding women in the field.

 Minority Business Entrepreneur (MBE), by Ginger Conrad, Ed., bimonthly, ISBN: 1048-0919, $12.00/yr. Minority Business Entrepreneur, 924 N. Market St., Inglewood, CA 90302. (213) 673-9398; (213) 673-0170 (fax). This magazine is specifically designed to reach entrepreneurs of color and focuses on issues of interest to minority-owned businesses.

 Minority Business Today, quarterly, free. U.S. Department of Commerce, Minority Business Development Agency, Rm. 7607, Washington, DC 20230. (202) 377-2678. This publication deals with issues of concern to potential or current minority business owners and is available at no charge.

 Minority Small Business and Capital Ownership Development Program, ©1990, 644 pp., ISBN: 0-16-027829-5, $33.00. U.S. Small Business Administration, New Orders, Superintendent of Documents, PO Box 371954, Pittsburgh, PA 15250-7954. (202) 783-3238; (202) 512-2250 (fax). This two-volume set explains everything you need to know about assistance programs available through the federal government for minority-based businesses, including information on management and technical assistance as well as procurement and subcontracting opportunities.

Office Design and Operation

*See also Managing Your Business; Office Supplies and Equipment;
Project Management; Time Management*

Seasoned solo entrepreneurs know that the physical layout of one's workspace can have a profound effect on personal productivity. Your office becomes a silent partner in all that you do—and it either supports or detracts from your efforts. Simple changes such as the location of equipment or telephones can conserve your energy and enable you to accomplish more each day. Investigate the following resources to see how your solo office might improve its operations from a better layout design or through the simple use of standard forms for repetitive paperwork. Over the course of weeks and months spent in your office, a simple idea can end up saving you hours of work.

AnthroCart, Anthro Corp., 3221 NW Yeon St., Portland, OR 97210. (800) 325-3841; (503) 241-7113; (503) 241-1619 (fax). The AnthroCart is a mobile, compact, and rugged workcart designed as an alternative desktop for computers and related equipment. Each cart comes standard with two adjustable shelves. More than 40 accessories are available to customize the cart to individual needs and office layouts.

Creating the Ergonomically Sound Workplace, by Lee T. Ostrom, ©1994, 172 pp., ISBN: 1-55542-621-2, $37.95. Jossey-Bass Publishers, 350 Sansome St., San Francisco, CA 94104-1310. (415) 433-1767; (415) 433-0499 (fax). This book helps you create a work environment that supports, rather than hinders, human performance. The author provides a systematic approach to assess ergonomic factors—including checklists and worksheets—and offers practical, cost-effective solutions for preventing work-related health problems.

Feng Shui, by Mark D. Marfori, ©1994, 192 pp., ISBN: 0-9637748-4-0, $13.95. Dragon Publishing, 1223 Broadway #231, Los Angeles, CA 90404. (310) 285-8616. Feng Shui is the ancient Asian philosophy of creating harmony and prosperity in living and working environments based on the alignment and arrangement of space. This book presents a solid overview of the art, and offers advice on how to enhance your workspace.

How to Conquer Clutter, by Stephanie Culp, ©1989, 184 pp., ISBN: 1-55870-569-8, $10.95. Betterway Books, 1507 Dana Avenue, Cincinnati, OH 45207. (800) 289-0963; (513) 531-4082 (fax). An A-to-Z guide for people who wake up and discover that clutter has once again taken over every inch of available space.

Kiplinger's Taming the Paper Tiger, by Barbara Hemphill, ©1990, 196 pp., ISBN: 0-938721-19-4, $11.95. Kiplinger Books & Tapes, 1729 H Street NW, Washington, DC 20006. (800) 462-6420; (202) 887-6431. Hemphill, an organizational consultant, leads you through simple, realistic steps to gain control over the paper in your life. Includes advice on tackling To-Do lists, developing an effective filing system, mastering the art of "wastebasketry," and more.

National Association of Professional Organizers (NAPO), Walter Schatz, Executive Director, 1604 N. Country Club Rd., Tucson, AZ 85716. (602) 322-9753. Members of this nonprofit national association include professionals who offer organization, time management, and productivity services and products. The association works to promote and educate the public about the professional organizing industry, and to provide support, education, and networking opportunities to members. An annual meeting is held in the spring, and a bimonthly newsletter is published. Dues are $120/year.

Organizing Your Workspace, by Odette Pollar, ©1994, 90 pp., ISBN: 0-56052-125-2, $8.95. Crisp Publications, 1200 Hamilton Ct., Menlo Park, CA 94025. (415) 323-6100; (415) 323-5800 (fax). This book focuses on organization and desk management, and presents techniques for paperwork control, fast filing, and creating a plan of action.

SOHO Adjustable Table, SOHO, 729 Boylston St., 4th fl., Boston, MA 02116. (617) 266-4004. This company manufactures adjustable tables for computers. A proprietary mechanism allows infinite and easy vertical adjustability of the unit's three shelves, allowing users to adapt it to meet their individual ergonomic needs and comfort.

 The Complete Guide to Building and Outfitting an Office in Your Home, by Jerry Germer, ©1994, 176 pp., ISBN: 1-55870-355-1, $18.99. Betterway Books, 1507 Dana Avenue, Cincinnati, OH 45207. (800) 289-0963; (513) 531-4082 (fax). In this book, architect Jerry Germer helps readers plan, design, and build efficient home-based offices. Includes details on handling zoning, determining space needs, layouts, utilities and communications planning, how to work with contractors, and the effect of the office on property and income taxes and home resale.

 Winning the Fight Between You and Your Desk, Your Office, and Your Computer, by Jeffrey J. Mayer, ©1994, 160 pp., ISBN: 0-88730-674-8, $18.00. HarperBusiness, 10 East 53rd St., New York, NY 10022-5299. (800) 982-4377; (212) 207-7000; (800) 822-4090 (fax). The author, known as "Mr. Clutterbuster," describes how to use computers to get organized, save time, and make more money. Also available on one 90-minute audiotape.

Systems Smooth the Way

In every business there are many activities performed repeatedly, such as capturing information from phone calls, making a marketing pitch for your product or service, or giving written or verbal explanations. Savvy entrepreneurs know that creating forms and systems to handle these tasks is key to saving time and energy. Once a system is established—whether on paper, computer, chalkboard, or other medium—your mind is free to focus on larger issues. Systems also allow for easy transition to delegating tasks to assistants, since your preferred method of tackling a business task is clearly presented.

Zap!: How Your Computer Can Hurt You and What You Can Do About It, by Don Sellers, ©1994, 150 pp., ISBN: 1-55609-021-0, $12.95. Peachpit Press, 2414 Sixth St., Berkeley, CA 94710. (800) 283-9444; (510) 548-4393; (510) 548-5991 (fax). This book tackles the critical—and rapidly growing—issues of computer-related health. In a comprehensive and even-handed survey, it covers everything from eyestrain to pregnancy issues to carpal tunnel syndrome to back problems. Filled with tips, exercises, illustrations, and dozens of resources.

Business Forms

Business Forms for the Fax and Copier, by Sharon Aselin-Kehr, 134 pp., ISBN: 0-56052-074-4, $9.95. Crisp Publications, 1200 Hamilton Ct., Menlo Park, CA 94025. (415) 323-6100; (415) 323-5800 (fax). A collection of quality photocopy-ready master forms to streamline your business operations.

Complete Book of Business Forms, ©1991, 234 pp., ISBN: 1-55571-107-3, $19.95. Oasis Press, 300 N. Valley Dr., Grants Pass, OR 97526. (800) 228-2275; (503) 479-9464; (503) 476-1479 (fax). Nearly 200 ready-to-use forms to assist in every aspect of day-to-day business operations.

Ready-To-Use Business Forms, ©1992, 128 pp., ISBN: 0-88908-997-3, $11.95. Self-Counsel Press, Inc., 1704 N. State St., Bellingham, WA 98225. (800) 663-3007; (206) 676-4530; (206) 676-4549 (fax). A selection of the most commonly used business forms such as inventory and requisition forms, service contracts, payroll sheets, invoices, and more.

Ten-Second Business Forms, by Robert L. Adams, ©1993, 208 pp., ISBN: 1-55850-307-2, $9.95. Bob Adams, Inc., 260 Center St., Holbrook, MA 02343. (800) 872-5627; (617) 767-8100; (800) 872-5628 (fax). More than 200 preprinted business forms for your most common needs.

Office Equipment and Supplies

See also Managing Your Business; Office Design and Operation

I'm convinced that most solo entrepreneurs view office-supply stores in the same way that home-improvement buffs enjoy a well-stocked hardware store. The daily tools of our work—from paper to pens to paper clips—can bring simple delights. A new office tool or an old standby in a different color or shape may elicit a cascade of fresh marketing concepts or ideas for expanded products or services. The growth of mail-order shopping has created an abundance of specialty catalog firms, all of which can deliver their innovative goods right to our doorstep. The resources presented in this section include mainstream office-supply companies as well as those selling more unusual selections. Happy browsing!

Buying Guides

 Should You Lease or Buy Equipment?, $0.50. U.S. Small Business Administration, SBA Publications, PO Box 30, Denver, CO 80201-0030. (800) 827-5722; (202) 205-6665. This booklet shows the pros and cons of leasing versus buying business equipment, and provides a format for comparing the costs of the two options.

 The Office Equipment Advisor, by John Derrick, ©1994, 624 pp., ISBN: 1-882568-57-5, $19.95. What to Buy for Business, Inc., 924 Anacapa St., Ste. 4G, Santa Barbara, CA 93101. (800) 247-2185; (805) 963-3539; (805) 963-3740 (fax). This comprehensive book explains and rates office equipment in an unbiased manner. Includes details on copiers, fax machines, computers, laser printers, telephones, voice mail, typewriters, postage meter systems, shredders, and more. The author also publishes a monthly consumer guide to office equipment (see related listing).

What to Buy for Business, by John Derrick, ISBN: 1-882568-24-9, $112.00/yr. What to Buy for Business, Inc., 1 Rebecca Lane, Pleasantville, NY 10570. (800) 247-2185; (914) 741-1367 (fax). This independent consumer guide to business equipment and services is published 10 times a year. Each report is between 40-90 pages long, and offers in-depth, easy-to-understand explanations and ratings of leading office equipment on a single topic, such as phone systems, portable cellular phones, or plain paper fax machines. Individual reports are $21.00.

 ## Mail-Order Office-Supply Firms

Penny Wise Office Products, 4350 Kenilworth Avenue, Edmonston, MD 20781. (800) 942-3311; (301) 699-1000 (in DC metropolitan area); (800) 622-4411 (fax).

Quill Corporation, 100 Schelter Rd., Lincolnshire, IL 60069-3621. (717) 272-6100; (708) 634-5708 (fax).

Reliable Office Supplies, 1001 W. Van Buren St., Chicago, IL 60607. (800) 735-4000; (800) 326-3233 (fax).

Viking Office Products, 13809 S. Figueroa St., Los Angeles, CA 90061. (800) 421-1222; (800) 762-7329 (fax).

 ## Labels and Tags

Kraftbuilt, PO Box 800, Tulsa, OK 74101-0800. (800) 331-7290; (918) 627-7138 (fax). Kraftbuilt's Scot-tags are coated aluminum tags which can be hand-engraved with a ballpoint pen. The soft surface will take the lettering and keep it permanently intact.

Laser Label Technologies, 1333 S. Jefferson St., Chicago, IL 60607-5099. (800) 882-4050; (800) 395-4721 (fax). This company offers more than 1,000 sizes of labels for laser, thermal, and pin-fed printers. Labels can also be preprinted for your business needs.

RapidForms Quality Business Forms, Inc., 301 Grove Rd., Thorofare, NJ 08086-9499. (800) 257-8354 (Samples); (800) 451-8113 (fax). RapidForms provides a variety of business labels, tags and forms printed with your firm's name and address.

Miscellaneous Equipment and Supplies

Business Envelope Manufacturers, Inc., 900 Grand Blvd., Deer Park, NY 11729. (800) 275-4400 (orders); (516) 667-8500 (in NY State); (800) 275-9600 (customer service); (516) 586-5988 (fax). This company sells quality envelopes and labels in bulk at reduced prices, and will imprint the envelopes if you wish.

Fidelity Graphic Products, 5601 International Parkway, PO Box 155, Minneapolis, MN 55440-9222. (800) 326-7555. Fidelity sells a full line of products for graphic designers as well as for other creative professionals such as architects, engineers and contractors.

Levenger, Inc., 420 Commerce Drive, Delray Beach, FL 33445-4696. (800) 544-0880; (407) 276-4141; (800) 544-6910 (fax). This mail-order firm offers many well-made, inventive tools for home and office reading.

Nelson Marketing, PO Box 320, Oshkosh, WI 54902-3020. (800) 5-IMPRINT. Nelson manufactures personalized or logo-decorated promotional items, such as pens, mugs, hats and tote bags for your business.

Pitney-Bowes, 40 Lindeman Dr., Trumbull, CT 06611-4785. (800) 672-6937 x5168. Pitney-Bowes is the leading manufacturer of postage meters and scales.

PSC Lamps, Inc., 435 W. Commercial St., E. Rochester, NY 14445-2298. (800) 772-5267; (800) 257-0760 (fax). This company offers replacement bulbs for a wide variety of lamps at a discount rate. They carry several name brands and guarantee their products.

SAGA, 400 Highway 169 South, Minneapolis, MN 55426-9829. (800) 328-0727; (612) 593-2345 (fax). SAGA offers professional drafting and design supplies, furniture, and equipment.

The Business Book, PO Box 8465, Mankato, MN 56002-8465. (800) 558-0220; (507) 388-6065 (fax). This company is a supplier of mailing labels, stationery, business forms, stamp pads, and other office supplies.

Packaging Supplies

Box-Board Products, Inc., PO Box 18863, Greensboro, NC 27419. (800) 234-5269; (910) 668-3347; (910) 665-0605 (fax). Box-Board sells a wide selection of boxes and packing materials as well as packing tools and machinery.

Chiswick Trading, Inc., 33 Union Ave., Sudbury, MA 01776-2267. (800) 225-9708; (800) 638-9899 (fax). This company offers a full line of packing materials, ranging from plastic bags and corrugated boxes in all sizes and shapes to bubble wrap, labels and dispensers, mailing bags, scales, and tape. Custom imprinting and quantity discounts are available.

Consolidated Plastics Company, Inc., 8181 Darrow Rd., Twinsburg, OH 44087. (800) 362-1000; (216) 425-3900 (in OH); (216) 425-3333 (fax). This company sells plastic bags, tapes, plastic wrapping, packing list envelopes, and more. Discounts for bulk orders.

Cornell Paper and Box Co, Inc., 162 VanDyke St., Brooklyn, NY 11231. (718) 875-3202; (718) 797-3529 (fax). This firm is a bulk outlet for corrugated boxes as well as packing and shipping materials such as tape, labels, bubble wrap, and foam chips.

National Bag Company, Inc., 2233 Old Mill Rd., Hudson, OH 44236. (800) 247-6000; (216) 425-2600. This company distributes nearly every variety of plastic bag. In addition, they sell tape, labels, envelopes, bubble wrap, packing peanuts, and boxes.

 ## Delivery Services

Airborne Express
(800) 222-3049

Federal Express
(800) 238-5355

DHL Worldwide Express
(800) 225-5345

Roadway Package System (RPS)
(800) 762-3725

Emery Worldwide
(800) 443-6379

United Parcel Service (UPS)
(800) 742-5877

Patents, Trademarks, and Copyrights

See also Legal Information

If your solo business creates or trades in intellectual property—including but not limited to work such as writing, art, design, music, inventions, or software—then you need to be aware of your legal rights to the protection of these ideas. Patents, trademarks, and copyrights are all distinct methods of protecting intellectual property, and each carries specific requirements and guidelines. The following resources can lead you step-by-step through the process, including analyzing what type of protection is appropriate for your needs, how to apply to the correct government agency, and what measures you need to take to ensure your ongoing protection.

Avoiding Patent, Trademark and Copyright Problems, $1.00. U.S. Small Business Administration, SBA Publications, PO Box 30, Denver, CO 80201-0030. (800) 827-5722; (202) 205-6665. This booklet teaches you how to protect your own rights and avoid infringing on those of others.

EUREKA! The Entrepreneurial Inventor's Guide to Developing, Protecting, and Profiting from Your Ideas, by Robert J. Gold, ©1994, 256 pp., ISBN: 0-13-011735-8, $16.95. Prentice Hall, Career & Personal Development, Paramount Publishing, 200 Old Tappan Rd., Old Tappan, NJ 07675. (800) 922-0579; (800) 445-6991 (fax). Written by a successful inventor, this book addresses everything from brainstorming a concept through development, financing, protecting, and marketing the final product or service.

Ideas into Dollars, $2.00. U.S. Small Business Administration, SBA Publications, PO Box 30, Denver, CO 80201-0030. (800) 827-5722; (202) 205-6665. This booklet helps identify the main challenges in product development. It lists a number of resources to help inventors and innovators get their ideas into the marketplace.

 Intellectual Property Owners, Katelyn M. Feeney, 1255 23rd St., N.W., Ste. 850, Washington, DC 20037. (202) 466-2396; (202) 833-3636 (fax). This association's primary concern is to keep members informed on patent, trademark, and copyright laws. A bimonthly newsletter reports on the latest legislation. An annual inventors' conference is held in July and an annual meeting takes place in December. Membership is $110/year (inventor) and $220/year (individual).

 Inventor Entrepreneur Network, Edward Zimmer, Ed., monthly, $10.00/yr. Edward Zimmer, 1683 Plymouth Rd. #K, Ann Arbor, MI 48105-1891. (313) 663-8000. Information, services, and resources for the inventor or entrepreneur. Full of stories and ideas regarding new inventions, information on licensing, and fundraising.

 Inventor's Digest, Joanne M. Hayes, Ed., bimonthly, $20.00/yr. Affiliated Inventors Foundation, 2132 E. Bijou St., Colorado Springs, CO 80909-5950. (800) 525-5885; (719) 635-1234; (719) 635-1578 (fax). This publication focuses on the process of invention, development, and marketing.

 Inventors Clubs of America, by Alexander T. Marinaccio, PO Box 450261, Atlanta, GA 31145-0261. (800) 336-0169; (404) 938-5089; (404) 355-8889 (call first) (fax). The oldest and largest inventors' group in the United States, with approximately 10,000 members. They sponsor the International Hall of Fame Awards each November and produce a monthly publication, *Inventors News*, which is included with membership. Dues range from $50–200/year.

 Licensing Art & Design, by Caryn R. Leland, ©1990, 112 pp., ISBN: 0-927629-04-6, $12.95. Allworth Press, 10 E. 23rd St., New York, NY 10010. (800) 247-6553; (212) 777-8395. This guide offers advice to designers, illustrators, photographers, and fine artists on how to increase income by licensing creative images. Includes: how to protect ideas; licensing agreements; how to maximize royalties; model agreements and checklists; how to find manufacturers and distributors; and more.

Patent, Copyright & Trademark: A Desk Reference to Intellectual Property Law, by Stephen Elias & Kate McGrath, ©1994, 256 pp., ISBN: 0-87337-236-0, $24.95. Nolo Press, 950 Parker St., Berkeley, CA 94710. (800) 955-4775; (510) 549-1976; (800) 645-0895 (fax). A guide for writers, programmers, publishers, musicians, inventors, and others who work with intellectual property and need to understand the concepts and their rights. Includes sample forms and listings of relevant government agencies and associations.

 Patent It Yourself, by David Pressman, ©1992, 480 pp., ISBN: 0-87337-167-4, $39.95. Nolo Press, 950 Parker St., Berkeley, CA 94710. (800) 955-4775; (510) 549-1976; (800) 645-0895 (fax). A state-of-the-art guide for all inventors interested in obtaining patents. The author is a former patent examiner, and presents the entire process from initial search to actual application and licensing. Includes all the necessary forms and instructions.

 Patent It Yourself, by David Pressman, ©1993, ISBN: 0-87337-249-2, $229.95. Nolo Press, 950 Parker St., Berkeley, CA 94710. (800) 955-4775; (510) 549-1976; (800) 645-0895 (fax). This disk-based version of the popular book takes users through the complicated patent process step-by-step. Includes all the forms needed, an electronic version of the book, and a 224-page users' guide. Available in Windows format only.

 Patents, Trademarks and Copyrights, by David G. Rosenbaum, ©1994, 128 pp., ISBN: 1-56414-085-7, $8.95. Career Press, 180 Fifth Ave., PO Box 34, Hawthorne, NJ 07507. (800) CAREER-1; (201) 427-2037 (fax). Details on what you need to know to protect your ideas and inventions, written in layman's language.

 Protecting Your Rights and Increasing Your Income, by Tad Crawford, ©1990, 60 min., ISBN: 0-9607118-0-5, $12.95. Allworth Audio, 10 E. 23rd St., New York, NY 10010. (800) 247-6553; (212) 777-8395. Targeted for authors, graphic designers, illustrators, and photographers, this audiotape features creative arts legal expert Tad Crawford presenting his advice on protecting and selling rights to visual work. Covers the basics of copyright law, dealing with changes and revisions, handling royalties, cancellation fees, advances, negotiation techniques, and more.

The Copyright Handbook: How to Protect and Use Written Works, by Stephen Fishman, ©1993, 320 pp., ISBN: 0-87337-130-5, $24.95. Nolo Press, 950 Parker St., Berkeley, CA 94710. (800) 955-4775; (510) 549-1976; (800) 645-0895 (fax). This book provides step-by-step instructions and many of the necessary forms to protect written expression under U.S. and International copyright laws. It also covers copyright protection for books produced on CD-ROM or on disk and electronic mail.

 The Game Inventor's Handbook, by Stephen Peek, ©1993, 192 pp., ISBN: 1-55870-315-2, $18.95. Betterway Books, 1507 Dana Avenue, Cincinnati, OH 45207. (800) 289-0963; (513) 531-4082 (fax). A comprehensive guide to inventing and publishing games, including selling to publishers, self-publishing, marketing, copyrights, patents, and trademarks.

 The Inventor's Desktop Companion, by Richard C. Levy, ©1991, 470 pp., ISBN: 0-8103-7943-0, $24.95. Visible Ink Press, PO Box 33477, Detroit, MI 48232-5477. (800) 776-6265; (800) 776-6265 (fax). A prolific toy inventor takes readers step-by-step through the inventing process, from how to protect an idea to tips on saving expensive legal fees. Includes dozens of reproducible forms.

 The Inventor's Handbook, by Robert Park, ©1990, 232 pp., ISBN: 1-55870-149-4, $14.95. Betterway Books, 1507 Dana Avenue, Cincinnati, OH 45207. (800) 289-0963; (513) 531-4082 (fax). Details on how to develop, market, and protect your invention.

 The Inventor's Notebook, by Fred Grissom & David Pressman, ©1993, 240 pp., ISBN: 0-87337-049-X, $19.95. Nolo Press, 950 Parker St., Berkeley, CA 94710. (800) 955-4775; (510) 549-1976; (800) 645-0895 (fax). This book helps the inventor document the process of independent inventing with the appropriate forms, instructions, and legal references.

 Trademark: How to Name Your Business and Product, by Kate McGrath & Stephen Elias, with Sharon Shena, ©1993, 352 pp., ISBN: 0-87337-151-7, $29.95. Nolo Press, 950 Parker St., Berkeley, CA 94710. (800) 955-4775; (510) 549-1976; (800) 645-0895 (fax). A comprehensive, do-it-yourself trademark book that includes information on conducting a trademark search, registering it with the U.S. Patent and Trademark Office, and steps needed to protect and maintain the mark.

Trademark Register of the United States, ©1994, 2,200 pp., $335.00. The Trademark Register, National Press Building 1297, Washington, DC 20045. (800) 888-8062; (202) 347-4408 (fax). This annual trademark directory contains more than 850,000 currently registered and renewed trademarks in effect in the U.S. Patent and Trademark Office from 1884. Includes a descriptive content section of each international class as well as a classification index of goods, products, and services.

 Trademarks and Business Goodwill, $1.00. U.S. Small Business Administration, SBA Publications, PO Box 30, Denver, CO 80201-0030. (800) 827-5722; (202) 205-6665. Learn how to protect your commercial name in addition to other details regarding the use and misuse of trademarks.

 U.S. Copyright Office, Library of Congress, Washington, DC 20559-6000. (202) 707-3000 (Public Information Office); (202) 707-9100 (Forms Hotline). General information on copyright matters can be obtained from the Public Information Office, which has recorded information available 24 hours a day, 7 days a week. Information specialists are on duty from 8:30am to 5:00pm ET, Monday-Friday, except holidays. Use the Forms Hotline (also available 24 hours a day) to request application forms for registration or informational circulars if you know which forms or circulars you want. If you are unsure of what forms you need, use the Public Information Office number.

U.S. Patent and Trademark Office, U.S. Department of Commerce, Washington, DC 20231. (703) 305-HELP (General Information); (703) 305-INFO (Recorded Line). General trademark or patent information can be obtained from the main helpline number. The recorded line provides answers to commonly asked questions 24 hours a day, 7 days a week. An automated line provides status information on pending trademark applications at (703) 305-8747.

 U.S. Patent and Trademark Office BBS, U.S. Department of Commerce, Washington, DC 20231. (703) 440-6236 (voice); (703) 305-8950 (data/modem). This computer bulletin board system provides details on recently issued patents and other government publications and resources related to patent and trademark issues. Set your telecommunications software to 8 data bits, 1 stop bit, no parity.

Printing and Desktop Publishing

See also Advertising; Direct Marketing; Marketing; Promotion and Public Relations

Whether it's a simple business card or a slick four-color brochure, the image presented in print about a solo business has a powerful impact. Positive or negative, the impression is immediate—and often enduring. A printed image can linger long after personal interaction, or it can be passed along or sent in the mail. Fortunately, today's desktop publishing (DTP) technology using computers and laser printers enables even design novices to create professional-looking printed pieces. The resources included in this section have been gathered to assist you in producing a polished graphic image for your solo business—while still maintaining your budget.

General Printing and DTP Resources

 Before & After, bimonthly, $36.00/yr. 1830 Sierra Garden Dr., Ste. 30, Roseville, CA 95661-2912. (916) 784-3880; (916) 784-3995 (fax). This magazine of design and page layout for desktop publishers is subtitled "How to design cool stuff," which sums up its approach. Articles, lessons, and projects guide readers through every step of the electronic design process, and each issue is filled with professional tips, useful ideas, and time-saving techniques.

 Desktop Publisher, James S. Pennybacker, Ed., monthly, $18.00/yr. Fox Pond Communications, 1841 Norristown Rd. PO Box 3200, Maple Glen, PA 19002. (215) 643-5940; (215) 641-9521 (fax). This newspaper-type publication is designed for users of desktop publishing systems.

Desktop Publishing by Design, by Ronnie Shushan & Don Wright, ©1994, 490 pp., $29.95. Microsoft Press, Microsoft Corp., One Microsoft Way, Redmond, WA 98052. (800) MS-PRESS. This best-selling design guide is three books in one: an intro to good design, a portfolio of DTP projects, and a hands-on software tutor.

 Electronic Design and Publishing: Business Practices, by Liane Sebastian, ©1994, 144 pp., ISBN: 1-880559-22-6, $19.95. Allworth Press, 10 E. 23rd St., New York, NY 10010. (800) 247-6553; (212) 777-8395. This book explains the rights and responsibilities of the parties involved in electronic design and publishing—client, designer, prepress house, and printer. Covers ethics, roles, legal issues, procedures, policies, ownership, and more. Also includes information on the new areas of multimedia and interactivity.

 Flyers That Work, by Sophia Tarila, ©1994, 106 pp., ISBN: 0-944773-09-5, $10.95. First Editions, PO Box 2578, Sedona, AZ 86339. (800) 870-4050; (602) 282-9574; (602) 282-9730 (fax). A guide to creating effective flyers, including what to put in or leave out, designing memorable and effective layouts, how to talk to printers to get desired results, when and where to mail or post your flyers, and how to be ready when your responses come in.

 Getting It Printed, by Mark Beach, ©1993, 208 pp., ISBN: 0-89134-510-8, $29.95. North Light Books, 1507 Dana Ave., Cincinnati, OH 45207. (800) 289-0963; (513) 531-4082 (fax). This practical, hands-on guide to working with printers and graphic arts service providers can help both newcomers and design pros alike ensure quality, meet deadlines, and control costs.

 HOW, bimonthly, $35.00/yr. HOW, PO Box 5250, Harlan, IA 51593-2750. (800) 365-0963. This magazine presents creative ideas, professional techniques, and money-saving tips for individuals involved in the world of desktop publishing. Includes news on electronic tools and trends, software reviews, and articles showing how professional designers produce newsletters, brochures, flyers, self-promotions, and other printed materials.

In-Plant Production, by Judy Bocklage, Ed., monthly, North American Publishing, Co., 401 N. Broad St., Philadelphia, PA 19108. (215) 238-5300; (215) 238-5457 (fax). This controlled-circulation magazine covers issues and resources pertinent to electronic publishing and printing, prepress, and bindery.

Digital Logos

When it comes time to design a graphic look or logo for your company, it pays to work with a computer-literate designer. Once in digital form, the graphic image can be translated into any printed format, from business cards to billboards. To retain its impact at different sizes, however, the logo must be originally conceived with that flexibility in mind. With the increase in electronic communication, it's also important that your logo reads well on computer screens. All these challenges make today's electronic designer an important partner for the solo entrepreneur.

 Looking Good in Print, by Roger C. Parker, ©1993, 412 pp., ISBN: 1-56604-047-7, $24.95. Ventana Press, PO Box 2468, Chapel Hill, NC 27515. (919) 942-0220; (919) 942-1140 (fax). Recognized as the classic guide for desktop publishers, this book covers the fundamentals of professional-quality design. Presents tips, techniques, and guidance on producing attractive and effective newsletters, advertisements, brochures, manuals, correspondence, and other communication pieces.

 National Association of Desktop Publishers (NADTP), Noel Ward, 462 Old Boston Rd., Topsfield, MA 01983-1232. (508) 887-7900; (508) 887-6117 (fax). NATDP informs and educates on developments in the desktop publishing industry. Members receive a monthly magazine and discounts on books and educational opportunities. Membership is $95/year (individual).

 Publishing and Production Executive, Rose Blessing, Ed., monthly, North American Publishing Company, 401 N. Broad St., Philadelphia, PA 19108. (215) 235-5100; (215) 238-5457 (fax). This controlled-circulation trade publication for individuals in the publishing and printing industry presents an overview of new products, technologies, and issues related to print production.

 Small Publisher, monthly, $12.00/yr. Nigel Maxey, Box 1620, Pineville, WV 24874-1620. (304) 732-8195. This newspaper-format publication provides the small publisher with information important to the field of small business and publishing.

Technique, bimonthly, $19.95/yr. Technique, PO Box 9164, Hyattsville, MD 20781-9164. This publication features the newest information for graphic designers and other desktop publishing-related professionals. Full of tips, ideas and resources.

 The Best of Business Card Design, ©1994, 160 pp., ISBN: 1-56496-045-5, $34.95. North Light Books, 1507 Dana Ave., Cincinnati, OH 45207. (800) 289-0963; (513) 531-4082 (fax). A collection of more than 1,000 business cards to help inspire your own design ideas.

 The Perfect Sales Piece, by Robert W. Bly, ©1994, 288 pp., ISBN: 0-471-00411-1, $14.95. John Wiley & Sons, Inc., 605 Third Ave., New York, NY 10158-0012. (800) CALL-WILEY; (212) 850-6000; (212) 850-8641 (fax). A do-it-yourself guide to creating brochures, catalogs, and flyers from initial concept to final publication.

Laser Printer Papers

The following companies offer specialty and preprinted papers that can turn your ink-jet printer, laser printer, or photocopier into an instant printing press. Their products enable you to create professional-looking brochures, business cards, letters, memos, signs, and other marketing materials inexpensively. Some also sell disk-based design templates that work with leading software packages so entrepreneurs with little design experience can create high-quality pieces quickly and easily.

BeaverPrints, 305 Main Street, Bellwood, PA 16617. (800) 923-2837; (800) 232-8374 (fax).

Idea Art, PO Box 291505, Nashville, TN 37229-1505. (800) 433-2278; (800) 435-2278 (fax).

Image Street, PO Box 5000, Vernon Hills, IL 60061-9926. (800) 462-4378.

Paper Access, 23 W. 18th St., New York, NY 10011. (800) 727-3701; (212) 463-7022 (fax).

Paper Direct, Inc., 205 Chubb Ave., Lyndhurst, NJ 07071. (800) 272-7377.

Queblo Papers, 1000 Florida Avenue, Hagerstown, MD 21741. (800) 523-9080; (800) 554-8779 (fax).

Printers

The printers listed below provide economical color printing services. Most can print product sheets, flyers, brochures, and catalogs in quantity at competitive prices. Some also print postcards and posters.

American Color Printing, 1731 NW 97th Ave., Plantation, FL 33322. (305) 473-4392; (305) 473-8621 (fax).

Carl Sebastian Colour, 436 E. Bannister Rd., Kansas City, MO 64131. (800) 825-0381. Also prints color postcards.

Econocolor, 7405 Industrial Rd., Florence, KY 41042-2997. (800) 877-7405; (605) 525-7654 (fax). Specializes in catalogs and product sheets.

Getz & McGrew Lithography, Inc., 14250 Santa Fe Trail Dr., Lenexa, KS 66215-1238. (913) 599-0707; (913) 599-1946 (fax).

McGrew Color Graphics, 1615 Grand Ave., Kansas City, MO 64108. (800) 877-7700; (816) 221-6560; (816) 221-3154 (fax). Also does color photo business cards.

Rapidocolor Printing, 705 E. Union St., West Chester, PA 19382-4937. (800) 872-7436. Also offers print-from-disk capabilities.

Triangle Printing Co., 325 Hill Ave., Nashville, TN 37210. (800) 843-9539; (615) 254-1879; (615) 256-5813 (fax). Specializes in inexpensive printing of forms, invoices, booklets, scratch pads, and envelopes.

U.S. Press, PO Box 640, Valdosta, GA 31603-0640. (800) 227-7377. Specializes in postcards, product sheets, and catalogs.

Gang Printing

If your printing schedule is flexible, you frequently can obtain reduced prices by participating in "ganged" print jobs. By grouping similar projects together, a printer often can run larger sheets of paper or eliminate press wash-ups. Their savings is passed on to you. Ask about it the next time you need something printed.

Binding, Laminating, Folding

Connecticut Laminating Company, Inc., 162 James St., PO Box 450, New Haven, CT 06513-0450. (800) 753-9119; (203) 2184; (203) 787-4073 (fax). CLC specializes in laminating services and printing on plastics.

General Binding Corporation (GBC), 1 GBC Plaza, Northbrook, IL 60062-9652. (800) 723-4000. This company produces a wide variety of binding solutions, from 19-hole professional plastic comb binding to thermal binding.

James Burn/American, Inc., 205 Cottage St., Box 430, Poughkeepsie, NY 12602. (914) 454-8200. This company manufactures wire binding machines, which enable you to create professional-looking wire-bound documents on your own.

Michael Business Machines, PO Box 40249, Charleston, SC 29423-9801. (800) 223-2508. This firm's Dyna-Fold folding machine can fold up to 15,000 sheets of paper per hour, in a variety of different folds.

USI Inc., PO Box 644, 33 Business Park Dr., Branford, CT 06405. (800) 243-4565; (203) 481-7508 (fax). USI offers a wide range of lamination equipment and supplies, ranging from luggage tag and business/ID card laminators to large-scale document laminating machines.

VeloBind, Inc., 47212 Mission Falls Ct., Fremont, CA 94539. (415) 657-8200; (415) 770-1227 (fax). This company markets a series of do-it-yourself binding machines and supplies that enables you to prepare professional-looking presentations. The DocuBind system offers 3-hole punching as well as 19-hole plastic comb binding capabilities. The VeloBind system is a plastic-strip system for documents up to 45 pages. Starter kits can often be found in office-supply stores.

Professional Associations

Successful solo entrepreneurs understand the value of personal networking, and nowhere can connections be made more easily than through a professional association. The collection of organizations listed below reflects only a tip of the iceberg of the more than 100,000 national and regional groups active in our country. Each association featured here responded to our call, and each specifically asked to be presented to solo entrepreneurs as a group that would welcome your participation. The listings here have been divided into two groups: general business/entrepreneurial groups, and associations devoted to specific industries. By browsing the listings, you can find groups that may spark your interest—or associations you may never have dreamed existed!

To locate other associations in a particular interest area or industry, check out the *Encyclopedia of Associations* published by Gale Research (listed in the *Research and Reference* chapter), available in most libraries. See also the listings elsewhere in the SOURCEBOOK that feature the networking icon with two clasped hands.

Guides to Networking

 It's Who You Know, by Cynthia Chin-Lee, ©1993, 125 pp., ISBN: 0-89384-223-0, $9.95. Pfeiffer & Company, 8517 Production Ave., San Diego, CA 92121-2280. (619) 578-5900; (619) 578-2042 (fax). This book explains the critical strategies of combining what you know with who you know, and shows how to make opportunities for yourself by developing networking skills.

 Organized Obsessions, by Deborah M. Burek & Martin Connors, ©1992, 288 pp., ISBN: 0-8103-9415-4, $9.95. Visible Ink Press, PO Box 33477, Detroit, MI 48232-5477. (800) 776-6265; (800) 776-6265 (fax). A collection of 1,001 offbeat and quirky associations, fan clubs, microsocieties, and other organizations you can join.

Power Schmoozing: The New Etiquette for Social & Business Success, by Terri Mandell, ©1993, 200 pp., ISBN: 0-9623062-9-0, $11.95. First House Press, 6671 Sunset Blvd., Ste. 1525, Los Angeles, CA 90028. (800) 626-4330; (213) 467-2898; (213) 466-4001 (fax). Advice on the art of mingling, so you can confidently connect with others in order to create a more productive business and social life. Includes dozens of real-life examples and practical ice-breaking and networking techniques that can be used in any business or social situation.

Teamworks!, by Barbara Sher & Annie Gottlieb, ©1989, 230 pp., ISBN: 0-446-39244-8, $12.95. Warner Books, Inc., 1271 Avenue of the Americas, New York, NY 10019. (800) 222-6747. From the author of *Wishcraft,* this book guides readers step-by-step in creating Success Teams to empower themselves and others in creating the life and work they want.

The New Network Your Way to Job and Career Success Book, by Drs. Ron and Caryl Krannich, ©1993, 168 pp., ISBN: 0-942710-86-X, $12.95. Impact Publications, 9104 N. Manassas Dr., Manassas Park, VA 22111. (800) 462-6420; (703) 361-7300; (703) 335-9486 (fax). This book provides practical guidance on how to create and organize job networks and prospect for job leads.

The Secrets of Savvy Networking, by Susan RoAne, ©1993, 224 pp., ISBN: 0-446-39410-6, $11.99. Warner Books, Inc., 1271 Avenue of the Americas, New York, NY 10019. (800) 222-6747. Practical advice and savvy strategies on the dos and don'ts of where to be seen, when to be heard, and how to be remembered—by the right people—that can make a difference in your career.

Capture the Details

When attending a professional network gathering, maximize the contacts you make by jotting brief notes on the back of their business cards. While a bit awkward at times, it certainly beats the experience of staring at a handful of cards back in your office and trying to remember important details or promises you made.

Business and Entrepreneurial Associations

 American Entrepreneurs Association, Lisa Holland, 2392 Morse Ave., Irvine, CA 92714. (800) 864-6888; (714) 261-2393. This association is owned by Entrepreneur Media, Inc. which also publishes *Entrepreneur* magazine.

 American Small Business Association, Vernon Castle, Executive Director, 1800 N. Kent St., Ste. 910, Arlington, VA 22209. (800) ASBA-911; (703) 522-2292; (703) 522-9789 (fax). This organization of more than 100,000 small business owners offers a wide range of services to its members, including: discounts on business products, credit cards, insurance, and travel; a college scholarship program for children of members; an online computer network via CompuServe; and more. The association has an active grassroots program to generate government change. Members also receive a bimonthly magazine. Annual membership dues are $210.00/year, plus a one-time initiation fee of $20.00.

 Global Entrepreneurs Network, Marguerite Ellen, PO Box 373229, Satellite Beach, FL 32937. (407) 799-9161; (407) 773-9557 (fax). This organization offers a network membership for leads, marketing resources, and online matching services for $189/year, which includes member discounts for advertising opportunities in print and online media. They also publish a monthly newsletter; subscriptions are $39/year. Free newsletter upon request.

 IDEA Association, John Wren, National Coordinator, 6900 W. Quincy Ave., Ste. 7E, Littleton, CO 80123. (303) 978-0335. This association is a support group for individuals starting new businesses. Its focus is on providing forums for networking and peer assistance. Three chapters are active in Colorado, and other chapters are forming nationwide. It also has an active information exchange on the Internet (telenet to freenet.hsc.colorado.edu, then go idea at main command prompt).

 Independent Workers Association (IWA), Ronald Brill, 488 Ignacio Blvd., Ste. 214, Novato, CA 94949. (415) 898-1580. This Bay Area network of independent professionals was formed in 1988 by Ronald Brill. It holds monthly luncheon meetings, publishes a membership directory, and sponsors an annual conference. Membership is open nationwide. For details, send a self-addressed stamped business envelope.

National Association for the Self-Employed (NASE), PO Box 612067, Dallas, TX 75261-2067. (800) 232-NASE; (800) 551-4446 (fax). NASE has more than 300,000 members and acts as a watchdog for the self-employed community. Members have access to more than 100 benefits, including business, personal, and health-related products and services, and receive a bimonthly publication, *Self-Employed America.* Memberships is $72/year.

 National Business Incubation Association, Dinah Adkins, 20. E. Circle Dr., Ste. 190, Athens, OH 45701. (614) 593-4331; (614) 593-1996 (fax). This organization involves managers and developers of business incubator sites, which provides small, entrepreneurial businesses with affordable space, and shared support and business development assistance. Membership is $175/year (individual); $300/year (company).

 National Business Owners Association (NBOA), Drew Hiatt, 1200 18th St. NW, Ste. 500, Washington, DC 20036. (202) 737-6501; (202) 737-3909 (fax). NBOA is an advocacy organization that represents more than 6,000 small companies. It publishes a monthly newsletter, the *Washington Report.*

 National Federation of Independent Business (NFIB), 600 Maryland Ave. SW, Ste. 700, Washington, DC 20024. (800) 634-2669; (202) 554-9000; (202) 554-0496 (fax). NFIB represents more than 600,000 small and independent business owners as an advocacy organization that lobbies to protect the interests of small business. It publishes a bimonthly magazine, *Independent Business,* and reports on legislative issues in its quarterly *Capitol Coverage.* Membership ranges from $75–1,000/year.

 National Small Business United, John Paul Galles, 1155 15th St., NW, Ste. 710, Washington, DC 20005. (202) 293-8830; (202) 872-8543 (fax). This national small business association represents more than 65,000 small businesses in its congressional lobbying efforts. Members receive a monthly publication, and can participate in special conferences and seminars. Semiannual meetings are held in May and November.

Industry-Specific Associations

 American Association of Healthcare Consultants, Vaughan A. Smith, 11208 Waples Mill Rd., Ste. 109, Fairfax, VA 22030. (703) 691-2242; (703) 691-2247 (fax). This organization consists of 65 member consulting firms. They publish an annual directory and hold triannual meetings. Dues are $395/year.

 American Association of Individual Investors, Laura A. Jajowski, 625 N. Michigan Ave., 19th fl., Chicago, IL 60611-3110. (312) 280-0170; (312) 280-9883 (fax). This nonprofit organization assists individuals in managing their financial portfolios through programs of education, information and research. They have 135,000 individual members, publish a monthly journal, and hold an annual meeting in the summer. Membership is $49/year.

 American Association of Professional Hypnotherapists, William S. Brink, PO Box 29, Boones Mill, VA 24065-0029. (703) 334-3035. More than 1,500 hypnotherapists, clinical social workers, marriage and family therapists, psychologists, physicians, pastoral counselors, and other individuals with suitable training or experience are members of this national network. An annual directory is produced. Dues are $55/year.

 American Association of Woodturners (AAW), Mary Redig, Administrator, 667 Harriet Ave., Shoreview, MN 55126-4085. (612) 484-9094; (612) 484-1724 (fax). The AAW is a nonprofit organization devoted to education and sharing information for those involved in woodturning. Members include hobbyists, professionals, gallery owners, collectors, and wood and equipment suppliers. Local chapters are active around the country. They publish a quarterly journal and hold an annual symposium.

 American Craft Council, Hunter Kariher, Executive Director, 72 Spring St., New York, NY 10012. (212) 274-0630; (212) 274-0650 (fax). This national, nonprofit educational organization founded in 1943 encourages American artists working in clay, wood, glass, metal, fiber, and other media and fosters an appreciation of their work. Programs of the council include the American Craft Association, American Craft Enterprises, American Craft Publishing, and the American Craft Information Center. There are more than 30,000 members. Dues are $40–1,000/year and include a subscription to the bimonthly magazine, *American Craft.*

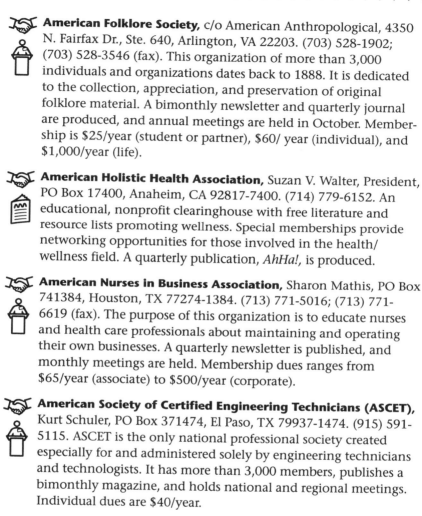

American Folklore Society, c/o American Anthropological, 4350 N. Fairfax Dr., Ste. 640, Arlington, VA 22203. (703) 528-1902; (703) 528-3546 (fax). This organization of more than 3,000 individuals and organizations dates back to 1888. It is dedicated to the collection, appreciation, and preservation of original folklore material. A bimonthly newsletter and quarterly journal are produced, and annual meetings are held in October. Membership is $25/year (student or partner), $60/ year (individual), and $1,000/year (life).

American Holistic Health Association, Suzan V. Walter, President, PO Box 17400, Anaheim, CA 92817-7400. (714) 779-6152. An educational, nonprofit clearinghouse with free literature and resource lists promoting wellness. Special memberships provide networking opportunities for those involved in the health/ wellness field. A quarterly publication, *AhHa!*, is produced.

American Nurses in Business Association, Sharon Mathis, PO Box 741384, Houston, TX 77274-1384. (713) 771-5016; (713) 771-6619 (fax). The purpose of this organization is to educate nurses and health care professionals about maintaining and operating their own businesses. A quarterly newsletter is published, and monthly meetings are held. Membership dues ranges from $65/year (associate) to $500/year (corporate).

American Society of Certified Engineering Technicians (ASCET), Kurt Schuler, PO Box 371474, El Paso, TX 79937-1474. (915) 591-5115. ASCET is the only national professional society created especially for and administered solely by engineering technicians and technologists. It has more than 3,000 members, publishes a bimonthly magazine, and holds national and regional meetings. Individual dues are $40/year.

American Society of Furniture Artists (ASOFA), Adam St. John, President/Executive Director, PO Box 270188, Houston, TX 77277-0188. (713) 660-8855. ASOFA is a nonprofit organization dedicated to the field of "art furniture." It has an artist slide registry available to members and the general public, sponsors an annual juried competition, and publishes a newsletter. Membership is open to anyone; dues are $40/year (individuals) and $100/year (businesses).

American Society of Home Inspectors, Joseph Martori, 85 W. Algonquin Rd., Ste. 360, Arlington Heights, IL 60005-4423. (800) 743-2744; (708) 290-1919; (708) 290-1919 (fax). The 3,200 members of this national association are professional home inspectors who have met the qualifications based on technical merit and experience. Membership is $250/year and includes an association publication. An annual meeting is held in January.

 Architectural Woodwork Institute (AWI), H. Keith Judkins, PO Box 1550, 13924 Braddock Rd., Ste. 100, Centreville, VA 22020. (703) 222-1100; (703) 222-2499 (fax). The AWI serves the construction industry as a voluntary association of professional woodworkers. They promote the use of fine woodwork through publications, education, and certification. A bimonthly journal and annual directory are produced. Annual meetings are held in the fall.

 Artist-Blacksmiths' Association of North America (ABANA), Janelle Franklin, Executive Secretary, PO Box 1181, Nashville, IN 47448. (812) 988-6919. ABANA is a nonprofit organization devoted to the art of blacksmithing. They help to serve and educate blacksmiths through resource lists of members and suppliers, a quarterly journal, a switchboard service to answer technical and safety questions, and an annual conference.

 Association of Bridal Consultants, Gerard J. Monaghan, 200 Chestnutland Rd., New Milford, CT 06776-2521. (203) 355-0464. This organization, composed of more than 1,300 independent consultants as well as owners and employees of wedding-related businesses, is dedicated to improving the recognition and professionalism of those in the weddings business worldwide. They publish a bimonthly newsletter and semiannual membership directory. Membership is $75–500/year.

 Association of Crafts and Creative Industries (ACCI), Walter E. Offinger, 1100-H Brandywine Blvd., PO Box 2188, Zanesville, OH 43702-2188. (614) 452-4541; (614) 452-2552 (fax). The purpose of ACCI is to offer a forum for information exchange to those engaged in the buying, selling, or manufacturing of crafts, art framing, notions, needlework, and floral design. They publish a bimonthly newsletter and sponsor semiannual trade shows and conventions in Chicago. Membership is $35–125/year.

Association of Independent Video and Filmmakers, Ruby Lerner, 625 Broadway, 9th fl., New York, NY 10012-2611. (212) 473-3400; (212) 677-8732 (fax). This membership organization includes 5,000 video and filmmakers working as independent professionals around the world. It publishes *The Independent* 10 times/year, and holds annual meetings. Membership is open to anyone involved in independent video and film. Dues are $45/year for regular members; $25/year for students.

Association of Professional Landscape Designers, Kibbe Turner, 420 E. Diamond Ave., Gaithersburg, MD 20877. (301) 216-2620; (301) 258-9544 (fax). More than 330 professional landscape designers are members of this organization, which publishes a newsletter and holds semiannual meetings in February and August. Membership is $125/year.

Association of Test Publishers (ATP), Lauren B. Scheib, 655 15th St. NW, Ste. 320, Washington, DC 20005. (800) 922-7343; (202) 857-8444; (717) 755-8962 (fax). This trade association represents the interests of educational, industrial, and clinical test publishers and providers of assessment products and services. Its mission is to encourage a high level of professionalism and business ethics, and to promote the ethical and effective use of tests through industry standards and guidelines. Annual meetings are held in August. Dues are based on a member-company's revenue.

Clowns of America International, David Barnett, Business Manager, PO Box 570, Lake Jackson, TX 77566-0570. (409) 297-6699 (phone & fax). More than 6,000 amateur, semi-professional, and professional clowns are members of this association. They produce one publication and hold annual meetings in April. Membership is $25/year (new member), $20/year (individual), $10/year (family).

Comedy Writers Association, Robert Makinson, PO Box 3304, Brooklyn, NY 11202-3304. (718) 855-5057. This association is open to anyone interested in the creation and marketing of comedy. They produce a semiannual comedy writers association newsletter (single issue $4), and hold an annual meeting. Membership is $24/year.

Dance Educators of America, Vickie Sheer, Box 509, Oceanside, NY 11572-0509. (516) 766-6615; (516) 536-6502 (fax). This nationwide organization of more than 2,000 dance professionals promotes the education of teachers in the performing arts. The group sponsors educational seminars and workshops as well as competitions and scholarships. Membership dues are $96/year.

Embroiderers' Guild of America, Inc. (EGA), Judy Jeroy, President, 335 W. Broadway, Ste. 100, Louisville, KY 40202. (502) 589-6956. The goal of the EGA is to set high standards of design, color, and workmanship in all kinds of embroidery and canvaswork. They offer lectures, exhibitions, competitions, and field trips, and produce a quarterly publication, *Needle Arts.*

 Garden Writers Association of America, Robert C. LaGasse, CAE, 10210 Leatherleaf Ct., Manassas, VA 22111. (703) 257-1032; (703) 257-0213 (fax). More than a thousand garden writers are members of this association which publishes a bimonthly newsletter and holds an annual meeting in the fall. Membership is $75/year (individual), $250/year (organization).

 Glass Art Society (GAS), Alice Rooney, Executive Director, 1305 4th Ave., Ste. 711, Seattle, WA 98101-2401. (206) 382-1305; (206) 382-2630 (fax). This international nonprofit organization promotes the appreciation, development, and understanding of the glass arts. Members are artists working in glass, as well as critics, collectors, educators, manufacturers, and gallery and museum personnel. The society publishes a quarterly journal and semiannual newsletter, and holds an annual conference in the spring. Membership ranges from $40–250/year.

 ## Maximize a Meeting

Before you attend a conference or seminar, establish three or four professional and personal goals for participating. They may include making new contacts, expanding your knowledge of a specific topic, exploring new business methods, and more. With a target in sight, you're more likely to accomplish what you want to achieve—and make your investment pay off.

Golf Course Builders Association of America, Phil Arnold, 920 Airport Rd., Ste. 210, Chapel Hill, NC 27514. (919) 942-8922; (919) 942-6955 (fax). This trade association represents all segments of the golf course construction industry. They publish a newsletter, *Earth Shaping News,* and hold an annual meeting in February. Membership ranges from $100–1,000/year.

 Graphic Artists Guild National, Paul Basista, CAE, 11 W. 20th St., 8th fl., New York, NY 10011-3704. (212) 463-7730; (212) 463-8779 (fax). The Guild is an advocacy labor organization dedicated to improving the economic and social conditions of professional artists and designers. Members are illustrators, graphic designers, surface designers, production artists, cartoonists, computer artists, and individuals allied to the field. The Guild publishes a biennial handbook on pricing and ethical guidelines, a quarterly newsletter, and hosts an annual meeting in June. Membership ranges from $55–245/year.

 Guild of Book Workers, Frank Mowery, 521 Fifth Ave., Ste. 1740, New York, NY 10175. (212) 757-6454. The purpose of this association is to continue and foster the growth of the hand book crafts, including binding, calligraphy, illumination, papermaking, and printing. They publish a semiannual journal, a bimonthly newsletter, and host an annual meeting in the fall. Dues are $40/year.

 Handweavers Guild of America, Inc. (HGA), Janet Huston, 120 Mountain Ave., B101, Bloomfield, CT 06002. (203) 242-3577; (203) 243-3982 (fax). The HGA promotes textile arts through education, scholarships, learning exchanges, and a biannual conference. They produce a quarterly magazine, *Shuttle, Spindle & Dyepot,* and host biennial national meetings in even-numbered years. Membership is $25/year.

 IDEA: International Association for Fitness Professionals, 6190 Cornerstone Court E., Ste. 204, San Diego, CA 92121-3772. (619) 535-8979; (619) 535-8234 (fax). More than 25,000 professionals involved with dance, exercise, and fitness training are members of this worldwide association. Three publications are produced ten times/year, and national meetings are held three times/year. Membership is $65/year (individual), $95/year (personal trainer), $145/year (business).

Visibility Through Volunteering

One of the best ways to build your skills and gain visibility among your peers is to volunteer in your professional organization. Step forward and get involved. The rewards will be yours.

Independent Automotive Damage Appraisers, Michael D. Hansen, 710 E. Ogden Ave., Ste. 113, Naperville, IL 60563-8603. (708) 369-2437; (708) 369-2488 (fax). This organization, founded by a group of independent appraisers, includes 125 companies who share information and network about their industry. They produce three publications and hold an annual meeting in June.

Indian Arts and Crafts Association, Helen Skredergard, 122 La Veta Dr., NE, Albuquerque, NM 87108-1613. (505) 265-9149. This association promotes, protects, and preserves Native American Indian arts and crafts. They produce a monthly newsletter, an annual directory, and host semiannual meetings in the spring and fall. Dues range between $50–175/year.

Industrial Designers Society of America, Kristina Goodrich, 1142-E Walker Rd., Great Falls, VA 22066. (703) 759-0100; (703) 759-7679 (fax). This national organization is dedicated to the advancement, education, and appreciation of industrial design. Regional chapters exist around the country. The organization produces three publications and holds an annual meeting in the summer. Membership is $136–219/year, plus chapter dues.

Institute of Diving, Dorothy Parkinson, 17314 Black Beach Rd., Panama City Beach, FL 32413-2020. (904) 235-4101; (904) 235-4101 (fax). Members of this association are individuals, organizations, and corporations interested in diving and diving-related activities. The institute operates a museum and library in Panama City Beach, produces a quarterly newsletter, and operates a diving information exchange program. Membership is $25/year.

Institute of Store Planners, Richard Byrne, 25 N. Broadway, Tarrytown, NY 10591-3201. (914) 332-1806; (914) 332-1541 (fax). Members of this organization are store planners, designers, visual merchandisers, educators, contractors, and suppliers. Members receive a quarterly newsletter and dues are $150–250/year.

International Association of Home Safety and Security Professionals, Bill Phillips, PO Box 2044, Erie, PA 16512-2044. (814) 456-2911; (814) 456-2911 (fax). Members of this association include retailers and wholesalers of safety and security products, writers, editors, researchers, security consultants, locksmiths, alarm-systems installers, and others with an interest in home safety and security. Members receive a monthly newsletter and access to an extensive database of statistical, technical, and product information. Membership is $75/year (associate), $100/year (professional), $200/year (allied).

 International Association of Lighting Designers (IALD), Maria Becerra, 18 E. 16th St., Ste. 208, New York, NY 10003-3193. (212) 206-1281; (212) 206-1327 (fax). This association of lighting professionals was established to develop a professional code of conduct and set guidelines. Members receive a bimonthly newsletter and annual directory, and annual meetings are held in the spring. Membership is $150/year (voting member), $60/year (associate), $35/year (educator), $15/year (student).

 International Association of Lighting Management Companies (NALMCO), Lynda J. Mastronordo, 34-C Washington Rd., Princeton Junction, NJ 08550-1028. (609) 799-5501; (609) 799-7032 (fax). This association involves companies that clean, repair, maintain, and manage commercial and industrial lighting fixtures. A monthly publication is produced and annual meetings are held in May.

 International Brotherhood of Magicians, Angie Nipper, PO Box 192090, St. Louis, MO 63119. (314) 638-6406; (314) 638-6708 (fax). More than 13,000 professional and amateur magicians and their suppliers are involved in this international organization. A monthly publication is produced. Membership is $35/year.

 International Cake, Candy, and Party Supply Association, Walter E. Offinger, 1100-H Brandywine Blvd., PO Box 2188, Zanesville, OH 43702-2188. (614) 452-4541; (614) 452-2552 (fax). This association involves individuals who create or market party supplies, cakes, candy, gifts, and crafts. A quarterly publication and annual directory is produced. Membership is $15–25/year.

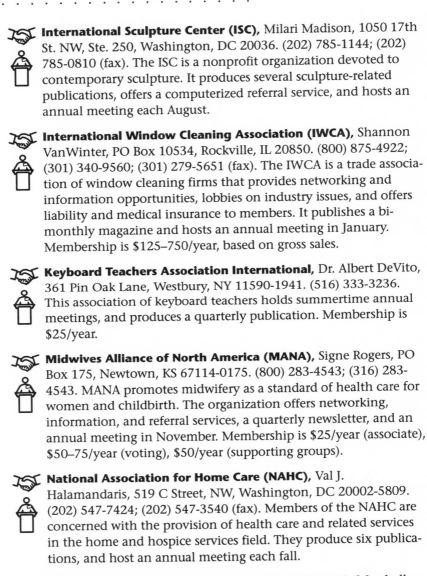

International Sculpture Center (ISC), Milari Madison, 1050 17th St. NW, Ste. 250, Washington, DC 20036. (202) 785-1144; (202) 785-0810 (fax). The ISC is a nonprofit organization devoted to contemporary sculpture. It produces several sculpture-related publications, offers a computerized referral service, and hosts an annual meeting each August.

International Window Cleaning Association (IWCA), Shannon VanWinter, PO Box 10534, Rockville, IL 20850. (800) 875-4922; (301) 340-9560; (301) 279-5651 (fax). The IWCA is a trade association of window cleaning firms that provides networking and information opportunities, lobbies on industry issues, and offers liability and medical insurance to members. It publishes a bi-monthly magazine and hosts an annual meeting in January. Membership is $125–750/year, based on gross sales.

Keyboard Teachers Association International, Dr. Albert DeVito, 361 Pin Oak Lane, Westbury, NY 11590-1941. (516) 333-3236. This association of keyboard teachers holds summertime annual meetings, and produces a quarterly publication. Membership is $25/year.

Midwives Alliance of North America (MANA), Signe Rogers, PO Box 175, Newtown, KS 67114-0175. (800) 283-4543; (316) 283-4543. MANA promotes midwifery as a standard of health care for women and childbirth. The organization offers networking, information, and referral services, a quarterly newsletter, and an annual meeting in November. Membership is $25/year (associate), $50–75/year (voting), $50/year (supporting groups).

National Association for Home Care (NAHC), Val J. Halamandaris, 519 C Street, NW, Washington, DC 20002-5809. (202) 547-7424; (202) 547-3540 (fax). Members of the NAHC are concerned with the provision of health care and related services in the home and hospice services field. They produce six publications, and host an annual meeting each fall.

National Association of Composers, USA (NACUSA), Marshall Bialosky, PO Box 49652, Los Angeles, CA 90049. (310) 541-8213. The members of this national association are composers, conductors, musicians, and other music-oriented professionals. They perform new American chamber music in concerts nationwide. The group publishes a regular newsletter, and sponsors an annual national composition competition. Membership is $35/year.

National Association of Environmental Professions (NAEP), Susan Eisenberg, 5165 MacArthur Blvd., N.W, Washington, DC 20016-3315. (202) 966-1500; (202) 966-1977 (fax). NAEP's multi-disciplinary focus brings together more than 4,000 environmental professionals who work in every field and provide access to the latest trends in environmental research, technology, law and policy. The organization publishes a bimonthly newsletter and hosts an annual meeting in the spring. Membership is $95/year; associate and student memberships are also available.

 National Association of Personal Financial Advisors (NAPFA), Margery Wasserman, Executive Director, 1130 Lake Cook Rd., Ste. 150, Buffalo Grove, IL 60089. (312) 537-7722; (312) 537-7740 (fax). The mission of this national membership organization is to advance the practice of fee-only financial planning, and to serve as an educational and networking forum for financial planning professionals. It hosts a national conference and regional events each year, and sponsors advanced seminars for professionals practicing at least five years. Local study and support groups are active in several areas around the country. A monthly newsletter is published. Dues range from $85–$240/year.

 National Association of Secretarial Services (NASS), Frank X. Fox, 3637 4th St., N. Ste. 330, St. Petersburg, FL 33704. (800) 237-1462; (813) 823-3646; (813) 894-1277 (fax). More than 1,500 independent secretarial, word processing, telephone answering, desktop publishing, transcription, and other related office support service firms belong to this association. Members receive a monthly newsletter (subscription available for $48/12 issues), discounts on office equipment and supplies, and an annual membership directory. An annual convention is held in June. Membership is $120/year, $70/six months.

 National Blacksmiths and Weldors Association, James Holman, PO Box 123, Arnold, NE 69120. (308) 848-2913. Blacksmiths, weldors, and individuals operating machine and general repair shops are members of this association. A quarterly publication is produced, and annual meetings are held the first week in December. Membership is $25/year.

National Child Care Association, Lynn White, 1029 Railroad St., N.W., Conyers, GA 30207-5275. (800) 543-7161; (404) 388-7772 (fax). This professional association represents more than 4,000 individuals involved with licensed private child care centers. The organization produces a quarterly publication and hosts an annual conference. Membership is $25/year (company).

 National Chimney Sweep Guild, John E. Bittner, 16021 Industrial Dr., Ste 8, Gaithersburg, MD 20877. (301) 963-5600; (301) 963-0838 (fax). Professional chimney service companies and their suppliers are members of this organization, which publishes a monthly magazine and hosts an annual meeting in the spring. Membership: $295/year (company), $495/year (supplier). The Guild is affiliated with the Chimney Safety Institute of America, an educational foundation that administers certification tests covering codes, standards, and practices of chimney sweeping.

 National Council on Education for the Ceramic Arts (NCECA), Regina Brown, Executive Secretary, PO Box 1677, Bandon, OR 97411. (503) 347-4394. NCECA is an international nonprofit organization devoted to the ceramic arts. Members include studio artists, teachers, students, collectors, gallery owners, critics, and others. NCECA sponsors an annual conference each spring, publishes a quarterly newsletter, annual directory, and annual journal, and organizes exhibitions and research projects on topics of interest to its members. Membership ranges from $25–200/year.

 National Guild of Professional Paperhangers, Daniel Lea, 136 S. Keowee St., Dayton, OH 45402. (513) 222-9252; (513) 222-5794 (fax). More than 1,000 professional paperhangers and wall-covering specialists are members of this association, which publishes a bimonthly publication and annual membership directory. Annual meetings are held in the summer. Membership is $125/year (individual); $250/year (organization/company).

 National Ornamental & Miscellaneous Metals Association, Barbara Cook, Executive Director, 804-10 Main St., Ste. E, Forest Park, GA 30050. (404) 363-4009. NOMMA is a trade organization for businesses who produce ornamental gates, furniture, and other metal products. Members receive a bimonthly magazine and newsletter, and can participate in an active educational program. NOMMA sponsors an annual awards competition, a trade show, and a national convention each winter.

Power Washers of North America (PWNA), Glenn Fellman, 1518 K. St., N.W., Ste. 503, Washington, DC 20005. (202) 393-7044; (202) 638-4833 (fax). PWNA is a nonprofit association dedicated to advancing the interests and concerns of individuals and companies performing both residential and commercial pressure washing services. Members receive a quarterly newsletter, access to a technical support network, training opportunities, and information on recycling and technology developments. Membership is $200–400/year.

 Professional Grounds Management Society (PGMS), John Gillan, 120 Cockeysville Rd., Ste. 104, Hunt Valley, MD 21030-2133. (410) 584-9754; (410) 584-9756 (fax). PGMS members are professionals involved in the management and maintenance of all types of grounds, including office parks, colleges and universities, hospitals, cemeteries, apartments/condos and residences. The organization produces a monthly publication and hosts an annual meeting in the fall. Membership is $125/year (individual), $400/year (organization).

 Professional Lawn Care Association of America, Ann E. McClure, 1000 Johnson Ferry Rd., N.E., Ste. C-135, Marietta, GA 30068-2112. (404) 977-5222; (404) 578-6071 (fax). This association serves as a national voice for the lawn care industry. It develops educational programs and training materials, defines industry standards, and disseminates business information to its members. Two quarterly newsletters are produced, and annual meetings are held in the fall. Membership fees are based on gross sales volume.

 Professional Picture Framers Association, Rex P. Boynton, 4305 Sarellen Rd., Richmond, VA 23231. (804) 226-0430; (804) 222-2175 (fax). The PPFA is a trade association of professionals involved in the art and picture framing industry. The organization provides members with technical support, education programs, resources, professional certification, business services, a specialty bookstore, local chapters, and national advertising and sales promotion tools. Meetings and trade shows are held three times a year. Membership: $45-75/year (individual), $100–1,000/year (organization).

Professional Plant Growers Association (PPGA), William Carlson, PO Box 275157, Lansing, MI 48909-0517. (517) 694-7700; (517) 694-8560 (fax). Members of the PPGA are growers, wholesalers, retailers, educators, and allied tradesmen of the flowering potted plant and the bedding plant industry. The organization publishes a monthly newsletter and hosts annual meetings in the fall.

 Registry of Interpreters for the Deaf (RID), Janet Bailey, 8719 Colesville Rd., Ste. 310, Silver Spring, MD 20910-3919. (301) 608-0050; (301) 608-0508 (fax). RID is a national association dedicated to the professional development of interpreters and transliterators for the deaf. The organization has developed the only national evaluation system of American Sign Language interpreters, and publishes a code of professional ethics. Members receive a monthly newsletter, an annual directory, discounts on publications and products, and networking opportunities through state and local affiliate chapters. A biennial conference is held in odd-numbered years. Membership is $85/year (certified), $70/year (associate). The TTY phone number is (301) 608-0562.

 Society of American Silversmiths (SAS), Jeffrey Herman, Director, PO Box 3599, Cranston, RI 02910. (401) 461-3156. SAS's aim is to preserve and promote contemporary silversmithing. It educates the public about the field through a free consulting service, and assists students who have a strong interest in becoming silver craftsmen through workshops, discounts, and access to technical and marketing expertise. Supporting membership is $40/year; Associate (full-time student) membership is $20/year.

For the Record

If you're unable to attend a conference, check to see if the organization offers audiotapes of the panels and presentations. While you won't be able to capture the energy of personal interchanges in the hallways, you can enjoy the program's content on your own schedule. For conference participants, tapes offer an ideal way to reinforce ideas and material over time.

Society of Children's Book Writers and Illustrators (SCBWI), Lin Oliver, 22736 Vanowen, Ste. 106, West Hills, CA 91307. (818) 888-8760. More than 9,000 writers, illustrators, TV producers, magazine editors, agents, librarians, teachers, bookstore owners, and others involved in children's literature are members of the SCBWI. The guild hosts meetings and educational workshops throughout the country, sponsors financial grants, and presents annual awards. A bimonthly newsletter is published, and annual meetings are held in August. Membership is $40/year.

 Society of Collision Repair Specialists (SCRS), John Loftus, 131 N. Tustin Ave., Ste. 210, PO Box 3765, Tustin, CA 92680. (714) 835-3110; (714) 835-3118 (fax). Members of the SCRS are owners of auto collision repair shops, suppliers, insurance, and educational associates. Membership is $300/year (individual).

 Society of Craft Designers, Nancy Horne, 6175 Barfield Rd., Ste. 220, Atlanta, GA 30328. (404) 252-2454; (404) 252-0215 (fax). Designers of craft items and writers for the craft industry are members of this association. The group publishes a bimonthly newsletter, and an annual journal of cost analysis. Annual meetings are held in the summer. Membership: $100/year (individual), $200/year (company).

 Society of North American Goldsmiths (SNAG), Robert E. Mitchell, 5009 Londonderry Dr., Tampa, FL 33647. (813) 977-5326; (813) 977-8462 (fax). SNAG promotes contemporary metalwork and jewelry, and is dedicated to the aesthetic, educational, and scientific aspects of this art field. The organization publishes a quarterly magazine, *Metalsmith,* a bimonthly newsletter, and an annual membership directory. Annual meetings are held in spring or summer. Membership is $55/year (individual).

 Songwriters Guild of America, Lewis M. Bachman, 1500 Harbor Blvd., Weehawken, NJ 07087-6732. (201) 867-7603; (201) 867-7535 (fax). This guild is a voluntary songwriters association run by and for songwriters. It is devoted exclusively to providing songwriters with the services and activities they need to succeed in the business of music. Other offices are located in New York, (212) 768-7902; Nashville, (615) 329-1782; and Los Angeles, (213) 462-1108. They publish a quarterly bulletin and hold annual meetings in the spring.

Souvenirs and Novelties Trade Association, Scott C. Borowsky, 7000 Terminal Sq., Ste. 210, Upper Darby, PA 19082. (610) 734-2420; (610) 734-2423 (fax). More than 20,000 individuals involved in the souvenir and novelty industry are members of this association. It publishes a member magazine seven times a year, and produces a publication on tourist attractions and parks. Annual meetings are held in January. Membership is $25/year.

 Surface Design Association, Joy Stocksdale, PO Box 20799, Oakland, CA 94620. (510) 841-2008; (707) 829-1756; (707) 829-3285 (fax). SDA members include professionals involved in printing, designing, and dyeing art fabrics, fibers, and other materials. The organization promotes the field of surface design by educating the public and improving professional opportunities and communication among its members and the industry. SDA publishes a quarterly journal and newsletter, and hosts national biennial conferences in odd-numbered years. Membership is $45/year.

 Teachers of English to Speakers of Other Languages (TESOL), Susan C. Bayley, 1600 Cameron St., Ste. 300, Alexandria, VA 22314-2751. (703) 836-0774; (703) 518-2505; (703) 836-7864 (fax). This international association promotes instruction and research in the teaching of English to speakers of other languages. TESOL produces several publications, including a bimonthly newsletter, a quarterly journal, a bimonthly placement bulletin, and a membership directory. Annual meetings are held in spring.

 USA Toy Library Association, Judith Q. Iacuzzi, 2530 Crawford Ave., Ste. 111, Evanston, IL 60201. (708) 864-3330; (708) 864-3331 (fax). Members of this organization are individuals, libraries, or organizations who have set up toy lending facilities. The association offers a video and set of instructions on how to establish a library, publishes a toy report, and a directory of toy libraries nationwide. Members also receive a quarterly newsletter. Membership is $50/year (basic), $150/year (comprehensive).

Project Management

See also Managing Your Business; Office Design and Operation

Even if a solo business does not focus specifically on project-based work, project management skills can bring a better sense of order and flow to the company. The resources in this chapter can show you how to accurately estimate the time, staff, and money needed for a project. You can also discover methods to chart your progress and ways to ensure that each project phase stays on track. Perhaps most importantly for independent entrepreneurs, you can learn how to juggle multiple complex projects simultaneously and keep them all headed toward successful completion.

High Performance Teamwork, by Doug Jones, $59.95. Nightingale Conant, 7300 N. Lehigh Ave., Niles, IL 60714. (800) 525-9000 (orders); (800) 323-3938; (708) 647-7145 (fax). In this six-volume set, Doug Jones, an internationally renowned management expert, shows how to design, train, cultivate, motivate, and reward a high-performance team. Includes workbook.

How to Manage Projects, 1 day, $149.00. SkillPath, Inc., 6900 Squibb Rd., PO Box 2768, Mission, KS 66201-2768. (800) 873-7545; (913) 677-3200; (913) 362-4241 (fax). This seminar presents a thorough overview of what it takes to guide a project from idea through final results. Participants learn management skills such as how to plan projects, establish time lines, keep things moving, monitor and control progress, solve problems, and manage multiple projects at once. Presented in selected cities nationwide.

How to Manage Projects, by Reich Gardner, $69.95. SkillPath, Inc., 6900 Squibb Rd., PO Box 2768, Mission, KS 66201-2768. (800) 873-7545; (913) 677-3200; (913) 362-4241 (fax). Based on the live seminar, this audio program describes in detail how to plan, staff, monitor, control, and solve the problems faced in managing any project. Includes six cassettes and a workbook.

Managing Multiple Projects, Objectives & Deadlines, 1 day, $99.00. SkillPath, Inc., 6900 Squibb Rd., PO Box 2768, Mission, KS 66201-2768. (800) 873-7545; (913) 677-3200; (913) 362-4241 (fax). A seminar that teaches how to gain control of your workday, handle competing priorities, get organized, increase your productivity through planning, manage people for results, and control stress. Offered in cities nationwide.

Managing Projects, Priorities & Deadlines, by Jim Temme, $59.95. SkillPath, Inc., 6900 Squibb Rd., PO Box 2768, Mission, KS 66201-2768. (800) 873-7545; (913) 677-3200; (913) 362-4241 (fax). This six-tape set teaches how to make every minute count by learning how to organize yourself and your priorities. A workbook is included.

On Time/On Budget, by Sunny Baker & Kim Baker, ©1993, ISBN: 0-13-633447-4, $39.95. Prentice Hall, 15 Columbus Circle, New York, NY 10023. (800) 223-1360. This book offers step-by-step guidance on managing all types of projects, from the simplest to most complex.

Project Management Seminar, 1 day, $195.00. Fred Pryor Seminars, 2000 Shawnee Mission Pkwy., Shawnee Mission, KS 66205. (800) 938-6330; (913) 722-8580 (fax). This seminar teaches strategies that ensure excellent, on-time, on-budget results for special projects of all sizes and complexity. Also available on six audiotapes for $59.95.

Promotion
and Public Relations

See also Communication Skills; Direct Marketing; Marketing; Sales

The areas of promotion and public relations (PR) fall under the larger umbrella of marketing but carry subtle distinctions. Promotion is generally understood to be anything that establishes or positions your business in the marketplace or develops new business contacts for you. Examples include special coupons or offers, bundling additional items at no extra cost, or "freebies" that accompany your product or service. PR is the process of creating a positive public image for your business, typically through media coverage in newspapers or magazines or on radio or television. Best of all, promotion and PR can bring widespread visibility for your solo business at little or no cost. Use the resources listed here to guide you in maximizing your marketing impact.

 Bulletproof News Releases: Practical, No-Holds-Barred Advice for Small Business From 135 American Newspaper Editors, by Kay Borden, ©1994, 176 pp., ISBN: 0-9637477-0-3, $16.95. Franklin-Sarrett Publishers, 3761 Vinyard Trace #100, Marietta, GA 30062. (800) 444-2524; (404) 578-9410; (800) 777-2525 (fax). This guide includes tips from 135 professional journalists who were surveyed on publicity for small businesses. Includes advice on where to send your release, how to plan a successful news release campaign, and when to use releases for the greatest impact.

 Creating Customers, by David H. Bangs, Jr., ©1992, 176 pp., ISBN: 0-936894-27-X, $19.95. Upstart Publishing Co., Inc., 12 Portland St., Dover, NH 03820. (800) 235-8866; (603) 749-5071; (603) 742-9121 (fax). This book, based on real-world experience and practical techniques, helps the reader create an action plan for maximizing sales, promotion, and publicity for their business.

Getting Publicity, by Tana Fletcher & Julia Rockler, ©1990, 144 pp., ISBN: 0-88908-890-X, $12.95. Self-Counsel Press, Inc., 1704 N. State St., Bellingham, WA 98225. (800) 663-3007; (206) 676-4530; (206) 676-4549 (fax). This book provides readers with inside advice on how to get media attention and how to profit from other forms of free publicity.

Guerilla PR: How To Wage an Effective Publicity Campaign, by Michael Levine, ©1994, 256 pp., ISBN: 0-88730-664-0, $10.00. HarperBusiness, 10 E. 53rd St., New York, NY 10022-5299. (800) 982-4377; (212) 207-7000; (800) 822-4090 (fax). Levine teaches low-cost tips and techniques on how to create memorable, effective PR campaigns that don't require large budgets.

How to Publicize High Tech Products & Services, by Dan Janal, ©1992, 180 pp., ISBN: 1-879572-00-1, $24.95. Janal Communications, 657 Doral Dr., Danville, CA 94526-6206. (510) 831-0900; (510) 831-2446 (fax). Written by an experienced PR professional, this guide is a valuable hands-on tool for solo businesses in high tech fields. Anecdotes, sample materials, and thought-provoking worksheets help readers create professional materials that will gain favorable attention from editors. Covers how to write effective press releases, talk to reporters, position products for editors, publicize products at trade shows, and more.

How to Sell & Promote Your Idea, Project, or Invention, by Reece A. Franklin, ©1994, 272 pp., ISBN: 1-55958-295-2, $16.95. Prima Publishing, PO Box 1260, Rocklin, CA 95677-1260. (916) 632-7400; (916) 632-7668 (fax). This book stresses how to promote an invention rather than how to get it patented. It leads readers from start-up through trade shows and selling techniques, including tips on media methods and financing.

Producing a First-Class Video for Your Business, by Dell Dennison, Don Doman, & Margaret Doman, ©1992, 176 pp., ISBN: 0-88908-527-7, $14.95. Self-Counsel Press, Inc., 1704 N. State St., Bellingham, WA 98225. (800) 663-3007; (206) 676-4530; (206) 676-4549 (fax). This book gives readers a variety of tips on the planning and production of a business-related video, including worksheets and sample scripts, as well as advice on how to integrate graphics, special effects, props, voiceovers, and music.

Promotion: Solving the Puzzle, $30.00. U.S. Small Business Administration, SBA Publications, PO Box 30, Denver, CO 80201-0300. (800) 827-5722; (202) 205-6665. This video helps small business owners see the individual pieces of the promotional puzzle, and teaches them how to put them together in a coherent, productive way to create a sound promotional plan.

 Publicity Builder, by Daniel S. Janal, $139.00. JIAN Tools for Sales, 1975 W. El Camino Real, #301, Mountain View, CA 94040-2218. (800) 346-5426; (415) 254-5600; (415) 254-5640 (fax). This disk/book combination enables you to create a PR campaign to promote your business. Disk-based templates work with any word processor. Available for DOS, Windows, or Macintosh formats.

 Six Steps to Free Publicity and Dozens of Other Ways to Win Free Media Attention for You and Your Business, by Marcia Yudkin, ©1994, 192 pp., ISBN: 0-452-27192-4, $9.95. Plume, 120 Woodbine St., Bergenfield, NJ 07621. (800) 253-6476. This lively and inspirational guide shows how to get more than your 15 minutes of fame—and fortune—through free media publicity. Dozens of real-life stories and examples demonstrate how to create low-cost media impact for your business.

 The Do-It-Yourself Business Promotions Kit, by Jack Griffin, ©1994, 300 pp., ISBN: 0-13-106006-6, $18.95. Prentice Hall, Career & Personal Development, Paramount Publishing, 200 Old Tappan Rd., Old Tappan, NJ 07675. (800) 922-0579; (800) 445-6991 (fax). Hundreds of ready-to-use models of effective and affordable communications, including personal letters, direct mail, telephone solicitations, print ads, press releases, and radio and TV spots.

Easy Does It

A golden rule in dealing with the media is to "make life easy" for them. Realize they are providing valuable visibility for your business. In exchange, assist them with well-written materials, clearly labeled photographs, quick responses to phone calls, and overall professionalism. That way, they can do their job well and everyone looks good.

The Unabashed Self-Promoter's Guide, by Jeffrey Lant, ©1992, 363 pp., ISBN: 0-940374-18-8, $39.50. JLA Publications, PO Box 38-2767, Cambridge, MA 02238. (617) 547-6372; (617) 547-0061 (fax). A step-by-step guide on how to get the media to promote your business for free, from one of the all-time masters of self-promotion. Includes a comprehensive list of media resources.

 Writing Effective News Releases, by Catherine V. McIntyre, ©1992, 176 pp., ISBN: 0-941599-19-1, $17.95. Picadilly Books, P.O. Box 25203, Colorado Springs, CO 80936. (719) 548-1844. Written in easy-to-understand language by a newspaper reporter and columnist, this book shows you how to create effective news releases to generate free publicity for your business. Includes practice exercises and dozens of examples.

 Zen of Hype: An Insiders Guide to the Publicity Game, by Raleigh Pinskey, ©1991, 171 pp., ISBN: 0-8065-1239-3, $10.95. Carol Publishing Group, 600 Madison Ave., New York, NY 10022. (800) 447-2665; (212) 736-1141. A practical, no-nonsense overview of understanding and using PR techniques to promote your business. Filled with "insider" tips from a successful PR professional.

 Zen of Hype Seminars, by Raleigh Pinskey, ©1993, $149.95. Raleigh Group, Ltd., 1223 Wilshire Blvd. #502, Santa Monica, CA 90403-5400. (310) 998-0055; (310) 998-0034 (fax). This series of eight audiotapes is based on the author's popular-selling book and seminar series on PR. Topics covered include: public relations and the media; how to make yourself media friendly; planning a media campaign; compiling a media kit; mailing lists; pitching your product; the art of following up; and media conferences and interviews.

Exhibiting and Displays

 Clear Solutions, Inc., Box 2460, West Brattleboro, VT 05301. (800) 257-4550; (802) 257-7052. Clear Solutions sells a wide selection of transparent acrylic book and card stands for display purposes. They also make risers and cubes and can work to specification.

 Downing Displays, 115 West McMicken Ave., Cincinnati, OH 45210. (800) 883-1800; (513) 621-7888; (513) 621-1069 (fax). Downing supplies portable trade-show exhibits, folding frames, pop-up panels, show services, rentals, and leasings.

Siegel Display Products, PO Box 95, Minneapolis, MN 55440. (612) 340-9235; (800) 230-5598 (fax). Metal and wire product displays are the primary focus of this firm.

 Successful Exhibiting, by James W. Dudley, 252 pp., ISBN: 1-55850-867-8, $12.95. Bob Adams, Inc., 260 Center St., Holbrook, MA 02343. (800) 872-5627; (617) 767-8100; (800) 872-5628 (fax). Advice for companies of all sizes to maximize their opportunities at exhibitions and trade shows.

 The Successful Exhibitor's Handbook, by Bary Siskind, ©1993, 256 pp., ISBN: 0-88908-528-5, $10.95. Self-Counsel Press, Inc., 1704 N. State St., Bellingham, WA 98225. (800) 663-3007; (206) 676-4530; (206) 676-4549 (fax). This book helps small businesses and entrepreneurs get more from their trade show participation and offers fresh ideas for the promotional plan.

Writing/Editing Services

 Editing-by-Fax Service, Marcia Yudkin, PO Box 1310, Boston, MA 02117. (617) 266-1613; (617) 438-7830 (fax). Author and writing consultant Marcia Yudkin can make intelligent line-by-line corrections and suggestions for your press releases, marketing materials, articles and business reports, all through the fax machine. Editing is done within two business days, and a typical charge is $40.00. Call to arrange editing by mail for documents longer than eight pages.

 National Marketing Center, Dan McComas, 11409 Catalina Terrace, Silver Spring, MD 20902. (301) 946-4284; (301) 946-4104 (fax). This professional service can write and edit your ads, flyers, sales letters, or other PR materials. It can also provide ghostwriting services for articles or other business presentation documents. Pricing is on a fee basis, with affordable small business rates. A free initial consultation is available.

Research and Reference

Experienced entrepreneurs know that gathering top-notch information is an important preliminary step to making intelligent business decisions. This chapter of the WORKING SOLO SOURCEBOOK features valuable reference tools that can aid you in guiding your business to success. To access the expensive volumes published annually, visit your local public library. Another option is to check out the research tools available via online computer networks (see the *Computers and Technology* chapter for listings of online services) or on CD-ROM disks. The listings below also include guides that teach how to do research, and they provide tips on the best ways to gather business information.

How to Conduct Research

 Business Research, by Paul R. Timm & Rick Farr, ©1994, 90 pp., ISBN: 0-56052-249-6, $8.95. Crisp Publications, 1200 Hamilton Ct., Menlo Park, CA 94025. (415) 323-6100; (415) 323-5800 (fax). This book focuses on primary research and helps the reader develop skills to find answers to business questions successfully.

 Researching Your Market, $1.00. U.S. Small Business Administration, SBA Publications, PO Box 30, Denver, CO 80201-0030. (800) 827-5722; (202) 205-6665. This booklet provides inexpensive and uncomplicated methods for doing market research.

 The Entrepreneur's Guide to Business Information, by Jim Lea, ©1994, 224 pp., ISBN: 1-56414-128-4, $14.95. Career Press, 180 Fifth Ave., PO Box 34, Hawthorne, NJ 07507. (800) CAREER-1; (201) 427-2037 (fax). How to identify the most useful sources of business information, gather it economically, and strategically use it to run your company more efficiently and profitably.

General Business Research Tools

 Association of Independent Information Professionals (AIIP), Stephanie Ardito, president, Ardito Information Research, Inc., 1019 Sedgwick Dr., Wilmington, DE 19803. (302) 479-5373; (302) 479-5375 (fax). AIIP members are owners of firms providing information-related services such as online and manual research, document delivery, database design, library support, consulting, writing, and publishing. Benefits include a quarterly newsletter, access to a private electronic bulletin board, and an annual meeting. Membership is $165/year (full); $85/year (associate).

 Breakaway Careers, by Bill Radin, ©1994, 224 pp., ISBN: 1-56414-121-7, $12.95. Career Press, 180 Fifth Ave., PO Box 34, Hawthorne, NJ 07507. (800) CAREER-1; (201) 427-2037 (fax). Billed as "a self-employment sourcebook for freelancers, consultants, and corporate refugees," this book contains practical information for individuals who want to work independently.

 Business Library, ©1993, $59.95. Allegro New Media, 387 Passaic Ave., Fairfield, NJ 07004. (800) 424-1992; (201) 808-1992; (201) 808-2645 (fax). This CD-ROM reveals the impressive amount of material that can be compiled on a single disk: it includes the complete text of 12 best-selling business books, and three complete business videos. Users can easily access marketing, sales, finance, management, real estate, career development, and business travel information. Available in Windows format only.

 Directory of Special Libraries and Information Centers, ©1994, 2,100 pp., annual, ISBN: 0-8103-8524-4, $475.00. Gale Research, Inc., 835 Penobscott Bldg., Detroit, MI 48226-0260. (800) 877-GALE; (313) 961-2242. A two-volume reference on special information sources maintained by government agencies, business, industry, newspapers, educational institutions, and societies.

 Encyclopedia of Associations, ©1994, 3,500 pp., annual, ISBN: 0-8103-9246-1, $415.00. Gale Research, Inc., 835 Penobscott Bldg., Detroit, MI 48226-0260. (800) 877-GALE; (313) 961-2242. This classic reference tool includes details on more than 110,000 U.S. and worldwide associations, including professional, trade, and business associations, labor unions, cultural organizations, chambers of commerce, and other groups of all types, sizes, and focus. Available in a three-volume printed version or on CD-ROM.

Entrepreneur's Small Business Encyclopedia, $149.00. Entrepreneur Magazine Group, 2392 Morse Ave., PO Box 57050, Irvine, CA 92619-7050. (800) 421-2300; (714) 851-9088 (fax). This binder contains 1,650 pages of advice and answers to the most frequently asked questions regarding small business. It is designed to be a hand-on business tool and includes categories such as advertising, pricing, security, start-up financing, and more.

 Gale Research Business Catalog, Gale Research, Inc., 835 Penobscott Bldg., Detroit, MI 48226-0260. (800) 877-GALE; (313) 961-2242. Gale publishes hundreds of research and reference volumes, most updated annually and available in a variety of printed and electronic formats. Call for a copy of their free business catalog to discover the wealth of information available to you.

 Information Industry Association (IIA), Terri Lageman, 555 New Jersey Ave., NW, Ste. 800, Washington, DC 20001. (202) 639-8262; (202) 638-4403 (fax). IIA's mission is to promote, enhance, and strengthen the business environment within which information companies exist, grow, and prosper by bringing together information providers, equipment vendors, consultants, and others. Publications and seminars are produced, and an annual meeting is held each fall. Membership fees start at $500.

 InKnowVation Newsletter, Innovation Development Institute, 45 Beach Bluff Ave., Ste. 300, Swampscott, MA 01907. (617) 595-2920. This newsletter discusses the possibilities of innovative research for small businesses and provides resource information for high-risk and development ventures.

Meet the "Cybrarian"

The explosive growth of online data banks has given birth to a new breed of researcher: cybrarians, or librarians who roam cyberspace, ferreting out information from electronic networks. As comfortable behind a computer terminal as they are flipping through hardbound reference tomes, these hip information professionals can be valuable allies to solo entrepreneurs. In our booming Information Age, they are the masters. Check 'em out!

Insider's Guide to Book Editors, Publishers, and Literary Agents, by Jeff Herman, ©1994, 450 pp., ISBN: 1-55958-344-4, $19.95. Prima Publishing, Inc., PO Box 1260, Rocklin, CA 95677-1260. (916) 632-7400; (916) 632-7668 (fax). Of particular interest to aspiring writers, this book offers a comprehensive listing of individuals and companies involved in the book acquisition process. Also includes details on proposals and manuscript submissions, ghostwriting, and collaboration.

 Lesko's Info-Power II, by Matthew Lesko, ©1993, 1,600 pp., ISBN: 0-8103-9485-5, $29.95. Visible Ink Press, PO Box 33477, Detroit, MI 48232-5477. (800) 776-6265; (800) 776-6265 (fax). A mind-boggling compendium of more than 45,000 free and low-cost sources of information from government agencies, associations, private organizations, and more.

 Small Business Sourcebook, by Kathleen Maki, Ed., ©1993, 3,000 pp., ISBN: 0-8103-8904-5, $235.00. Gale Research, Inc., 835 Penobscott Bldg., Detroit, MI 48226-0260. (800) 877-GALE; (313) 961-2242. This is perhaps the most comprehensive sourcebook on small business, published annually in two volumes. It includes listings of government agencies, business-related publications, a glossary of small business terms as well as details on hundreds of specific small businesses.

 Small Business Trends and Entrepreneurship, by the editors of *Business Week,* ©1994, 192 pp., ISBN: 0-07-009424-1, $12.95. McGraw-Hill, Inc., 11 W. 19th St., New York, NY 10011. (800) 822-8158. Insights, interviews, case studies, graphics, and more are featured in this book that takes a look at key techniques and trends in entrepreneurship in the mid-1990s. More than 100 staffers of *Business Week* magazine contributed to the special issue that formed the basis for this book.

 The Artist's Resource Handbook, by Daniel Grant, ©1994, 176 pp., ISBN: 1-880559-17- X, $12.95. Allworth Press, 10 E. 23rd St., New York, NY 10010. (800) 247-6553; (212) 777-8395. This sourcebook explains how artists can benefit from the extensive resources available to them at little or no cost. Includes a listing of organizations offering career advice, advice on working with umbrella organizations, sources of public and private support, artist-in-residency programs, tips on obtaining low-cost materials and studio space, advice on networking, and more.

The Crafts Fair Guide, quarterly, ISSN: 0273-7957, $42.50/yr. Lee Spiegel, PO Box 5508, Mill Valley, CA 94942. (415) 924-3259. This publication offers an evaluation of craft fairs around the country, with ratings compiled from participants at past events on topics such as site, cost, attendance, and sales. It also includes details on upcoming shows, including dates and deadlines.

 The Crafts Supply Sourcebook, by Margaret Boyd, ed., ©1994, 288 pp., ISBN: 1-55870-355-1, $16.99. Betterway Books, 1507 Dana Avenue, Cincinnati, OH 45207. (800) 289-0963; (513) 531-4082 (fax). A comprehensive, shop-by-mail guide to thousands of craft resources, including tools, accessories, books, magazines, associations, videos, databases, display items, and other resources of interest to professional craftspeople.

 The Information Please Business Almanac & Desk Reference, by Seth Godin, Ed., ©1994, 768 pp., ISBN: 0-395-70110-4, $21.95. Houghton Mifflin Company, Wayside Rd., Burlington, MA 01803. (800) 225-3362. This handy, all-in-one volume of business information includes names, address, phone/fax numbers, and other details on more than 700 topics, structured in ten key areas: marketing, finance, international, human resources, corporate planning, personal computing, manufacturing, communications, office management, and legal issues and government.

 The Information Please Women's Sourcebook, by Lisa Dimona & Constance Herndon, ©1994, 640 pp., ISBN: 0-395-70067-1, $13.95. Houghton Mifflin Company, Wayside Rd., Burlington, MA 01803. (800) 225-3362. This directory contains an extensive collection of information on opportunities, resources, and organizations for women, presented in a visually appealing style. Facts and commentary scattered throughout the book provide fuller insights into the data and statistics.

 The Vest-Pocket Entrepreneur, by David E. Rye, ©1995, 400 pp., ISBN: 0-13-158510-X, $17.95. Prentice Hall, Career & Personal Development, Paramount Publishing, 200 Old Tappan Rd., Old Tappan, NJ 07675. (800) 922-0579. This small-format reference guide provides hundreds of answers and strategies for entrepreneurial success, including researching and testing ideas, obtaining financing, developing marketing concepts, and managing an ongoing business.

. . . .

 The Whole Career Sourcebook, by R.M. Kaplan, ©1991, 225 pp., ISBN: 0-8144-0464-3, $16.95. AMACOM Books, PO Box 1026, Saranac Lake, NY 12983. (800) 262-9699; (518) 891-3653 (fax). A combination how-to guide and resource directory for career builders at every level.

 Women's Business Resource Guide, by Barbara Littman & Michael Ray, ©1994, 144 pp., ISBN: 1-884565-01-8, $21.95. The Resource Group, PO Box 25505, Eugene, OR 97402. (503) 683-5330. This comprehensive directory brings a wide range of valuable information specifically targeted to women business owners. Includes thousands of details on: training, technical assistance, and counseling opportunities; federal and state information sources; publications, books, magazines, and online services; business and professional organizations; and more.

Marketing Research Tools

 All-in-One Directory, ©1994, 500 pp., $80.00. Gebbie Press, PO Box 1000, New Paltz, NY 12561-0017. (914) 255-7560. This annual directory includes details on more than 19,000 PR outlets, including daily and weekly newspapers, radio and TV stations, general consumer magazines, business and trade publications, news syndicates, and more. An electronic version of the directory is available on computer disk, and selected lists can be obtained on pressure-sensitive mailing labels.

Bacon's Media Directories, Bacon's Information, Inc., 323 S. Michigan Ave., Chicago, IL 60604. (800) 621-0561; (312) 922-2400; (312) 922-3127 (fax). Bacon's publishes five annual directories with up-to-date media contact information. The Newspaper/Magazine Directory has information on U.S. and Canadian daily newspapers, U.S. weeklies, and more than 9,500 business, trade, and consumer magazines (2 volumes, $270.00). The Radio/TV/Cable Directory covers U.S. radio and TV stations (2 volumes, $270.00). The Media Calendar Directory contains editorial profiles for more than 1,500 major magazines and top daily newspapers ($250.00). The Business Media Directory provides more than 8,000 business and financial editorial contacts for top newspapers, magazines, radio, and TV shows ($250.00). The International Media Directory covers more than 22,000 trade and consumer magazines plus more than 1,000 newspapers in 15 Western European countries ($270.00).

Chases' Annual Events, © 1994, 592 p., ISBN: 0-8092-3732-6, $45.95. Contemporary Books, Inc., Two Prudential Plaza, Ste. 1200, Chicago, IL 60601-6790. (312) 540-4500; (312) 540-4687. This annual directory of thousands of commemorative holidays and special events is a useful resource in planning PR campaigns.

 Hudson's Subscription Newsletter Directory, Howard Penn Hudson, Ed., © 1994, 450 pp., ISBN: 0-9617642-4-4, $140.00. The Newsletter Clearinghouse, 44 W. Market St., PO Box 311, Rhinebeck, NY 12572. (914) 876-2081; (914) 876-2561 (fax). Details on more than 4,800 subscription newsletters in 52 subject headings and 169 categories. Includes alphabetical and geographical indexes.

 Know Your Market, by David B. Frigstad, ©1994, 209 pp., ISBN: 1-55571-333-5, $19.95. Oasis Press, 300 N. Valley Dr., Grants Pass, OR 97526. (800) 228-2275; (503) 479-9464; (503) 476-1479 (fax). A practical guide to low-cost market research, this book shows how to gather, analyze, and present information on products, markets, market segments, market potentials, and market shares. Includes forms, worksheets, checklists, tables, and charts.

 Newsletter Sourcebook, by Mark Beach, ©1993, 144 pp., ISBN: 0-89134-469-1, $26.95. North Light Books, 1507 Dana Ave., Cincinnati, OH 45207. (800) 289-0963; (513) 531-4082 (fax). Everything a designer, editor, or even a novice needs to know to produce an effective newsletter. Includes more than 100 newsletter examples to inspire your own efforts.

 Oxbridge Directory of Newsletters, annual, $395.00. Oxbridge Communications, 150 Fifth Ave., New York, NY 10011. (800) 955-0231; (212) 633-2938 (fax). Information on more than 20,000 U.S. and Canadian newsletters in 168 categories. Includes contact details, circulation, ad rates, mailing list rental rates, and more.

 Standard Periodical Directory, annual, $495.00. Oxbridge Communications, 150 Fifth Ave., New York, NY 10011. (800) 955-0231; (212) 633-2938 (fax). Details on more than 85,000 North American periodicals, including magazines, newsletters, newspapers, journals, and directories. Features data on publishing, circulation, production, and advertising. Also available in CD-ROM format for $695.00.

Standard Rate and Data Services (SRDS), 3004 Glenview Rd., Wilmette, IL 60091. (800) 851-SRDS; (708) 256-6067; (708) 441-2522 (fax). SRDS is the leading publisher of advertising media and marketing data. They publish nearly two dozen different subscription-based directories and databases to assist businesses in locating appropriate advertising vehicles in print, radio, and TV.

The Guild, Kraus Sikes Inc., 228 State St., Madison, WI 53703-2215, (800) 969-1556; (608) 256-1938 (fax). This company publishes two annual full-color directories of work by contemporary artisans, with detailed contact information for purchases or commissions. The Designer's Edition features furniture, accessories, lighting, and works for the wall. The Architect's Edition showcases public art, sculpture, and architectural glass, ceramics, and metal. Each volume is $35.00.

Address and Telephone Resources

Fax U.S.A., ©1994, 455 pp., ISBN: 0-7808-0030-3, $58.00. Omnigraphics, Inc., Penobscot Bldg., Detroit, MI 48226. (800) 234-1340; (313) 961-1340; (800) 875-1340 (fax). This directory lists more than 85,000 fax numbers for businesses and organizations nationwide. Each listing also provides the complete mailing address and telephone number.

Government Directory of Addresses and Telephone Numbers, ©1994, 1,350 pp., ISBN: 0-7808-0017-6, $150.00. Omnigraphics, Inc., Penobscot Bldg., Detroit, MI 48226. (800) 234-1340; (313) 961-1340; (313) 961-1383 (fax). This comprehensive guide to federal, state, country and local government offices in the U.S. provides easy access to names, address, offices, and telephone, fax, and toll-free numbers.

National Directory of Addresses and Telephone Numbers, ©1994, 1,500 pp., ISBN: 0-7808-0039-7, $95.00. Omnigraphics, Inc., Penobscot Bldg., Detroit, MI 48226. (800) 234-1340; (313) 961-1340; (800) 875-1340 (fax). Nearly 125,000 listings of the largest and most important corporations, organizations, government offices, and institutions in the U.S. are included in this directory. Includes names, addresses, as well as telephone, fax, toll-free numbers, and Internet addresses. Also available in CD-ROM format for $150.00

ProPhone, Pro CD, Inc., 222 Rosewood Dr., Danvers, MA 01923-4520. (800) 99-CD-ROM; (508) 750-0000; (508) 750-0060 (fax). This company produces a variety of telephone directories on CD-ROM disks, allowing users to access more than 80 million listings in seconds. Includes autodial capability for use with a computer modem, and searches can be output to paper lists or mailing labels. Five directories are currently available: Direct Phone listings can be searched by name; Select Phone listings can be searched by any field, including phone number, address, city, state, Zip code, area code, business heading, or SIC code; Free Phone features nationwide toll-free listings; Canada Phone features Canadian listings; and Euro Pages gives access to Europe's top 150,000 buyers and suppliers classified by individual country. Prices range from $49.00–$299.00, and are available for DOS, Windows, and Macintosh computers. Updates are available at a discounted fee.

The Address Book, by Michael Levine, ©1993, 284 pp., ISBN: 0-399-51793-6, $9.95. Putnam Publishing Group, 200 Madison Ave., New York, NY 10016. (800) 631-8571; (212) 951-8400. Mailing addresses of more than 3,500 celebrities, corporate executives, and other VIPs.

Technology Reference Tools

CD-ROMs in Print, annual, $100.00. Meckler Corp., 11 Ferry Lane W., Westport, CT 06880. (203) 226-6967; (203) 226-5840 (fax). This directory, published on CD-ROM, features more than 6,000 CD-ROM titles.

CompuServe Companion: Finding Newspapers and Magazines Online, by Glenn S. Orenstein & Ruth M. Orenstein, ©1994, 198 pp., ISBN: 1-879258-10-2, $29.95. BiblioData, PO Box 61, Needham Heights, MA 02194. (800) 247-6553; (617) 444-1154; (617) 449-4584 (fax). A guide to the more than 3,300 magazines, journals, newsletters, and newspapers on CompuServe, with tips on how to retrieve them quickly, inexpensively, and efficiently.

Computer Industry Almanac, by Karen Petska Juliussen and Egil Juliussen, ©1994, 816 pp., ISBN: 0-942107-05-5, $50.00. Computer Industry Almanac, Inc., 225 Allen Way, Incline Village at Lake Tahoe, NV 89451-9608. (702) 831-2288; (702) 831-8610 (fax). This annual reference includes thousands of entries on every facet of the computer industry, including details on: computer companies; magazines, newspapers, and newsletters; market research companies; associations and user groups; computer book publishers; conferences; online service providers; and industry leaders. Also includes salary and wealth rankings of the top computer people as well as the average salaries for various computer-related occupations. Also available on CD-ROM for DOS-compatible PCs.

 Gale Directory of Databases, ©1994, 2,356 pp., annual, ISBN: 0-8103-5747-X, $290.00. Gale Research Inc., PO Box 33477, Detroit, MI 48232-5477. (800) 877-4253; (313) 961-6083 (fax). This directory profiles more than 8,800 databases available worldwide in a variety of formats, including CD-ROM, online, disk-based, magnetic tape, and handheld products. Published as a two-volume set each January and July. Also available on a single CD-ROM disk for $600.00.

 Macintosh Product Registry, quarterly, $40.00. Redgate Communications Corporation, 600 Beachland Blvd., Vero Beach, FL 32963. (800) 333-8760. A comprehensive quarterly directory of more than 7,000 products for Macintosh computers, including software, hardware, accessories, training, and other technical solutions. Each issue averages at least 500 pages.

 Secrets of the Super Searchers, by Reva Basch, ©1993, 235 pp., ISBN: 0-910965-12-9, $39.95. Online Inc., 462 Danbury Rd., Wilton, CT 06897-2126. (800) 248-8466; (203) 761-1444 (fax). A collection of interviews with experienced online researches who reveal their tips, techniques, secrets, mistakes, and more. A question-and-answer format allows readers to compare how veteran online searchers attack their quests, and understand how these pros get the most out of electronic databases.

Sales

*See also Communication Skills; Direct Marketing; Marketing;
Promotion and Public Relations*

Making a direct connection with a customer and asking him or her to buy your product or service is the heart of the sales process. For most solo entrepreneurs, selling brings either a rush of adrenaline or a compulsion to flee. Unfortunately, most opinions about selling are based on past negative buying experiences—with poor salespeople. It's up to you to overcome these negative feelings, in both yourself and your prospects. Even if a solo business relies primarily on an outside sales force, this is an area in which all independent entrepreneurs can improve. Sales greats are quick to point out that selling is a skill that improves with time and experience. Let the resources in this chapter help you hone your sales abilities—and improve your company's bottom line.

 Cold Calling Techniques, by Stephan Schiffman, ©1992, ISBN: 1-55850-860-0, $7.95. Bob Adams, Inc., 260 Center St., Holbrook, MA 02343. (800) 872-5627; (617) 767-8100; (800) 872-5628 (fax). This concise book provides the reader with effective, easy-to-implement techniques for making important sales calls.

 Creative Selling: The Competitive Edge, $0.50. U.S. Small Business Administration, SBA Publications, PO Box 30, Denver, CO 80201-0030. (800) 827-5722; (202) 205-6665. This pamphlet explores creative selling techniques that can benefit any business.

 Five Steps to Successful Selling, by Zig Ziglar, 81 min., $69.95. Nightingale Conant, 7300 N. Lehigh Ave., Niles, IL 60714. (800) 525-9000 (orders); (800) 323-3938; (708) 647-7145 (fax). Master motivator Zig Ziglar presents five basic steps that cover every aspect of the selling process, showing viewers how to create satisfied customers and a satisfying income for themselves.

Guerrilla Selling, by Jay Conrad Levinson, Bill Gallagher, & Orvel Ray Wilson, ©1992, 288 pp., ISBN: 0-395-57820-5, $9.95. Houghton Mifflin Company, Wayside Rd., Burlington, MA 01803. (800) 225-3362. Expanding on his guerrilla philosophy, Levinson presents unconventional sales ideas that are easy, accessible, and effective for entrepreneurs at every level and in every type of business.

 How To Master the Art of Selling Anything, by Tom Hopkins, $165.00. CareerTrack, 3085 Center Green Dr., Boulder, CO 80301-5408. (800) 334-1018; (800) 832-9489 (fax). These tapes feature Tom Hopkins, master salesman and author of several business books, sharing his approach to making sales and improving the productivity of your own business.

 How to Sell More Than 75% of Your Freelance Writing, by Gordon Burgett, ©1994, 240 pp., ISBN: 1-55958-035-6, $12.95. Prima Publishing, Inc., PO Box 1260, Rocklin, CA 95677-1260. (916) 632-7400; (916) 632-7668 (fax). This book is directed at writers of all kinds and focuses on learning how to sell an article before it is written, and how to spin one idea into several well-paying articles.

  Is the Independent Sales Agent for You?, $0.50. U.S. Small Business Administration, SBA Publications, PO Box 30, Denver, CO 80201-0030. (800) 827-5722; (202) 205-6665. This pamphlet helps you decide if your business would benefit from a sales agent and provides tips on choosing the right one.

 Letters That Sell, by Edward W. Werz, ©1987, 163 pp., ISBN: 0-8092-4684-8, $9.95. Contemporary Books Inc., Two Prudential Plaza, Ste. 1200, Chicago, IL 60601. (312) 540-4500; (312) 540-4657 (fax). A collection of 90 easy-to-use sample letters covering every business situation, from direct-sell to customer service, with marginal notes to assist readers in tailoring them to specific needs.

No B.S. Sales Success, by Dan Kennedy, ©1994, 176 pp., ISBN: 0-88908-769-5, $8.95. Self-Counsel Press, Inc., 1704 N. State St., Bellingham, WA 98225. (800) 663-3007; (206) 676-4530; (206) 676-4549 (fax). Pragmatic advice from the "Professor of Harsh Reality" on what selling is really all about: selling yourself.

Prospecting and Networking for Qualified Sales Leads, by Mark Victor Hansen, 94 min., $79.95. CareerTrack, 3085 Center Green Dr., Boulder, CO 80301-5408. (800) 334-1018; (800) 832-9489 (fax). This video program explains some of the complexities involved in making sales and offers a variety of solutions for making the process easier, more profitable, and more enjoyable.

 Relationship Selling, by Karen Johnston and Jean Withers, ©1992, 120 pp., ISBN: 0-88908-529-3, $12.95. Self-Counsel Press, Inc., 1704 N. State St., Bellingham, WA 98225. (800) 663-3007; (206) 676-4530; (206) 676-4549 (fax). This book is for people who don't think of themselves as salespeople, and don't want to. It focuses on building trust and serving customers' needs as the primary tools to selling your service.

 Retailing Today, monthly, $48.00/yr. Robert Kahn & Associates, PO Box 249, Lafayette, CA 94549. (510) 254-4434; (510) 284-5612 (fax). This publication provides general information about the retail industry, comments on current trends, customer service, and company policy.

 S.P.I.N. Selling, by Neil Rackham, ©1988, 224 pp., ISBN: 0-07-051113-6, $22.95. McGraw-Hill, Inc., 11 W. 19th St., New York, NY 10011. (800) 822-8158. Details on an effective sales method developed from research studies of 35,000 sales calls. The SPIN approach focuses on Situation, Problem, Implication, and Need—and how to generate sales success.

 Sales Magic, by Steve Bryant, ©1992, 151 pp., ISBN: 0-936262-24-9, $12.95. Amherst Media, PO Box 586, Amherst, NY 14226. (716) 874-4450. Tips and techniques on delivering powerful sales presentations, from a leading sales expert who is a show host on the QVC network. Focuses on highlighting the "benefit of the benefit" to create loyal customers and win more sales.

 Secrets of the World's Top Sales Performers, by Christine Harvey, ©1990, 156 pp., ISBN: 1-55850-852-X, $6.95. Bob Adams, Inc., 260 Center St., Holbrook, MA 02343. (800) 872-5627; (617) 767-8100; (800) 872-5628 (fax). This book presents tips, advice and insights on sales success from top sales professionals.

Sell Your Way to the Top, by Zig Ziglar, $59.95. Nightingale Conant, 7300 N. Lehigh Ave., Niles, IL 60714. (800) 525-9000 (orders); (800) 323-3938; (708) 647-7145 (fax). This set of six audiotapes is a high-energy, no-holds-barred look at selling, including Ziglar's 12 keys to successful selling plus 44 winning techniques for closing sales.

 Selling the Dream, by Guy Kawasaki, ©1991, 320 pp., ISBN: 0-06-092212-5, $10.00. HarperBusiness, 10 East 53rd St., New York, NY 10022-5299. (800) 982-4377; (212) 207-7000; (800) 822-4090 (fax). The former director of software marketing for Apple Computer and member of the original Macintosh computer team presents an innovative approach to sales, marketing, and management called evangelism—using fervor, zeal, guts, and cunning to mobilize your customers and staff into becoming as passionate about a cause as you are.

 Selling: The Mother of All Enterprise, by William H. Blades, ©1994, 152 pp., ISBN: 0-9624798-7-X, $12.95. Marketing Methods Press, 2811 N. 7th Ave., Phoenix, AZ 85007. (800) 745-5047. An internationally recognized sales trainer shares tips and tactics to improve selling skills without resorting to high pressure closes or silly gimmicks. Shows how to develop a strategy that focuses on an organized, efficient approach that emphasizes doing the little things in the selling process that produce big results.

 Selling to VITO, by Anthony Parinello, ©1994, 276 pp., ISBN: 1-55850-386-2, $10.95. Bob Adams, Inc., 260 Center St., Holbrook, MA 02343. (800) 872-5627; (617) 767-8100; (800) 872-5628 (fax). A book which will help you sell to the VITO (very important top officer) of many companies. Improve your sales and save the time you would spend asking questions of the wrong people.

 Selling Your Ideas, by Mike McCaffrey, $99.95. Center for Video Education, PO Box 635, North White Plains, NY 10603. (800) 621-0043; (914) 428-0180 (fax). This workshop is predicated on the establishment of a need or want—at the right time and in the best way—so that you can connect with your customers. It shows how to create specific objectives for each sales presentation, and how to follow through to achieve them. Includes 24-page manual.

Seven Pillars of Sales Success, by Jonathan Evetts, ©1990, 192 pp., ISBN: 0-8069-7204-1, $12.95. Sterling Publishing Co., Inc., 387 Park Ave. South, New York, NY 10016-8810. (800) 367-9692; (212) 532-7160; (800) 542-7567 (fax). This informative book offers minute-by-minute, word-for-word solutions for every part of the selling process, from first moments to closing the deal. Includes advice and strategies on listening, setting up your pitch, using testimonials, ways to polish telephone presentations, and more.

 Smart Salespeople Sometimes Wear Plaid, by Barry Graham Munro, ©1994, 304 pp., ISBN: 1-55958-422-X, $12.95. Prima Publishing, PO Box 1260, Rocklin, CA 95677-1260. (916) 632-7400; (916) 632-7668 (fax). Used as a sales tool at leading companies, this book covers issues such as attitude, competition, organization, presentation, and closing the sale.

 Soft Sell: The New Art of Selling, Self-Empowerment, and Persuasion, by Tim Connor, ©1994, 224 pp., ISBN: 0942061-64-0, $9.95. Sourcebooks, PO Box 372, Naperville, IL 60566. (800) SBS-8866; (708) 961-3900. This book presents a new approach to selling, one that stresses motivation, relationship-building, communication, and self-image psychology to boost your personal sales success.

 Solution Selling: A Grid Science Approach, by Robert R. Blake & Rachel K. McKee, ©1994, 192 pp., ISBN: 0-88415-161-1, $29.95. Gulf Publishing Company, PO Box 2608, Houston, TX 77252-2608. (713) 520-4444; (713) 525-4647 (fax). This book uses an innovative grid diagram approach to plan targets and strategies for the professional who wants to increase sales effectiveness.

Solutions, Not Sales

By focusing on offering solutions to customer problems in your sales process, you change the selling relationship. Instead of standing across from customers stating, "Here's a product or service I'm selling," you're standing next to them explaining, "Here's how we can solve your problem together." It's a subtle but powerful shift that can have a dramatic impact on your sales success.

Successful Cold Call Selling, by Lee Boyan, ©1989, 225 pp., ISBN: 0-8144-7718-6, $16.95. AMACOM Books, PO Box 1026, Saranac Lake, NY 12983. (800) 262-9699; (518) 891-3653 (fax). More than 100 ideas, scripts and examples from one of the nation's foremost sales trainers.

 The Competitive Advantage, by James F. Moran, monthly, ISSN: 0886-1994, $99.00/yr. Moran Publishing Company, PO Box 10828, Portland, OR 97210. (800) 722-9221; (503) 274-2953; (503) 274-4349 (fax). This monthly newsletter for sales and marketing professionals highlights professional tips for maximizing time, energy, and money gathered from leading business books and magazines. Discounts for multiple subscriptions are available.

 The Greatest Salesman in the World, by Og Mandino, ©1968, 112 pp., ISBN: 0-553-27757-X, $4.99. Bantam Books, Inc., 1540 Broadway, New York, NY 10036. (800) 323-9872; (212) 354-6500. This best-selling inspirational classic teaches sales principles through the story of ten ancient scrolls that contain selling wisdom.

 The "I Hate Selling" Book, by Allan Boress, ©1994, 224 pp., ISBN: 0-8144-0245-3, $24.95. AMACOM Books, PO Box 1026, Saranac Lake, NY 12983. (800) 262-9699; (518) 891-3653 (fax). Business-building advice for consultants, accountants, attorneys, and other professionals.

 The Joy of Selling, by J.T. Auer, ©1993, 180 pp., ISBN: 1-55850-011-1, $7.95. Bob Adams, Inc., 260 Center St., Holbrook, MA 02343. (800) 872-5627; (617) 767-8100; (800) 872-5628 (fax). Learn (or relearn!) the basics of good selling in order to maintain a winning edge.

 The Psychology of Selling, by Brian Tracy, $70.00. Brian Tracy International, 462 Stevens Ave., Suite 202, Solana Beach, CA 92075. (800) 542-4252; (619) 481-2977; (619) 481-2445 (fax). This series of six audiotapes and workbook includes a collection of comprehensive techniques, secrets, and action-oriented ideas on how to join the top 10% of all salespeople.

 The Selling Starts When the Customer Says No, by Richard S. Seelye & O. Willliam Moody, ©1993, 250 pp., ISBN: 1-55738-446-0, $21.95. Probus Publishing, Inc., 1925 N. Clyburn Ave. #401, Chicago, IL 60614. (800) PROBUS-1; (312) 868-6250 (fax). The 12 toughest sells and how to overcome them.

Twenty-Five Sales Habits of Highly Successful Salespeople, by Stephan Schiffman, ©1991, 144 pp., ISBN: 0-685-50188-4, $5.95. Bob Adams, Inc., 260 Center St., Holbrook, MA 02343. (800) 872-5627; (617) 767-8100; (800) 872-5628 (fax). Schiffman's 25 simple "sales keys" don't require large investments of energy or time—but they can pay enormous dividends when they become second nature.

 Words That Sell, by Richard Bayan, ©1984, 127 pp., ISBN: 0-8092-4799-2, $13.95. Contemporary Books, Inc., Two Prudential Plaza, Ste. 1200, Chicago, IL 60601. (312) 540-4500; (312) 540-4657 (fax). A comprehensive list of more than 2,500 high-powered words, phrases, and slogans, arranged by category, that can enhance sales materials.

Starting a Business

See also Business Planning; Choosing a Business; General Business Information; Managing Your Business

The steps taken in the early stages of any business are like laying the foundation of a high-rise building. If the base is level and solid, the walls can soar to great heights. If, however, the construction is done with poor planning or shoddy workmanship, small errors will become amplified and problems will emerge as the building rises. So it is, too, with beginning a business. Preparation pays off and ensures that the business is sound and can reach the high-rise heights of success.

The resources featured here all focus on the critical early phases of a company. Use them to guide you through the maze of start-up details and gain the confidence that your business adventure is off to a great launch.

Engineering Your Start-Up: A Guide for the High-Tech Entrepreneur, by Michael L. Baird, ©1992, 294 pp., ISBN: 0-912045-48-5, $19.95. Professional Publications, Inc., 1250 5th Ave., Belmont, CA 94002. (415) 593-9119. This book provides a no-nonsense approach to the problems and issues involved in starting a high-technology company in the 1990s. Covers financing, planning, management, and business strategy.

Entrepreneur Magazine Group's Business Start-Up Guide Series, $79.50. Entrepreneur Magazine Group, 2392 Morse Ave., PO Box 57050, Irvine, CA 92619-7050. (800) 421-2300; (714) 851-9088 (fax). The Entrepreneur Magazine Group offers a series of more than 180 different start-up guides for specific businesses, such as mail order, gift basket services, information brokerage, desktop publishing, event planning, medical claims processing, janitorial service, and others. Each guide features step-by-step details in a 3-ring binder, interactive financial templates on disk, and membership in the American Entrepreneur Association.

Getting Into Business Guides, by Dan Kennedy, ©1991, 456 pp., ISBN: 0-88908-980-9, $29.95. Self-Counsel Press, Inc., 1704 N. State St., Bellingham, WA 98225. (800) 663-3007; (206) 676-4530; (206) 676-4549 (fax). This series of four books (also available individually) is designed to help prospective entrepreneurs through the challenging start-up stages. Titles include: *Getting Ready, Getting Started, Getting Money, and Getting Sales.*

 How to Be a Weekend Entrepreneur, by Susan Ratliff, ©1991, 112 pp., ISBN: 0-9624798-2-9, $9.95. Marketing Methods Press, 2811 N. 7th Ave., Phoenix, AZ 85007. (800) 745-5047. A step-by-step guide to building a profitable weekend business by exhibiting and selling at craft fairs and trade shows. Includes checklists and illustrations to help both beginners and veterans.

 How to Become Successfully Self-Employed, by Brian R. Smith, ©1993, 304 pp., ISBN: 1-55850-248-3, $9.95. Bob Adams, Inc., 260 Center St., Holbrook, MA 02343. (800) 872-5627; (617) 767-8100; (800) 872-5628 (fax). This comprehensive guide helps streamline the decision-making process and removes the myths associated with self-employment.

 How to Bring a Product to Market for Less than $5,000, by Don Debalak, ©1994, 288 pp., ISBN: 0-471-53279-7, $17.95. John Wiley & Sons, Inc., 605 Third Ave., New York, NY 10158-0012. (800) CALL-WILEY; (212) 850-6000. Details on developing a product-based business on a limited budget, including testing your product in the marketplace, how to market your product to keep costs low, and how to prepare a business plan to get financing.

 How to Really Start Your Own Business, 2 hrs., $59.95. Inc. Business Resources, 350 N. Pennsylvania Ave., PO Box 1365, Wilkes-Barre, PA 13703-1365. (800) 468-0800 x4760; (717) 822-8899. This video features an all-star team of entrepreneurs sharing their thoughts on starting and growing a business, including getting the idea, trusting your gut, and going for it. Humorous and revealing personal stories show how these entrepreneurs turned their dreams into reality.

How to Start a Business Without Quitting Your Job, by Philip Holland, ©l994, 192 pp., ISBN: 0-89815-449-9, $9.95. Ten Speed Press, PO Box 7123, Berkeley, CA 94707. (800) 841-BOOK; (510) 845-8414; (510) 524-1052 (fax). The moonlighting entrepreneur's guide to launching a business while working for someone else.

 How to Start and Run a Small Company, 82 min., $59.95. Inc. Business Resources, 350 N. Pennsylvania Ave., PO Box 1365, Wilkes-Barre, PA 18703-1365. (800) 468-0800 x4760; (717) 822-8899. This is a subscription series of four videos featuring in-depth interviews with entrepreneurs discussing key issues facing small business owners. Parts 2, 3, and 4 are each $39.95 and are shipped every 90 days.

 How to Start and Succeed in Your Own Business, by Brian Tracy, $60.00. Brian Tracy International, 462 Stevens Ave., Suite 202, Solana Beach, CA 92075. (800) 542-4252; (619) 481-2977; (619) 481-2445 (fax). This series of six audiotapes and a workbook focuses on key ingredients for starting, managing, or turning around a small business, including establishing a solid foundation, strategic marketing, and facing the challenges of leadership.

 How to Start, Finance, & Manage Your Own Small Business, by Joseph R. Mancuso, ©1993, ISBN: 0-679-74639-0, $45.00. Random House, Inc., 201 E. 50th Street, New York, NY 10022. (800) 726-0600; (212) 751-2600. This book/disk package offers advice on building an entrepreneurial team, finding financial resources, building management skills, and planning a small business. It features Andrew Tobias' *Managing Your Money* software.

 How to Start, Run, and Stay in Business, by Gregory F. Kishel, ©1993, 240 pp., $12.95. John Wiley & Sons, Inc., 605 Third Ave., New York, NY 10158-0012. (800) CALL-WILEY; (212) 850-6000. This guide offers down-to-earth advice on every aspect of starting and running a business in an interactive handbook format. It takes you step-by-step through each decision, from accounting and advertising to inventory and staffing.

 New Business Opportunities, by Rieva Lesonsky, Ed., monthly, $11.97/yr. Entrepreneur, Inc., 2392 Morse Ave., Irvine, CA 92714. (714) 261-2083. Produced by the same company as *Entrepreneur* magazine, this publication offers advice and ideas for those exploring the start-up of a new business.

Nobody Gets Rich Working for Somebody Else, by Roger Fritz, ©1993, 175 pp., ISBN: 1-879590-19-4, $15.95. Crisp Publications, 1200 Hamilton Ct., Menlo Park, CA 94025. (415) 323-6100; (415) 323-5800 (fax). Numerous case studies, worksheets, checklists, examples, and questions provide guidance for start-up business strategies and success.

 Start Your Business: A Beginner's Guide, by Oasis Press, ©1993, 200 pp., ISBN: 1-55571-198-7, $8.95. Oasis Press, 300 N. Valley Dr., Grants Pass, OR 97526. (800) 228-2275; (503) 479-9464; (503) 476-1479 (fax). A user-friendly workbook designed to help beginning business owners organize and track all the activities necessary for a strong business launch. Numerous checklists and worksheets.

 Start Your New Business Now!, by Arlene Appelbaum, ©1994, ISBN: 1-883678-52-8, $39.95. Devine Multi-Media Publishing, Inc., 346 Chester St., St. Paul, MN 55107. (612) 699-5436; (612) 221-9722 (fax). This multimedia package includes a 110-page book, a 25-minute video, a 45-minute audiotape, worksheets, a filing system, and software, all on the topic of small business start-up. The company's philosophy is to offer an integrated educational experience through a variety of media, allowing each user to adapt the program to his or her personal learning style. Software is available for Windows-based computers only.

 Start Your Own Business for $1,000 or Less, by Will Davis, ©1994, 280 pp., ISBN: 0-936894-70-9, $17.95. Upstart Publishing Co., Inc., 12 Portland St., Dover, NH 03820. (800) 235-8866; (603) 749-5071; (603) 742-9121 (fax). Davis shows how to start a "mini-business"—one that minimizes the experience required, the start-up funding needed, and the paperwork, debt, and risk.

 Start-Up: An Entrepreneur's Guide to Launching and Managing a New Business, by William J. Stoltz, ©1994, 288 pp., ISBN: 1-56414-092-X, $16.95. Career Press, 180 Fifth Ave., PO Box 34, Hawthorne, NJ 07507. (800) CAREER-1; (201) 427-0229; (201) 427-2037 (fax). This comprehensive, concise guide is designed for anyone who is ready to launch a new business or individuals who have started a business in the past few years. Includes sample business plans.

Where to Begin?

When faced with a bewildering number of start-up activities, many entrepreneurial newcomers quickly become overwhelmed. Some, not knowing what to do first, simply freeze and do nothing —and their businesses fizzle before they've begun.

It's important to realize that there is no single "right" way to launch a business. Yes, there are some steps that must proceed in a certain order, such as obtaining legal business papers before opening a business checking account. But no magic domino must fall to set a chain of events in motion. In fact, many start-up tasks are tackled best in tandem, since they feed the business momentum. So, take a deep breath and dive in. Let start-up resources guide you, and know that each business birth is unique.

Starting and Operating a Business in... (series), $21.95. Oasis Press, 300 N. Valley Dr., Grants Pass, OR 97526. (800) 228-2275; (503) 479-9464; (503) 476-1479 (fax). This series presents a one-stop resource to current federal and state laws and regulations that affect businesses. It guides new entrepreneurs in launching a business, and keeps seasoned owners up to date on changing laws. Includes checklists and worksheets. Available for every state in the United States, plus the District of Columbia. Also available in binder workbook format.

Starting on a Shoestring, by Arnold S. Goldstein, ©1991, 284 pp., ISBN: 0-471-52455-7, $14.95. John Wiley & Sons, Inc., 605 Third Ave., New York, NY 10158-0012. (800) CALL-WILEY; (212) 850-6000; (212) 850-8641 (fax). How to plan and begin operating a small business with a very modest budget.

The Closet Entrepreneur, by Neil Balter & Carrie Shook, ©1994, 224 pp., ISBN: 1-56414-138-1, $14.95. Career Press, 180 Fifth Ave., PO Box 34, Hawthorne, NJ 07507. (800) CAREER-1; (201) 427-2037 (fax). The founder of the California Closet Company shares his thoughts on how to start a successful business with little or no money.

The Mid-Career Entrepreneur, by Joseph R. Mancuso, ©1993, 235 pp., ISBN: 0-7931-0719-9, $17.95. Dearborn Trade, 520 N. Dearborn St., Chicago, IL 60610-4354. (800) 245-2665; (312) 836-4400; (312) 836-1021 (fax). Mancuso, a longtime entrepreneur and respected business consultant, explores the experience of starting a business in mid-career from three different angles: starting a new business from scratch; buying a franchise; and acquiring a business someone else has already started.

 The Start Up Guide: A One-Year Plan for Entrepreneurs, by David H. Bangs, Jr., ©1994, 192 pp., ISBN: 0-936894-57-1, $19.95. Upstart Publishing Co., Inc., 12 Portland St., Dover, NH 03820. (800) 235-8866; (603) 749-5071; (603) 742-9121 (fax). This book is designed as a first-year guide to starting a successful business for individuals with little or no formal training. The author provides a realistic timetable for covering all the basics before opening a new business.

 Winning the Entrepreneurial Game, by David E. Rye, ©1994, 300 pp., ISBN: 1-55850-345-5, $10.95. Bob Adams, Inc., 260 Center St., Holbrook, MA 02343. (800) 872-5627; (617) 767-8100; (800) 872-5628 (fax). This guide answers the many questions entrepreneurs face when starting a new venture, from how to finance it to what to do to survive tough times.

 You Can Start Your Own Business, by Arnold Sanow & Jeff Davidson, ©1991, 212 pp., ISBN: 0-925052-02-7, $14.95. The Business Source, Inc., 2810 Glad Vale Way, Vienna, VA 22181. (703) 255-3133. This book presents an overview of what you need to know to start a business, from the characteristics of winning entrepreneurs to step-by-step strategies for making it a success. The text is lively, with plenty of examples and graphics that keep your interest and make important information easy to grasp. Forms, checklists, and agreements are also included.

Taxes

See also Financial Matters; Government Resources

Taxes are a fact of life of any small business. Savvy entrepreneurs know, however, that working within the limits of tax laws can be a creative process that profoundly affects a company's profits. Even if you rely on outside financial professionals, understanding tax matters increases the control—and chances for success—you can exert over your business's future. The following resources can guide you in learning the full extent of your rights as a taxpayer, including ways to maximize deductions to achieve financial benefits and how to incorporate year-round tax planning into your business activities.

IRS Information and Programs

 Small Business Tax Education Program (STEP) Brochure, Internal Revenue Service, (800) TAX-FORM (829-3676). Through a unique partnership between the IRS and many community and junior colleges, universities, and business associations across the country, small business owners have an opportunity to learn about taxes. Educational programs often are offered in conjunction with a variety of federal and state agencies, providing small business owners with one-stop assistance. Contact your local IRS office to find out about other tax services available for small businesses, such as Community Outreach Tax Education. For details, see IRS Publication 910, *Guide to Free Tax Services.*

 Your Business Tax Kit (YBTK), Internal Revenue Service, (800) TAX-FORM (829-3676). The IRS has compiled a collection of tax-related publications and forms into a single kit to assist new business owners in understanding their tax responsibilities. Individual publications are also available upon request (see the separate listings on the next page).

IRS Tax Forms

The following business-related tax publications and forms can be obtained free from the IRS by calling (800) TAX-FORM (829-3676).

Publication 334, *Tax Guide for Small Business*

Publication 463, *Travel, Entertainment and Gift Expenses*

Publication 505, *Tax Withholding and Estimated Tax*

Publication 508, *Taxable and Non-Taxable Income*

Publication 529, *Miscellaneous Deductions*

Publication 533, *Self-Employment Tax*

Publication 535, *Business Expenses*

Publication 538, *Accounting Periods and Methods*

Publication 541, *Tax Information on Partnerships*

Publication 542, *Tax Information on Corporations*

Publication 544, *Sales and Other Dispositions of Assets*

Publication 551, *Basis of Assets*

Publication 552, *Recordkeeping for Individuals*

Publication 560, *Retirement Plans for the Self-Employed*

Publication 583, *Taxpayers Starting a Business*

Publication 587, *Business Use of Your Home*

Publication 589, *Tax Information on S Corporations*

Publication 590, *Individual Retirement for Direct Sellers*

Publication 911, *Tax Information for Direct Sellers*

Publication 917, *Business Use of a Car*

Publication 937, *Employment Taxes and Information Returns*

Publication 946, *How to Begin Depreciating Your Property*

Tax Information Resources

Being Self-Employed, by Holmes F. Crouch, ©1994, 224 pp., ISBN: 0-944817-06-8, $16.95. Allyear Tax Guides, 20484 Glen Brae Dr., Saratoga, CA 95070. (408) 867-2628. Written by a 20-year tax specialist who has prepared nearly 9,000 returns, this book highlights ways to keep federal, state, and self-employment taxes to a minimum.

Confessions of a Tax Accountant, by Noelle Allen, ©1993, 136 pp., ISBN: 1-884221-00-9, $6.95. Canyon View Institute, 11475 Canyon View Circle, Cupertino, CA 95014. (800) 252-5007; (408) 252-1367; (408) 252-5624 (fax). In her practice as a CPA, Noelle Allen has encountered numerous "creative" approaches to tax deductions. In this lighthearted book, she has collected the most outrageous, hilarious, and totally true stories. Since entrepreneurs are by nature inventive individuals, many of the stories involve innovative uses of the IRS Schedule C (Profit or Loss from a Business).

 Dealing with the IRS, by Scott Miller & Thomas Guy, ©1992, 70 pp., ISBN: 0-9631941-0-0, $8.95. Creek Bend Publishing Company, 410 Seafarer Dr., Carolina Beach, NC 28428-4625. This concise book provides insights into dealing effectively and efficiently with the IRS.

 Disagreeing with the IRS, by Holmes F. Crouch, ©1993, 224 pp., ISBN: 0-944817-16-5, $16.95. Allyear Tax Guides, 20484 Glen Brae Dr., Saratoga, CA 95070. (408) 867-2628. An experienced tax preparer who has represented hundreds of taxpayers before the IRS presents all the proper corrective actions you can take against erroneous assertions by the IRS. Includes details on appealing audit results, claiming refunds, the pros and cons of Tax Court litigation, directing complaints to your Congressperson, and more.

 Kiplinger's Sure Ways to Cut Your Taxes, by Kevin McCormally, ©1995, 476 pp., ISBN: 0-938721-36-4, $13.95. Kiplinger Books & Tapes, 1729 H Street NW, Washington, DC 20006. (800) 462-6420; (202) 887-6431. Details on how to take advantage of opportunities to make the tax law work for you, including year-round planning and how to survive an audit. Features real-life tax scenarios in question-and-answer format, with the primary focus on personal finance.

Stand Up to the IRS, by Frederick Daily, ©1994, ISBN: 0-87337-240-9, $21.95. Nolo Press, 950 Parker St., Berkeley, CA 94710. (800) 955-4775; (510) 549-1976; (800) 645-0895 (fax). Full of "insider" tips from a seasoned tax attorney, this book provides advice on how to prepare and handle an IRS audit successfully. It includes techniques on how to challenge a tax bill, appeal an IRS decision, avoid property seizures, get a long-term payment plan for a tax bill, and how to represent yourself in Tax Court.

Starting Your Business, by Holmes F. Crouch, ©1993, 224 pp., ISBN: 0-944817-10-6, $16.95. Allyear Tax Guides, 20484 Glen Brae Dr., Saratoga, CA 95070. (408) 867-2628. A professional tax consultant with more than 20 years experience preparing small business returns covers the pros, cons, and tax forms of choosing a proprietorship, partnership, or corporation when launching your business. Includes an in-depth synopsis on determining the cost of goods and services, depreciation, operating expenses, business auto deductions, and more.

 Tax Loopholes, by Martin Edelston, $35.00. Boardroom Classics, PO Box 11401, Des Moines, IA 50336-1401. (800) 274-5611. More than 1,200 neglected tax strategies that are absolutely legal, ranging from legal and travel expenses to daily business deductions.

 Tax Planning for the One-Person Business, by James Bucheister, ©1994, 135 pp., $14.95. Rayve Productions, Inc., PO Box 726, Windsor, CA 95492. (800) 852-4890; (707) 838-2220 (fax). This easy-to-understand guide shows you how current tax laws can benefit your solo business. It covers tax-related topics such as recordkeeping requirements, hobby loss provisions, independent contractor tax issues, and retirement benefits.

Timing for Tax Benefits

As the final months of each year approach, it's not unusual for the telephone lines to be buzzing between solo entrepreneurs as they project their annual tax bill and discuss potential equipment purchases to make before December 31. These tax-savvy business owners know that investments made in office equipment can perform double duty: add value to their businesses while at the same time reduce their tax liability.

Of course, investing in equipment that brings marginal productivity gains to your operations is false economy. Purchases must also be used exclusively for business purposes. Entrepreneurs who reap the greatest benefits understand that tax planning is a year-round activity—best guided by a tax professional.

Tax Savvy for Small Business, by Frederick W. Daily, ©1994, 320 pp., ISBN: 0-87337-262-X, $26.95. Nolo Press, 950 Parker St., Berkeley, CA 94710. (800) 955-4775; (510) 549-1976; (800) 645-0895 (fax). This book tells business owners what they need to know about federal taxes and how to make the best decisions for their business, maximize profits, and stay out of trouble in dealing with the IRS.

 Taxes for the Self-Employed, by Noelle Allen, ©1993, 3 hrs., ISBN: 1-884221-01-7, $49.95. Canyon View Institute, 11475 Canyon View Circle, Cupertino, CA 95014. (800) 252-5007; (408) 252-1367; (408) 252-5624 (fax). In this audiotape program, former IRS auditor and successful CPA Noelle Allen takes the subject of taxes and makes it clear—and entertaining! Covers the details of deductions, filing requirements, independent contractor rules, a Schedule C audit, and more. Includes three one-hour audiotapes and a 70-page workbook.

 The Successful Audit, by Felix Pomeranz, ©1991, 350 pp., ISBN: 1-55623-391-4, $65.00. Irwin Professional Publishing, Inc., 1333 Burr Ridge Pkwy., Burr Ridge, IL 60521. (800) 634-3961; (708) 789-4000. This book provides readers with tips that will help them facilitate and survive an audit by the IRS.

 Top Tax Saving Ideas for Today's Small Business, by Thomas J. Stemmy, ©1994, 312 pp., ISBN: 1-55571-313-0, $14.95. Oasis Press, 300 N. Valley Dr., Grants Pass, OR 97526. (800) 228-2275; (503) 479-9464; (503) 476-1479 (fax). Solutions and strategies for effective tax planning, including tips on choosing the appropriate business structure, current tax saving trends, maximizing deductions, recordkeeping techniques, and more.

 Winning Your Audit, by Holmes F. Crouch, ©1993, 224 pp., ISBN: 0-944817-15-7, $16.95. Allyear Tax Guides, 20484 Glen Brae Dr., Saratoga, CA 95070. (408) 867-2628. An experienced tax preparer who has represented more than 500 taxpayers before the IRS explains the selection process for audits, the various types of audits, your rights as an auditee, the importance of good preparation, and more.

Time Management

See also Managing Your Business; Office Design and Operation

The difference between successful independents and their failed counterparts often is not a matter of money, luck, or talent. What successful solo entrepreneurs know is the value of time and how to use it effectively. Everyone is given the same amount of this important ingredient. Those who reach the top realize that small actions—completed daily—build into patterns of accomplishment over weeks, months, years, and a business lifetime. Let the resources featured here empower you to focus your direction, prioritize your tasks, and get the most out of every single day.

 How to Gain an Extra Hour Every Day, by Ray Josephs, ©1992, 350 pp., ISBN: 0-452-26783-8, $11.00. Dutton, 120 Woodbine St., Bergenfield, NJ 07621. (800) 253-6476. This book focuses on time management skills and teaches readers to use the day more efficiently.

 How to Get Control of Your Time and Your Life, by Alan Lakein, ©1973, 160 pp., ISBN: 0-451-16772-4, $4.99. Penguin Group, 120 Woodbine St., Bergenfield, NJ 07621. (800) 253-6476. Lakein, a guru of time management, has written this practical, no-nonsense guide to help individuals manage personal and business time. He offers simple, effective techniques on how to set short-term goals, establish priorities, defeat unpleasant tasks, and ways to work smarter, not harder.

  How to Get Things Done, 48 min., $95.00. Fred Pryor Seminars, 2000 Shawnee Mission Pkwy., Shawnee Mission, KS 66205. (800) 938-6330; (913) 722-8580 (fax). This program includes a video, audiotape, and book that focus on fresh new ideas and techniques on mastering time, avoiding procrastination, and achieving meaningful goals.

How to Manage Priorities and Meet Deadlines Seminar, 1 day, $59.00. Fred Pryor Seminars, 2000 Shawnee Mission Pkwy., Shawnee Mission, KS 66205. (800) 938-6330; (913) 722-8580 (fax). This intensive seminar helps you gain control over your time and prioritize the many things that lie before you. Participants learn to create a personalized action plan and organize their schedule to suit their natural energy cycles. Also available on six audiotapes with a workbook for $59.95.

If You Haven't Got the Time To Do it Right, When Will You Find the Time to Do it Over?, by Jeffrey J. Mayer, ©1990, 157 pp., ISBN: 0-671-73364-8, $9.00. Fireside, Simon & Schuster Bldg., Rockefeller Center, 1230 Avenue of the Americas, New York, NY 10020. (800) 223-2336; (212) 698-7000. A collection of ideas and strategies on making your desk and your day work for you, from a popular authority on time management.

Manage Your Time, Your Work, Yourself, by Merill E. & Donna N. Douglass, ©1993, 176 pp., ISBN: 0-8144-7825-5, $15.95. AMACOM Books, PO Box 1026, Saranac Lake, NY 12983. (800) 262-9699; (518) 891-3653 (fax). A guide to maximizing your energy and efforts in both personal and business settings.

Managing Your Time and Priorities, by Reich Gardner, $69.95. SkillPath, Inc., 6900 Squibb Rd., PO Box 2768, Mission, KS 66201-2768. (800) 873-7545; (913) 677-3200; (913) 362-4241 (fax). This fast-paced training video teaches viewers how to gain control of their workday, get organized, and increase their productivity.

Personal Time Management, by Brian Tracy, 1 hr., $60.00. Brian Tracy International, 462 Stevens Ave., Suite 202, Solana Beach, CA 92075. (800) 542-4252; (619) 481-2977; (619) 481-2445 (fax). In this video Brian Tracy presents his practical advice for overcoming procrastination and teaches viewers how to create a blueprint for their days that will benefit them and their work.

Practical Time Management, by Bradley C. McRae, ©1992, 144 pp., ISBN: 0-88908-281-2, $7.95. Self-Counsel Press, Inc., 1704 N. State St., Bellingham, WA 98225. (800) 663-3007; (206) 676-4530; (206) 676-4549 (fax). This book is designed to help the overly busy person take charge of their tasks, prioritize, and manage time more effectively.

Practical Time Management, by Marion E. Haynes, ©1991, 138 pp., ISBN: 1-56052-018-3, $13.95. Crisp Publications, 1200 Hamilton Ct., Menlo Park, CA 94025. (415) 323-6100; (415) 323-5800 (fax). A guide to learning how to make the most out of each day and accomplish self-directed tasks.

Productivity Power: 250 Great Ideas for Being More Productive, by Jim Temme, ©1994, 185 pp., $15.95. SkillPath, Inc., 6900 Squibb Rd., PO Box 2768, Mission, KS 66201-2768. (800) 873-7545; (913) 677-3200; (913) 362-4241 (fax). This book is full of innovative and helpful ideas which will help you be more productive in your life and your work.

Seize the Day, by Danny Cox & John Hoover, ©1994, 224 pp., ISBN: 1-56414-134-9, $21.95. Career Press, 180 Fifth Ave., PO Box 34, Hawthorne, NJ 07507. (800) CAREER-1; (201) 427-2037 (fax). How to make high performance a regular, daily occurrence, from one of the nation's leading business speakers.

Setting Priorities and Meeting Deadlines Seminar, 1 day, $59.00. CareerTrack, 3085 Center Green Dr., Boulder, CO 80301-5408. (800) 334-1018; (800) 832-9489 (fax). In this seminar, participants learn to organize their time and energy better so that they can be more productive and have more time left for themselves.

Electronic Organization

A new category of computer technology called PIMs— Personal Information Managers—is making it a lot easier for solo entrepreneurs to maintain their appointment calendars, To-Do lists, contact lists, and address books. Available for all major computer systems and in every price range, these electronic assistants bring exceptional power to the desktop. The best programs have sophisticated integration capabilities. For example, a calendar entry that says "Lunch with Susan" automatically links to Susan's complete contact history, making it easy to review pending business details to discuss over lunch. Many PIMs also offer versatile printing options. Getting organized has never been simpler—or more fun.

Taking Control of Your Workday, by Dick Lohr, 4 hrs., $59.95. CareerTrack, 3085 Center Green Dr., Boulder, CO 80301-5408. (800) 334-1018; (800) 832-9489 (fax). This program teaches how to accomplish top-priority tasks without ignoring the demands of others. Also on video (3 volumes, 3.5 hrs.) for $199.95. Both formats come with 24-page workbook.

 TalKit, by Sherle Adams, 2 hrs., $29.95. Stimulus, Ten Oak Creek Dr., Ste. 1013, Buffalo Grove, IL 60089. (800) 566-1411; (708) 520-1411; (708) 520-1471 (fax). These two 60-minute cassettes are "idea-a-minute" tapes, filled with tips and techniques on managing your business and personal time more efficiently. Includes a booklet highlighting key points of the program.

 Up Your Productivity, by Kurt Hanks, ©1994, 100 pp., ISBN: 0-931961-49-1, $11.95. Crisp Publications, 1200 Hamilton Court, Menlo Park, CA 94025. (415) 323-6100; (415) 323-5800 (fax). A friendly, fun and practical book that teaches you how to motivate yourself and others to become more productive. Visual images help explain concepts at a glance.

 Where Did the Time Go?, by Ruth Klein, ©1994, 250 pp., ISBN: 1-55958-492-0, $10.95. Prima Publishing, PO Box 1260, Rocklin, CA 95677-1260. (916) 632-7400; (916) 632-7668 (fax). After polling women about their specific lifestyle goals, the author used the results to develop a practical three-part system to organize the hours women juggle between career, personal, and family needs.

 ## Time Management Systems

The following companies manufacture and market personal organizers and datebooks.

Day Runner, Inc.
(800) 635-5544

Rolodex Corporation
(800) 727-7656

Day-Timers, Inc.
(800) 225-5005

Time Design
(800) 637-9942

filofax
(800) 345-6798

Write Track
(800) 331-4159

Lefax
(800) 783-9590

Travel Resources

I f you've ever longed to have a directory of all the important telephone numbers you need to make your business travel plans, here is your dream come true. We've gathered toll-free telephone numbers for major hotels, car rental agencies, and airlines all in one convenient spot. Making travel arrangements can now be simpler and speedier. Don't you wish hustling through airports was this easy?

 Jobs for People Who Love to Travel, by Ron and Caryl Krannich, ©1993, 256 pp., ISBN: 0-942710-62-2, $12.95. Impact Publications, 9104 N. Manassas Dr., Manassas Park, VA 22111. (800) 462-6420; (703) 361-7300; (703) 335-9486 (fax). This book surveys hundreds of jobs in business and government which allow the individual to travel both internationally and locally.

 Savvy Business Travel, by Darryl Jenkins, ©1993, 307 pp., ISBN: 1-55623-752-9, $25.00. Irwin Professional Publishing, Inc., 1333 Burr Ridge Pkwy., Burr Ridge, IL 60521. (800) 634-3961; (708) 789-4000. This book provides advice in regard to safer, more economical, and stress-free business travel.

 ## Airlines

Air Canada
(800) 776-3000

Air France
(800) 237-2747

Alaska Airlines
(800) 426-0333

America West
(800) 235-9292

American Airlines
(800) 433-7300

British Airways
(800) 247-9297

Continental Airlines
(800) 525-0280

Delta Airlines
(800) 221-1212

Airlines *(continued)*

Japan Airlines
(800) 525-3663

Kiwi International Airlines
(800) 538-5494

Lufthansa
(800) 645-3880

Midwest Express
(800) 452-2022

Northwest Airlines
(800) 225-2525

Reno Air
(800) 736-6747

Southwest Airlines
(800) 435-9792

Trans World Airlines
(800) 221-2000

United Airlines
(800) 241-6522

USAir
(800) 428-4322

 ### Car Rental Agencies

Alamo
(800) 327-9633

Allstate
(800) 634-6186

Avis
(800) 331-1212

Budget
(800) 527-0700

Dollar
(800) 800-4000

Enterprise
(800) 325-8007

Hertz
(800) 654-3131

National
(800) 227-7368

Thrifty
(800) 367-2277

U-Save
(800) 438-2300

 ### Hotels

Adams Mark Hotels
(800) 231-5858

**Best Western
International, Inc.**
(800) 528-1234

Budgetel Inns
(800) 428-3438

Canadian Pacific Hotels
(800) 828-7447

Hotels *(continued)*

Choice Hotels International
(800) 424-6423

Clarion Hotels and Resorts
(800) 424-6423

Comfort Inns
(800) 424-6423

Courtyard by Marriot
(800) 321-2211

Days Inn
(800) 325-2525

Dillon Inns
(800) 253-7503

Doubletree, Inc.
(800) 528-0444

Downtowner/Passport Motor Inns
(800) 238-6161

Drury Inn
(800) 325-8300

Econo Lodges
(800) 424-6423

Embassy Suites
(800) 362-2779

Excel Inns of America
(800) 356-8013

Fairfield Inn
(800) 228-2800

Forté Hotels
(800) 225-5843

Four Seasons Hotels and Resorts
(800) 332-3442
(800) 268-6282 (Canada)

Friendship Inns
(800) 424-6423

Guest Quarters Suite Hotel
(800) 424-2900

Hampton Inns
(800) 426-7866

Harley Hotels
(800) 321-2323

Helmsley Hotels
(800) 221-4982

Hilton Hotels
(800) 445-8667

Holiday Inns, Inc.
(800) 465-4329

Homewood Suites
(800) 225-5466

Hospitality International
(800) 251-1962

Howard Johnson Lodges
(800) 654-2000

Hyatt Hotels Corporation
(800) 233-1234
(800) 228-9005 (Alaska)
(800) 228-3366 (Nebraska)

Inter-Continental Hotels
(800) 327-0200

Hotels *(continued)*

Knights Inn
(800) 772-7220
(800) 243-7220 (Canada)

LaQuinta Motor Inns, Inc.
(800) 531-5900

Loews Hotels
(800) 235-6397

Luxbury Hotels
(800) 252-7748

Marriot Hotels & Resorts
(800) 228-9290

Master Hosts
Meridien
(800) 534-4300

Omni Hotels
(800) 843-6664

Preferred Hotels
(800) 323-7500

Quality Inns
(800) 424-6423

Radisson Hotel
Corporation
(800) 333-3333

Ramada Inns, Inc.
(800) 228-2828

Red Carpet Inns
Red Lion Inns
(800) 547-8010

Red Roof Inns
(800) 843-7663

Regal Inns
(800) 851-8888
(800) 541-5005 (Canada)

Regent International
Hotels
(800) 545-4000

Residence Inn by Marriott
(800) 331-3131

Rodeway Inns
(800) 424-6423

Scottish Inns
Sheraton Hotels &
Motor Inns
(800) 325-3535

Shoney's Inn
(800) 222-2222

Sleep Inns
(800) 424-6423

Sonesta Hotels
(800) 766-3782

Stouffer Hotels-Inns
(800) 468-3571

Super 8 Motels, Inc.
(800) 848-8888

Susse Chalet
(800) 258-1980

The Ritz-Carlton
(800) 241-3333

Travelodge & Viscount
Hotels
(800) 255-3050

Hotels *(continued)*

Treadway Inns Corporation
(800) 873-2392

Vagabond Inns, Inc.
(800) 522-1555
(800) 468-2251 (Canada)

West Coast Hotels
(800) 426-0670

Westin Hotels & Resorts
(800) 228-3000

**Wyndham Hotels &
Resorts**
(800) 822-4200
(800) 631-4200 (Canada)

Trends

One of the strategic advantages of working solo is that a one-person business can stay flexible and responsive to changes in customer needs and requests. Independent entrepreneurs can add a new product or service, or shift a marketing approach, much more quickly than a larger business can. Using the resources in this section of the WORKING SOLO SOURCEBOOK, you can peek into the future and see what professionals think is on the economic, cultural, and business horizon. By staying aware of new trends and applying the futurists' insights on anticipated shifts in consumer interest, you can establish better plans for solo business growth.

 American Demographics, Brad Edmonsdon, Ed., monthly, $69.00/yr. American Demographics, PO Box 68, Ithaca, NY 14851-0068. (800) 828-1133; (607) 273-6343. This magazine presents insights, interpretations, and information regarding consumer buying behavior, trends, and other statistics.

 Future Now, by Joline Godfrey, ©1994, 256 pp., ISBN: 0-88730-659-4, $22.00. HarperBusiness, 10 East 53rd St., New York, NY 10022-5299. (800) 982-4377; (212) 207-7000. A respected businesswoman and author offers insights on how women entrepreneurs are creating new paradigms that will revolutionize the businesses of the future. Includes stories of successful entrepreneurs who understand the power of emphasizing the "human" aspects—allowing for head, heart, and hand—in creating a new vision for work and life.

 Future Vision, by the editors of *Research Alert,* ©1994, 256 pp., ISBN: 0942061-16-0, $12.95. Sourcebooks, PO Box 372, Naperville, IL 60566. (800) SBS-8866; (708) 961-3900. A guide to the 189 most important trends of the 1990s, and the impact they will have on your business and personal life.

John Naisbitt's Trend Letter, biweekly, $195.00/yr. The Global Network, 1101 30th St. NW, Ste. 130, Washington, DC 20007. (800) 368-0115; (202) 337-5960; (202) 333-5198 (fax). Written by a leading futurist, this newsletter focuses on advance business trend forecasting. Each issue presents news and trend information on business and industry, communications, marketing, managing, education, and a host of other areas.

 Megatrends 2000: Ten New Directions for the 1990's, by John Naisbitt & Patricia Aburdene, ©1990, 416 pp., ISBN: 0-380-70437-4, $5.95. Avon Books, 1350 Avenue of the Americas, New York, NY 10019. (800) 238-0658; (800) 6633-1607 (in TN); (212) 261-6800. Futurists and social forecasters Naisbitt & Aburdene, co-authors of the 1980s classic *Megatrends,* take a look at the trends that will define the 1990s, and what they will mean for individuals, nations, and the global economy.

 The Next Economy, by Paul Hawken, ©1983, 242 pp., ISBN: 0-345-31392-5, $3.50. Ballantine Books, 201 East 50th St., New York, NY 10022. (800) 733-3000; (212) 751-2600. Hawken presents his ideas about America's shift from a mass economy to an information economy, and what implications it has for both small and large businesses.

 The Popcorn Report, by Faith Popcorn, ©1991, 268 pp., ISBN: 0-88730-594-6, $11.00. HarperBusiness, 10 East 53rd St., New York, NY 10022-5299. (800) 982-4377; (212) 207-7000. One of the nation's leading trend forecasters shares her insights on the coming changes in America's lifestyle, and the impact it will have on businesses and individuals. Tips on how to chart the future of a business, how to capitalize on new trends, and the coming changes in marketing.

 Trend Tracking, by Gerald Celente & Tom Milton, ©1990, 303 pp., ISBN: 0-446-39287-I, $12.99. John Wiley & Sons, Inc., 605 Third Ave., New York, NY 10158-0012. (800) CALL-WILEY; (212) 850-6000. Trends analyst Celente offers easy-to-follow techniques that allow readers to foresee major trends, and position themselves and their businesses to benefit from change. Includes an A-to-Z directory of profit opportunities.

Women-Owned Businesses

See also General Business Information; Managing Your Business; Starting a Business

By the year 2000, it is estimated that half of all American businesses will be owned by women. Millions of these ventures will be solo endeavors, since this flexible business structure enables women to balance home, children, and work responsibilities. The mid-1990s are a time when women are discovering the joys and challenges of running their own companies, and the resources have never been more plentiful to help them achieve their dreams. In this chapter you'll find top-notch information to guide your business from start-up to success—no matter what your gender! The resources in general, however, highlight the specific needs of women-based entrepreneurs.

 American Business Women's Association (ABWA), Carolyn B. Elman, 9100 Ward Pkwy., Box 8728, Kansas City, MO 64114. (816) 361-6621. The mission of ABWA is to bring together businesswomen of diverse backgrounds and to provide opportunities for them to help themselves and others grow personally and professionally through leadership, education, networking, and national recognition. Members include 90,000 individuals and 8,000 small business owners. Membership is $27/year. An annual convention as well as regional small business seminars are held.

 American Women's Economic Development Corporation (AWED), 71 Vanderbilt Ave., 3rd fl., New York, NY 10169. (800) 222-AWED. This nonprofit organization provides management training and business counseling for women-owned businesses in both the start-up and growth stages. A major conference is held in New York City each spring. Regular membership is $55/year.

Assertive Communication Skills for Women, by Chris Abiera, $69.95. SkillPath, Inc., 6900 Squibb Rd., PO Box 2768, Mission, KS 66201-2768. (800) 873-7545; (913) 677-3200; (913) 362-4241 (fax). This video/workbook program teaches women how to project a powerful, positive impression. It teaches both verbal and nonverbal communication skills that can be applied to achieving both personal and professional goals.

Business Matters, National Education Center for Women in Business (NECWB), Seton Hill College, Seton Hill Dr., Greensburg, PA 15601-1599. (800) NECWB-4-U; (412) 830-4625; (412) 834-7131 (fax). This four-part educational series focuses on women starting or managing their own business and is sponsored by the NECWB. Sessions take place on the Seton Hill College campus in Greensburg, PA, or in downtown Pittsburgh. A self-study option, with full-length videos of the programs and a workbook, includes one hour of telephone consultation with an instructor. Fees are $150 for each of the four parts.

Congratulations! You've Been Fired, by Emily Koltnow & Lynne S. Dumas, ©1990, 260 pp., ISBN: 0-449-90443-1, $8.95. Ballantine Books, 201 East 50th St., New York, NY 10022. (800) 733-3000; (212) 751-2600. A successful entrepreneur shares her experiences about the journey after employment, and how being fired may be the perfect opportunity for women to begin a new way of thinking about their careers—including the possibility of starting a business.

Enterprising Women, by A. David Silver, ©1994, 224 pp., ISBN: 0-8144-0226-7, $21.95. AMACOM Books, PO Box 1026, Saranac Lake, NY 12983. (800) 262-9699; (518) 891-3653 (fax). Revealing profiles of 100 top entrepreneurs that show readers how to use nontraditional techniques to raise capital and overcome obstacles in starting a business.

Everything My Father Told Me About Business, by Dr. Cynthia Iannarelli & Pamela Gilberd, ©1994, 160 pp., ISBN: 1-885043-01-5, $15.00. National Education Center for Women in Business (NECWB), Seton Hill College, Seton Hill Dr., Greensburg, PA 15601-1599. (800) NECWB-4-U; (412) 830-4625; (412) 834-7131 (fax). A collection of memorable quotes from women business owners recalling the advice their fathers gave them about being in business.

For Women: Managing Your Own Business, a Resource and Information Handbook, ©1983, 230 pp., ISBN: 0-16-026609-2, $13.00. U.S. Small Business Administration, New Orders, Superintendent of Documents, PO Box 371954, Pittsburgh, PA 15250-7954. (202) 783-3238; (202) 512-2250 (fax). This easy-to-read volume, prepared at the Wharton Entrepreneurial Center, provides an overview of the basics of running a successful business, including financial planning, marketing, employees, insurance, accounting, international operations, and more.

Hers: The Wise Woman's Guide to Starting a Business on $2,000 or Less, by Carol Milano, ©1991, 208 pp., ISBN: 0-9607118-7-2, $12.95. Allworth Press, 10 E. 23rd St., New York, NY 10010. (800) 247-6553; (212) 777-8395. This book offers brief descriptions of more than 100 businesses than can be started for $2,000 or less, and includes interviews with many women who successfully built their own business. Also includes tips on getting started, secrets of low-cost marketing, resources, and more.

Homeworking Mothers, Georganne Fuimarra, Ed., quarterly, Included with organization membership. Mother's Home Business Network, PO Box 423, East Meadow, NY 11554. (516) 997-7394; (517) 997-0839 (fax). This publication is designed to inform and inspire mothers who work at home or are thinking of doing so. It often features articles written by women who successfully combine motherhood and home business.

How to Succeed on Your Own, by Karin Abarbanel, ©1994, 320 pp., ISBN: 0-8050-3555-9, $12.95. Henry Holt and Company, Inc., 115 W. 18th St., New York, NY 10011. (800) 488-5233; (212) 886-9200; (212) 633-0748 (fax). This book serves as a guide to overcoming the emotional roadblocks women face on the way from corporation to cottage, from being an employee to becoming an entrepreneur. Features interviews with 30 female business owners discussing the psychological pitfalls and payoffs that women encounter in starting their own businesses.

National Association for Female Executives (NAFE), Leslie Smith, 30 Irving Pl., New York, NY 10003. (800) 634-NAFE; (212) 477-2200; (212) 477-8215 (fax). This national organization operates in cooperation with 250 active local affiliates to provide women with information and networking opportunities to achieve career success. Members receive a bimonthly magazine, *Executive Female*, as well as discounts on conferences, training, and business-related products and services. Membership dues are $29/year, plus chapter fees.

National Association of Women Business Owners (NAWBO), 1377 K St. NW, Ste. 637, Washington, DC 20005. (301) 608-2590. NAWBO promotes business ownership by women and serves as a forum for education and professional development. More than 50 active local chapters throughout the country provide networking and business development opportunities. The organization publishes a monthly magazine and hosts an annual meeting in the summer. Membership is $75/year, plus local chapter dues.

The Master Jugglers

After years of being in the workplace or at home and juggling activities involving professional duties, husbands, children, pets, sports competitions, PTA meetings, household tasks, and numerous other responsibilities, it's no wonder many women find running a business to be second nature. While the specific activities may differ, the same skills of keeping many operations going simultaneously are central to business success. Others observe that women often have valuable experience in working with teams and soliciting a consensus among widely differing viewpoints (just ask any mother with more than two children!).

Perhaps most of all, today's female solo entrepreneur finds satisfaction in knowing that her business can be one part of a multidimensional career. Whatever their structure or focus, women-based businesses are bringing a new dimension to the lives of their owners—and to the landscape of American business.

National Business Woman, by Maryanne S. Costa, Ed., 4x/yr., $10.00/yr. National Federation of Business & Professional Women's Clubs, 2012 Massachusetts Ave. NW, Washington, DC 20036. (202) 293-1100. This magazine is aimed at working women and deals with issues related to equity in the workplace.

 National Women's Economic Alliance Foundation (NWEAF), Beth Woodman, 1440 New York Avenue NW, #300, Washington, DC 20036. (202) 393-5257. This Foundation's goal is to improve career and economic opportunities for women worldwide by increasing the number of women serving on corporate boards. Associates can attend workshops on leadership and corporate board service. The organization holds networking meetings with guest speakers, and sponsors annual meetings in December in Washington, DC.

 Network of Enterprising Women, Inc. (NEW), Lisa M. Aldisert, President, PO Box 480, Midtown Station, New York, NY 10018. (212) 502-1186; (212) 840-3522 (fax). NEW is a nonprofit organization and affiliate of the National Association for Female Executives (NAFE) that promotes the advancement of New York-area women-owned businesses through the exchange of ideas, resources, and experience. Members receive a quarterly newsletter, a free listing in the annual membership directory, and can attend monthly dinner meetings with guest speakers. Dues are $60/year, or $75/year with a discounted membership to NAFE.

 Offices of Women's Business Ownership, U.S. Small Business Administration, Betsy Myers, Assistant Administrator, 409 Third St. SW, 6th Fl., Washington, DC 20416. (800) U-ASK-SBA; (202) 205-6673; (202) 205-7287 (fax). This office coordinates programs for women business owners through the U.S. Small Business Administration, a government agency.

 On Your Own: A Woman's Guide to Building a Business, by Laurie B. Zuckerman, ©1993, 224 pp., ISBN: 0-936894-52-0, $19.95. Upstart Publishing Co., Inc., 12 Portland St., Dover, NH 03820. (800) 235-8866; (603) 749-5071; (603) 742-9121 (fax). This book offers practical advice on starting and growing a business, including sample business plans and examples of successful women-owned businesses.

Orange County Women Networkers (OCWN), Dr. Leora Baron, PO Box 18456, Irvine, CA 92713. (714) 285-1927. This association is a group of professional and entrepreneurial women, and is an affiliate of the National Association for Female Executives (NAFE). Membership is $40/year. Networking meetings with guest speakers are held monthly.

 Our Wildest Dreams: Women Entrepreneurs Making Money, Having Fun, Doing Good, by Joline Godfrey, ©1993, 272 pp., ISBN: 0-88730-633-0, $11.00. HarperBusiness, 10 East 53rd St., New York, NY 10022-5299. (800) 982-4377; (212) 207-7000; (800) 822-4090 (fax). Godfrey, one of the leading spokespersons for the women-owned business movement, talks about the special qualities that women bring to business, and the new definition of success they are creating.

 Stress Management for Women, by Nancy Sullivan, $19.95. SkillPath, Inc., 6900 Squibb Rd., PO Box 2768, Mission, KS 66201-2768. (800) 873-7545; (913) 677-3200; (913) 362-4241 (fax). This audio/workbook program teaches women how to take command of stress and regain control of their live. The audiotape is designed for quiet relaxation, and the book is full of effective stress relieving exercises.

 The Entrepreneurial Woman's Guide to Owning a Business, $74.50. Entrepreneur Magazine Group, 2392 Morse Ave., PO Box 57050, Irvine, CA 92619-7050. (800) 421-2300; (714) 851-9088 (fax). This guide, packaged in a loose-leaf binder, provides more than 300 pages of information for women planning to be—or already in—business for themselves. Includes strategies for writing a business plan, financing, product development, marketing, advertising, and staffing.

 The Female Entrepreneur, by Connie Sitterly, ©1993, 200 pp., ISBN: 1-56052-207-0, $15.95. Crisp Publications, 1200 Hamilton Ct., Menlo Park, CA 94025. (415) 323-6100; (415) 323-5800 (fax). A step-by-step guide that addresses the special challenges women face in the business world.

The National Education Center for Women in Business (NECWB), Seton Hill College, Seton Hill Dr., Greensburg, PA 15601-1599. (800) NECWB-4-U; (412) 830-4625; (412) 834-7131 (fax). This national nonprofit organization promotes women and business ownership and serves as an information clearinghouse for women entrepreneurs. It sponsors educational programs, conducts research, and provides curriculum development. Members receive a quarterly journal, a bimonthly newsletter, and discounts on education products and programs. Membership is $49 (full partner); $19 (student partner).

 The Self-Employed Woman, by Jeannette R. Scollard, ©1985, 298 pp., ISBN: 0-671-63052-0, $6.95. Pocket Books, Simon & Schuster, Inc., 1230 Avenue of the Americas, New York, NY 10020. (800) 223-2336; (212) 698-7000. This guidebook is targeted to women who want to create their own solo businesses. It spans every step of the process, from making the transition to self-employment, finding funding, growing the business, and dealing with the stress to considering the possibilities of franchising or taking the company public.

 The Smart Woman's Guide to Starting a Business, by Vickie L. Montgomery, ©1994, 224 pp., ISBN: 1-56414-129-2, $14.95. Career Press, 180 Fifth Ave., PO Box 34, Hawthorne, NJ 07507. (800) CAREER-1; (201) 427-2037 (fax). A former banker shares tips on dealing with start-up, daily business operations, marketing, research, and financial planning.

 The Woman Entrepreneur: 33 Personal Stories of Success, by Linda Pinson & Jerry Jinnett, ©1994, 244 pp., ISBN: 0-936894-18-6, $14.00. Upstart Publishing Co., Inc., 12 Portland St., Dover, NH 03820. (800) 235-8866; (603) 749-5071; (603) 742-9121 (fax). Written accounts by 33 women business owners about how they overcame hardships in order to make their lives and their businesses a success.

 The Woman's Guide to Starting a Business, by Claudia Jessup & Genie Chipps, ©1991, 414 pp., ISBN: 0-8050-1140-4, $14.95. Henry Holt & Co., 115 W. 18th St., New York, NY 10011. (800) 488-5233; (212) 886-9200. This book presents a comprehensive overview of small business in straightforward, nontechnical language, and specifically addresses the many challenges faced by women entrepreneurs.

Women Business Owners: Selling to the Federal Government,
©1990, 74 pp., ISBN: 0-16-025264-4, $3.25. U.S. Small Business
Administration, New Orders, Superintendent of Documents,
PO Box 371954, Pittsburgh, PA 15250-7954. (202) 783-3238;
(202) 512-2250 (fax). This publication provides women business
owners with information about marketing their products and
services to the federal government. It includes information on the
basics of government contracting, and details on bids, proposals,
and contracts.

Women In Business, 70 min., $39.95. Inc. Business Resources, 350
N. Pennsylvania Ave., PO Box 1365, Wilkes-Barre, PA 13703-1365.
(800) 468-0800 x4760; (717) 822-8899. In this video, successful
women discuss a wide range of issues, including how to start a
business, find support, raise money, attract and manage employees, build credibility, and deal with success.

Women in Communications, Inc. (WIC), Roni D. Posner, 3717
Columbia Pike, Ste. 310, Arlington, VA 22204. (703) 920-5555;
(703) 920-5556 (fax). More than 10,000 women belong to this
national organization which seeks to improve women in their
communications careers. Nearly 200 local and regional chapters
provide networking opportunities. The organization publishes
The Professional Communicator five times/year, and annual meetings are held in the fall. Membership is $90/year, plus local
chapter dues.

Women in Film, Harriet Silverman, Executive Director, 6464
Sunset Blvd., Ste. 530, Hollywood, CA 90028. (213) 463-6040;
(213) 463-0963 (fax). Women and men working in the film and
television industries with a minimum of three years of professional experience are members of this national association. The
group sponsors workshops, seminars, and scholarships. A film
festival is held in the fall, and the organization's Crystal Awards
are presented each June. Members receive a monthly newsletter
and annual directory. Membership is $125/year.

Women's Exchange (WE), Beth Gulas, 37 Upwey Rd., Wellesley,
MA 02181. (617) 235-0035; (617) 431-2341 (fax). This association
provides and promotes comprehensive business services, career
direction, and entrepreneurial counseling to women in business.
Monthly meetings are held.

Working Woman, by Lynn Povich, Ed., monthly, ISSN: 0145-5761, $11.97/yr. Working Woman, Inc., 230 Park Ave., New York, NY 10169. (800) 234-9675; (212) 551-9500. This monthly magazine is devoted to women in the workplace, and consistently features insightful and informative articles on women entrepreneurs and their business experiences.

 Work of Her Own: A Woman's Guide to Success off the Fast Track, by Susan Wittig Albert, ©1994, 272 pp., ISBN: 0-87477-767-4, $12.95. Jeremy P. Tarcher, Inc., Putnam Publishing Group, 200 Madison Ave., New York, NY 10016. (800) 631-8571; (212) 951-8400. This book presents inspiring stories and practical advice from women who have left positions of leadership and authority in search of deeper fulfillment in work and life. It draws upon case studies and interviews with 80 women who have successfully made the change to create work of their own.

Youthful Entrepreneurs

As entrepreneurship expands to be an exciting career option for millions of Americans, a remarkable parallel development is occurring: a surge of interest among the younger generation. As a result, a wide range of innovative programs and resources are springing up around the country specifically designed for youthful entrepreneurs. As current business leaders pass on their entrepreneurial passion to their offspring—through both genetics and their family environment—it seems certain that this area will show significant expansion in the coming years.

ACE Action Newsletter, quarterly, Association of Collegiate Entrepreneurs, 1845 N. Fairmount, Box 147, Wichita, KS 67208. (316) 689-3000; (316) 689-3687 (fax). This publication is the communication vehicle for the national college-age entrepreneurial association and provides international networking and information resources.

A Teen's Guide to Business, by Linda Menzies, Oren S. Jenkins, & Rickell R. Fisher, ©1992, ISBN: 0-942361-50-4, $7.95. MasterMedia Limited, 17 E. 89th St., Ste. 7D, New York, NY 10128. (800) 334-8232; (212) 260-5600; (212) 546-7638 (fax). Written by three experienced teenage entrepreneurs, this action-oriented guide is filled with tips and interactive quizzes to help young people understand and succeed in their own businesses. It features role models from all ethnic, economic, and geographic backgrounds, and includes an extensive resource list.

Better Than a Lemonade Stand!, by Daryl Bernstein, ©1992, 170 pp., ISBN: 0-941831-75-2, $7.95. Beyond Words Publishing, Inc., 13950 NW Pumpkin Ridge Rd., Hillsboro, OR 97123. (800) 284-9673; (503) 647-5109. Written by a 15-year-old entrepreneur (with seven years of business experience!), this book presents 51 easy-to-launch small businesses that require little or no start-up costs and are ideally suited for youthful entrepreneurs.

Camp Entrepreneur, Wendy Peters, Youth Program Coordinator, National Education Center for Women in Business (NECWB), Seton Hill College, Seton Hill Dr., Greensburg, PA 15601-1599. (800) NECWB-4-U; (412) 830-4625; (412) 834-7131 (fax). This week-long summer camp program teaches teen girls leadership, self-esteem, and self-confidence through entrepreneurship. Girls learn the business skills they need to run their own companies, meet women entrepreneurs with successful businesses, and interact with teens from around the country interested in entrepreneurship. Held on the campus of Seton Hill College, Camp Entrepreneur is designed for girls ages 15-19; Camp Entrepreneur Junior is for girls ages 10-14. Tuition is $395; room and board is $145. The program is also held at other college campuses around the country.

Entrepreneurship Camp, Arleen Banowetz, Center for Entrepreneurship, Wichita State University, 1845 N. Fairmount, Wichita, KS 67260-0147. (316) 689-3000. This week-long resident workshop for high school sophomores, juniors, and seniors is held in Kansas each June, and attracts participants from all over the United States.

The ABC's of Business, by Dr. Cynthia Iannarelli, Jodi-Lynn Iannarelli, & Pamela Brooks, ©1994, 36 pp., ISBN: 1-885043-88-7, $18.00. National Education Center for Women in Business (NECWB), Seton Hill College, Seton Hill Dr., Greensburg, PA 15601-1599. (800) NECWB-4-U; (412) 830-4625; (412) 834-7131 (fax). Using the adventures of young entrepreneur Emily and her friends (the Entrekids), readers discover basic business concepts from A-to-Z, ranging from advertising to zoning. Designed for ages 3-10, with colorful illustrations.

Actions Speak Louder

What's the best way to get young people enthused about entrepreneurship? Get them involved. Show them how your company works, invite them to participate, introduce them to the thrill of turning an idea into a business reality. Best of all, let them discover the joy of finding work they love. We can give no better gift.

The Adventure to Entrepreneurship, by Dr. Cynthia Iannarelli & Wendy Peters, ©1994, 250 pp., ISBN: 1-885043-02-3, $24.00. National Education Center for Women in Business (NECWB), Seton Hill College, Seton Hill Dr., Greensburg, PA 15601-1599. (800) NECWB-4-U; (412) 830-4625; (412) 834-7131 (fax). This innovative workbook helps young women explore entrepreneurship as a career option no matter what their field of interest. Based on the curriculum from NECWB's Camp Entrepreneur program (see related listing), the workbook is filled with activities and self-discovery questions.

The Entrepreneurial Spirit (NFTE Newsletter), by Steve Mariotti, President & CEO, 3x/yr., National Foundation for Teaching Entrepreneurship to Handicapped and Disadvantaged Youth, Inc., 64 Fulton St., Ste. 700, New York, NY 10038. (212) 233-1777; (212) 233-3992 (fax). The NFTE is a nonprofit organization that sponsors programs to help disadvantaged and physically challenged youth learn the fundamentals of entrepreneurship.

Young Entrepreneurs Mini-Camp, Tom Monroy, Executive Director, Baldwin-Wallace College Family/Small Business Institute, Baldwin-Wallace College, Berea, OH 44017. (216) 826-5927. This four-day nonresident program is designed for young entrepreneurs between the ages of 10 and 17, and is held in June. Each participant learns business basics, including how to develop a business plan and marketing strategy.

Youth Entrepreneurial Camp, Robert Keyser, Director, Small Business Development Center, Portland Community College, 123 NW 2nd Ave., Ste. 321, Portland, OR 97209. (503) 273-2828. This week-long nonresident camp in Oregon is designed for students aged 12 to 16. In addition to general entrepreneurial skills, participants learn about business presentations, computers, marketing, and management.

Index

This index features an alphabetical listing of every resource featured in the WORKING SOLO SOURCEBOOK as well as numerous topic headings. To locate information on a specific subject, you can also refer to the *Table of Contents* on pages 9–12.

I

U

V

Would you like to nominate a resource for
the WORKING SOLO SOURCEBOOK?
Here's how!

The WORKING SOLO SOURCEBOOK is designed to be an information bank of resources for independent entrepreneurs. As a dynamic collection, it will be updated on a regular basis—in both printed and electronic versions.

If you have a favorite entrepreneurial resource you'd like to share, we would enjoy hearing from you. To consider a resource for inclusion, here is the information we need:

1. Full title of resource

2. Author(s)

3. Format (book, audiotape, video, network, etc.)

4. Copyright date

5. Page count or Duration

6. ISBN/ISSN, if appropriate

7. Price or Membership dues

8. Publisher/Provider information, including full address and contact numbers (800 number, telephone, fax)

9. Description of the resource and its value to entrepreneurs (limit to 100 words)

After reviewing this preliminary information, we may ask for a review copy, sample product, or additional details.

Once you have gathered this information, send it to one of the addresses located on the back of this page.

To nominate a resource to be included in the WORKING SOLO SOURCEBOOK, complete the information listed on the previous page and send it to one of the addresses below:

- By mail: WORKING SOLO SOURCEBOOK
  Portico Press
  PO Box 190
  New Paltz, NY 12561-0190

- By fax: (914) 255-2116 (24 hours a day)

- By e-mail: America Online: LONIER
  CompuServe: 72630,3426
  eWorld: T.Lonier
  Internet: lonier@aol.com

Here's the book that started it all...

WORKING SOLO

The Real Guide to
Freedom & Financial Success
with Your Own Business
by Terri Lonier

If you've enjoyed the *WORKING SOLO SOURCEBOOK,* and you don't have a copy of its companion volume, you're missing out!

WORKING SOLO is a comprehensive, easy-to-read guide to self-employment for both newcomers and seasoned pros. This detailed road map takes you step-by-step through every twist and turn of your solo adventure. Its pages are jam-packed with professional hints, money-saving tips, and proven techniques to help you launch a successful solo business or improve and expand your current one. It includes more than 1,000 solo business ideas and a free trial subscription to the *WORKING SOLO Newsletter.*

This is the best-seller that *Inc.* magazine chose as *the #1 book for solo entrepreneurs!* To obtain your copy, visit your local book-store or use the convenient order form on the back of this page.

Paperback, 6x9, 400 pages, $14.95

Also...

The *WORKING SOLO Newsletter* is a quarterly publication that keeps solo entrepreneurs up to date on news, marketing, legal and tax issues, new products and services, resources and other opportunities affecting the self-employed community. Subscriptions are $24/year. A sample issue is $4.00.

To order, send a check or money order payable to Portico Press, Dept. WS-SB, PO Box 190, New Paltz, NY 12561-0190.

To buy additional copies of the *WORKING SOLO SOURCEBOOK* or *WORKING SOLO,* visit your local bookstore or photocopy the order form below.

ORDER FORM

Three convenient ways to order:

By phone: Call (800) 222-SOLO (orders only)
Please have your Visa or MasterCard ready.

By fax: (914) 255-2116 (24 hours a day)

By mail: Portico Press
PO Box 190
New Paltz, NY 12561-0190
(914) 255-7165

Please send me:

_____ copies of **WORKING SOLO** by Terri Lonier @ $14.95

_____ copies of the **WORKING SOLO SOURCEBOOK** by T. Lonier
____ Paperback edition @ $14.95
____ Hardcover edition @ $24.95

Name _____

Address _____

City/State/Zip _____

Daytime Phone _____

Sales Tax:
Please add 7.75% sales tax to total order for books shipped to New York State addresses.

Shipping:
Book Rate: $2.00 for the first book and 75 cents for each additional book. (Surface shipping may take 3–4 weeks.)

Air Mail: $3.00 for the first book and $1.00 for each additional book.

Payment:
____ Check   ____ Visa   ____ MasterCard

Card Number _____

Name on card _____ Exp. date: ____/____